AMERICAN

WILDFLOWERS

A

LITERARY

FIELD GUIDE

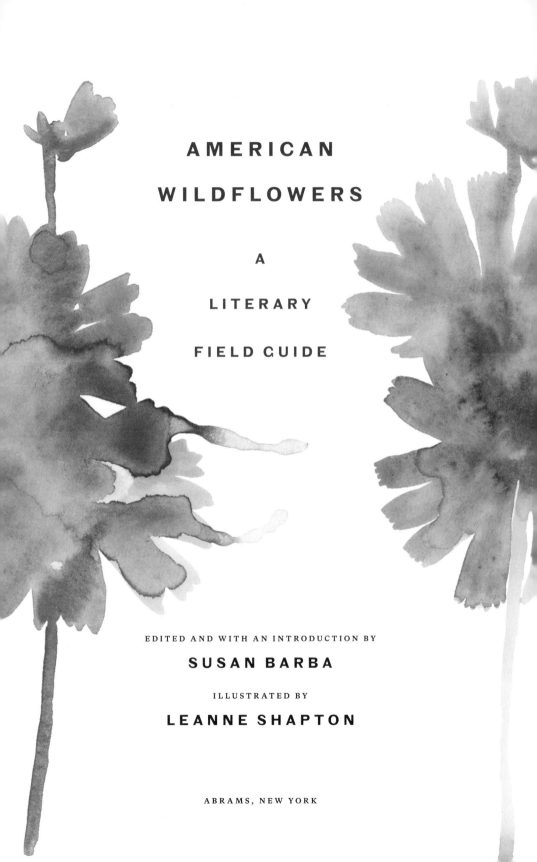

AMERICAN WILDFLOWERS

A

LITERARY

FIELD GUIDE

EDITED AND WITH AN INTRODUCTION BY

SUSAN BARBA

ILLUSTRATED BY

LEANNE SHAPTON

ABRAMS, NEW YORK

Editor: Michael Sand
Designer: Deb Wood
Design Manager: Heesang Lee
Managing Editor: Lisa Silverman
Production Manager: Larry Pekarek

Library of Congress Control Number: 202293217

ISBN: 978-1-4197-6016-7
eISBN: 978-1-64700-605-1

Selection and introduction copyright
© 2022 by Susan Barba
Illustrations copyright
© 2022 by Leanne Shapton
Additional credits on pages 323–329

Jacket © 2022 Abrams

Printed and bound in China
10 9 8 7 6 5 4 3 2 1

When foraging and using wild plants for
medicinal purposes, it is essential that readers
use extreme caution and consult physicians
or other medical professionals as needed. The
Author and Publisher disclaim any and all
liability in connection with information in this
book about the foraging and use of wild plants.

Abrams books are available at special discounts
when purchased in quantity for premiums and
promotions as well as fundraising or educational
use. Special editions can also be created to
specification. For details, contact specialsales@
abramsbooks.com or the address below.

Abrams® is a registered trademark of
Harry N. Abrams, Inc.

ABRAMS The Art of Books
195 Broadway, New York, NY 10007
abramsbooks.com

FOR LILLIAN AND PHILIP

The sky is falling, she says to him. Just yesterday I saw a piece of it hit the lake on the far side of town and land in the form of a cloud. The ground seizes up in drought. Just yesterday I saw cracks in the earth. Yesterday, brushfires followed by downpours, then immediate flooding. All the more reason to talk about flowers . . . I will make a bouquet of many colors for you to eat.

—KATIE PETERSON, from *Life in a Field*

CONTENTS

Introduction
9

A Note on the Illustrations
20

List of Illustrated Species
21

List of Texts, Arranged by Species
22

The Field Guide
29

Further Reading
320

Acknowledgments
322

Credits
323

Contributor Biographies
330

Aster
Asteraceae spp.

INTRODUCTION

BY SUSAN BARBA

Here on a hill in Massachusetts, the fog is lifting and the sun, still in the east, is turning the yellow leaves gold. The wind is from the east, too, and the clouds are rushing ahead of the bend of light. It is late October. Still in flower are the goldenrods and asters, now waving, now steady, at the edge of the grass. The view reminds me of Edna St. Vincent Millay's poem "Afternoon on a Hill," especially the first stanza:

> I will be the gladdest thing
> Under the sun!
> I will touch a hundred flowers
> And not pick one.

I've just rediscovered this poet, whose entire life's work I put away with childhood. I remember reading *Wine from These Grapes*, not knowing anything about wine, or women, or the work of being a poet, but feeling like I'd stumbled on some kind of secret ceremony. I was a girl then, in Morris County, New Jersey. My favorite day of the week was Thursday, when I had piano lessons in Florham Park, not because I loved the piano especially, but because we always had time to kill between school and my lesson, time my mother used instead to take me to the Frelinghuysen Arboretum, where we'd walk through the woodlands and meadows. What I liked about those afternoons was that it was just us and the flowers. After my lesson, we'd circle back to the library, across the street from the arboretum, and I would check out as many books as I could carry. Flowers-music-books, all within the same circumference, which I now recognize as a gift my mother gave me. She took me by the hand and introduced me to beauty, and while I put it off later in search of knowledge, I've come around to seeing that the two are related, that beauty is indispensable, and that books are the reproductive proof of it. This book is an attempt to reacquaint myself and others with the wild beauty we live with, to reclaim that beauty from sentimentality, consumerism, preciosity, and exclusivity.

I start with a story of my childhood because that is the origin of my feeling for flowers. I think it must be this way for many; beauty relieves us with its unexpected greeting and even integrates us. However, as a subject, beauty is often suspect. Even now writing about it causes me some embarrassment, some shame; when there is such suffering in the world, the thinking goes, how can you write about beauty? And yet beauty is linked to justice, as Elaine Scarry has argued persuasively, through an act that occurs involuntarily in its presence: "At the moment we see something beautiful, we undergo a radical decentering."[1] Scarry draws on Simone Weil, an ardent advocate for justice, to make her argument, Weil who described an encounter with beauty as a movement away from "our imaginary position as the center," which allows us "to discern that all points in the world are equally centers,"[2] and that the periphery is only a place of insufficient attention. In this way, the experience of beauty may be a beginning,[3] and a wildflower, that most common peripheral presence, a real vector for change in the world.

My hope is that this anthology, devoted to writing about American wildflowers, will counter the "plant blindness" of our dominant culture by exhibiting many of the flowers in the periphery of our vision, the flowers that have been written into our literature. I hope, too, that each of these radically decentering texts will prompt a consideration of that modifying term, "American." The language we use to describe people and plants often overlaps, with taxonomies that divide and place value on those divisions, words that actively discriminate. In the scientific literature and in common use, flowers are referred to as "native" (like sunflowers) or "alien" (like bluebells); they can be "naturalized" (like clover) or "invasive" (like purple loosestrife). There are "migrants" and "exotics," "escapes" and "refugees." The language expresses a position; it reveals a posture in regard to a species; it grants a plant its liberty or sanctions its eradication. The best writers closely observe not only the plant but our words in relation to it, and in doing so they focus our attention and clarify our intentions.

1   Elaine Scarry, *On Beauty and Being Just* (Princeton, NJ: Princeton University Press, 1999), 111.
2   Simone Weil, "Love of the Order of the World," in *Waiting for God* (New York: G. P. Putnam's Sons, 1951), 158–59.
3   "Beginning" in the political sense of the word, as Hannah Arendt uses it: "It is in the nature of beginning that something new is started which cannot be expected." *The Human Condition* (Chicago: The University of Chicago Press, 1958, 1998), 177–78.

According to the dictionary, the first usage of the word wildflower, defined as "the flower of a wild or uncultivated plant or the plant bearing it," occurred in 1620, the year the *Mayflower* landed on this continent.[4] In his poem of 1856, "The Mayflowers" (page 148), the Quaker poet and abolitionist John Greenleaf Whittier links the Pilgrim ship to a flower by the same name, the mayflower or trailing arbutus (*Epigaea repens*).[5] These "wild-wood" flowers grew abundantly around Plymouth, but they were a different flower from the one the ship had been named for, which, according to Whittier, is the English hawthorn (*Crataegus monogyna*). In the poem, the pilgrims mistake the native flower for their own mayflower, and its appearance is to them a sign of Providence. Does the origin story of a nation stem from the misidentification of a flower, from a naming that imposed a direct line where there was none? The English hawthorn is a small tree, anywhere from six to thirty feet tall, with flowers resembling apple blossoms. *Epigaea repens* is a creeping mat, four to six inches high, with trumpet-shaped flowers. Nostalgia is a contradictory longing for home that does not contain itself in the past but also projects itself into the future.[6]

Horticulture and botany in America have deep roots in the empire the *Mayflower* sailed from. The establishment of the legitimacy of a people was contingent on the establishment of dominion over the flora of this new continent. This process involved not only exporting specimens and inscriptions to Europe but importing a whole history from the Old World—the Greek and Roman herbals that identified the medicinal qualities of plants, the early botanists of the sixteenth century with their herbariums and schematizations—to the New. Thus the lineage continued: with John Bartram, born in 1699, hailed as the first American-born naturalist (and titled in 1765 by King George III as the "King's Botanist in North America"), whom Carl Linnaeus[7] called "the greatest natural botanist in the world" and whose colonial plant collection came from the Shenandoah Valley and Blue Ridge Mountains; with his son,

---

4   *Merriam-Webster's Collegiate Dictionary* (Springfield, MA: Merriam-Webster, 2014), 1432.
5   *Epigaea repens* became the state flower of Massachusetts in 1918. It is now rare.
6   See Svetlana Boym, *The Future of Nostalgia* (New York: Basic Books, 2001).
7   Carl Linnaeus was a Swedish botanist whose new classification system and identification of living organisms by genus and species formed the basis of modern taxonomy.

William Bartram (born 1739), whose travels in the South inspired the English Romantic poets, and who chronicled his discoveries of plants and peoples in his *Travels in the North and South*; with the publication of the first American flora, *Flora Virginica* (1762), written in Latin and published in Holland; with the establishment of the earliest institutions—the Massachusetts Horticultural Society in 1829, the Public Garden in Boston in 1837, and the Arnold Arboretum, America's first public collection of plants, in 1872.[8] Only now, in the twenty-first century, is the decolonization of botany beginning. Native botanical knowledge, which predated this imposed heritage, and continued to exist alongside it to the extent that teachings were not irrevocably lost in the genocide of the Native peoples, is at last being properly recognized by botanists and the wider public for its primacy, complexity, and necessity.

This short history of our knowledge of the native plants and wildflowers is a story of how the flowers, unwittingly, became American. Their growth preceded these events and proceeded apace. Henry David Thoreau, the most perspicacious of amateur botanists, wrote, "We find ourselves in a world that is already planted, but is also still being planted as at first."[9] Thoreau sought to create a "Kalendar" that would record the first flowerings of the hundreds of species he identified annually in Concord and its environs. He recognized the enduring power of their perennial presence. Even the most ephemeral wildflowers can assume outsize significance, for they are symbols of survival and subversion, of the triumph of the small and meek, of the virtues of the weedy, ugly, and malodorous. Like the birds, we rely on their regular return.

Yet despite their appeal, and perhaps because of their nature, wildflowers have no established field of their own in our literature. Thoreau again, in 1852:

> I asked a learned and accurate naturalist who is at the same time the courteous guardian of a public library to direct me to those works

---

8   At the Arnold Arboretum I once saw a Franklin tree in bloom. Native to Georgia but extinct in the wild, this tree (*Franklinia alatamaha*) was observed by the Bartrams, father and son, and named after their family friend Benjamin Franklin. If not for the seeds the son collected, the tree would be entirely extinct. The flowers of the Franklin tree are similar to a magnolia's but smaller, white-petaled with bright orange-yellow stamens at center, like a perfectly hardboiled egg.
9   Henry David Thoreau, *The Journal, 1837–1861*, ed. Damion Searls (New York: New York Review Books, 2009), 640.

which contained the more particular *popular* account or *biography* of particular flowers, from which the botanies I had met with appeared to draw sparingly—for I trusted that each flower had had many lovers and faithful describers in past times—but he informed me that I had read all, that no one was acquainted with them, they were only catalogued like his books.[10]

There are numerous volumes devoted solely to gardens, cultivated flowers, roses; to Shakespeare's flowers, English flowers, the language of flowers. Wildflowers alone are represented primarily by field guides. Frances Theodora Parsons's *How to Know the Wild Flowers* (1893) was one of the first.[11] Roused by the writings of the Transcendentalists and Darwin's plant-life revelations, Parsons commended the learning of flowers to the public as an intellectual activity and included in her identification aid not only the flower's physical characteristics but also the derivations of the Latin and common names, the flower's medicinal properties, Native usage, and presence in folklore and poetry.[12] It was a success in its time, and far from being quaint or shopworn, it is still a book of lasting value, a classic that belongs to a rich period in American horticultural writing, primarily by women.

At the turn of the last century, garden writers like Neltje Blanchan, Alice Lounsberry, and Mabel Osgood Wright contributed greatly to the limited bibliography of books about wildflowers by combining scientific knowledge with aesthetic appreciation; these literary narratives were in the spirit of the popular accounts Thoreau had wished for, written by "faithful describers" who had both personal and objective knowledge of their subjects. Later in the twentieth century, wildflowers were adopted by the ecological movement and appear as the heroes of books like Euell Gibbons's *Stalking the Wild Asparagus* (1962) and Sara B. Stein's *My Weeds* (1990). With recent efforts to rewild land in the service of conservation, an interest in wildflowers is waxing again. It

---

10   Henry David Thoreau, *Thoreau's Wildflowers*, ed. Geoff Wisner (New Haven and London: Yale University Press, 2016), 262.
11   Frances Theodora Parsons published initially under her married name, Mrs. William Starr Dana.
12   Her book was succeeded by terser pocket field guides, but some field guides follow her example by going beyond notations of color and form to describe the flowers' effects on the senses, or comparative beauty or rarity. *How to Know the Wild Flowers* went out of print until Frances Tenenbaum reissued it for HarperCollins in 1989. It is out of print again.

is high time. Wildflowers have never been more endangered and in need of our renewed attention.

As I write now, there are 4,400 imperiled native flora in the United States.[13] These plants are at risk because of climate change, loss of habitat, reductions in the numbers of pollinators, and the spread of non-native species. To protect these native species, a shift in terminology appears to be taking place. The term "wildflower" is falling out of favor, eclipsed by the term "native plant."[14] The new term represents a shift toward action, the conservation of native species, which are being lost at alarming rates. The imperilment of native plants is not in doubt, and yet I wonder what we lose by editing a word out of our language in order to protect a certain population. What happens to the idea of angiosperms, flowering plants, as a distinct category, flowers being one of the two defining features of the older term, if they are lumped together with gymnosperms, nonflowering plants? And where do the long-naturalized flowering plants—for instance, the common mullein (*Verbascum thapsus*), which the Anishinaabe include in their botanical teachings,[15] or red clover (*Trifolium pratense*), which Emily Dickinson favored—belong then?

I imagine that "native plant" is not intended to be a synonym but a more exact substitution, of better service to science and to advocacy. Still, the old term retains its significance, partly because we don't want to be told what we can and can't love, and partly because in any transition the past is present until it isn't anymore. The word wildflower has an aesthetic power that comes partly from the picture the word creates in the mind—that necessary quality of wildness—and partly from its sound. The long, sighing, stressed first syllable—*why*—the stress end-stopped by *-ld*, then relieved through the slower unfolding of *flower*, with its paired and unstressed syllables: a singing word, of significance to poets, if not to scientists. For this reason, and for the greater inclusiveness that wildflowers convey, I've chosen to retain the word for the purposes of this book.

---

13   "CPC Best Practices: Why Conserve Rare Plants?" Center for Plant Conservation, accessed November 20, 2021, https://saveplants.org/best-practices/why-conserve-rare-plants.
14   The New England Wildflower Society, for example, is now the Native Plant Trust. The Lady Bird Johnson Wildflower Center, which retains the wildflower designation, has a database of native-only plants, which is useful, and yet necessarily limited by design.
15   See Mary Siisip Geniusz, "Indigenous or Imported?" in *Plants Have So Much to Give Us, All We Have to Do Is Ask: Anishinaabe Botanical Teachings*, edited by Wendy Makoons Geniusz (Minneapolis, MN: University of Minnesota Press, 2015), 24–26.

American Wildflowers: A Literary Field Guide is a *florilegium*, the Latin word for a gathering of flowers, just as *anthology* is Greek for a bouquet. Instead of gathering flowers, I have been gathering stories about them, which are also stories about who we are and our relation to place. It is a book about nature and culture. It includes both native and non-native species, pristine and rambunctious definitions of nature.[16] It acknowledges the ways in which wildflowers are both threatened and resilient. The kinds of writing represented here are diverse: letters, reviews, bulletins, essays, excerpts from novels, reports from the field, and, most of all, poems. The main criterion for inclusion is that the writing represents an encounter with flowers more wild than cultivated, more self-determined than domesticated. Uncultivated multitudes of wildflowers are found not only in what wilderness is left, if any, but everywhere else; they have always frequented gardens, prairies, meadows, farms, and now, more often, vacant lots, roadsides, and median strips, also known (revealingly) as central reservations. Wildflowers extend from coast to coast, in rural, suburban, and urban ecosystems. The flowers are the bridgehead to America.[17]

The writers are equally diverse. There are foreign-born writers writing about American plants, American writers writing about non-native plants. They span the past three centuries, from the late 1700s to 2020. There are writers with deep regional knowledge of their country: from northern to southern Appalachia, the central plains, the southwest desert, Florida, California, and the Rocky Mountains, the White Mountains and the Green, the eastern coast and west. There are urban writers who are intimately acquainted with the nature that exists in their neighborhoods. There are female writers, Black writers, gay writers, Indigenous writers. There are botanists like William Bartram, George Washington Carver, and Robin Wall Kimmerer, and horticultural writers like Neltje Blanchan and Eleanor Perényi. There are versatile, various writers whose prose

---

16   Emma Maris, *Rambunctious Garden: Saving Nature in a Post-Wild World* (New York: Bloomsbury USA, 2011).
17   See James Fenton's "What I Mean by Mexico," in *The New York Review of Books*, February 25, 2015: "One says of any great subject as yet untackled—Mexico, for instance—Oh, that's such a big undertaking, that's going to need such preparation. Then something happens and you just have to go in there anyway, in all your ignorance. What happens next is you acquire a little piece of knowledge, a little amount of experience, and this experience is your bridgehead. Lawrence sits at his little onyx table, sniffing Mexico, listening to the birds, thinking about the Aztecs: he is creating his bridgehead."

pieces are included here, like Lydia Davis and Aimee Nezhukumatathil. And most of all, there are the poets: from Walt Whitman and Emily Dickinson, William Carlos Williams and T. S. Eliot to Allen Ginsberg and Robert Creeley, Lucille Clifton and Louise Glück, Natalie Diaz and Jericho Brown.

In these pages are to be found rare and endangered flowers like the *Iris prismatica* and the trout lily, or dogtooth violet (*Erythronium americanum*), and flowers that flourish here still, the asters and goldenrod, the waterlilies and lupine. But America's most celebrated wildflowers may be the tenacious dandelions and daisies, best known to some (those unfamiliar with their virtues) as weeds. There are flowers whose existence is central to story, like the Hawaiian 'ōhi'a lehua, and others whose existence is central to survival, like the sunflower. Reading these various accounts of wildflowers from different times and places is like reading the record of geological time in rock. One can see similar patterns and then seismic shifts. The biography of the flower depends on who is writing it. Where some see beauty, others see use. Where some see tradition, others see degradation. There is one constant, however: Every time we find a wildflower in literature, it is the result of reverie, not some kind of lazy daydream, but a spark, a kindling of the imagination, be it to praise or rage or make sense of the world.

I've arranged the book by the common names of species, in order to put the flowers first and to emphasize the sense of the book as a field guide. The species themselves are organized into families, which appear in alphabetical order of the Latin family name. My hope is that by grouping flowers together in this way, readers will recognize their family characteristics. Many writers, of course, do not refer to the flowers by their scientific names, which makes this kind of organization challenging, but usually the identity of the flower in question is clear enough; if the species is unclear, I use the botanical abbreviation "spp." which means multiple species. There are also works that make no specific reference to individual species but are about wildflowers in general; these works have their own section, which includes writing about multiple species.

My aim is to give a new presentation of the flowers for the general reader. For example, an actual field guide presentation of the western sunflower, whether organized by key or color, would be presented under the heading of the family's common name, the composite family, with the scientific name in parentheses (Compositae). Alongside the common name, western sunflower, would be its scientific name: *Helianthus occidentalis*. Perhaps a sketch or photograph would accompany this entry, along with a short report of its anatomy, locale, and time of bloom. The flower is one of thousands. Under the sunflower species here, you will find a painting of the flower by Leanne Shapton, Allen Ginsberg's "Sunflower Sutra," poems by Jill Bialosky and Henri Cole, and an essay by Gary Paul Nabhan. My intention is not to replace the invaluable work of scientific field guides, but to give a fuller picture of fewer flowers, alternate biographies of their lives, and to collect them in this panoramic field guide to the wildflowers writers have devoted chapters to.

One of the most important elements of this literary field guide has nothing to do with words and everything to do with flowers: the illustrations. The history of botanical illustration is a vast subject in itself, indispensable to botanical scholarship, exploration, and exploitation, and too vast to explicate further here. Leanne Shapton's illustrations are informed by this history, but like the texts in this book they are biographies of particular flowers, not botanies. They privilege aesthetic freedom over anatomical precision, and by doing so, they announce brightly and boldly the spirit of this anthology. They are painted from pressed flowers, mirroring the flowers printed in the text and pressed between these pages. Like pressed flowers, too, they gesture backward and forward; as Williams wrote in his poem "A Coronal":

Anemones sprang where she pressed
and cresses
stood green in the slender source—
And new books of poetry
will be written, leather-colored oakleaves
many and many a time.

Leanne's wildflowers have the feel of the wild about them still. You can see the wind, rain, clouds, and sun in various flowers, some appear as they must to pollinators (the clover!), or to other species with faster, broader-spectrum receptors than ours. And simultaneously the paintings make us aware of the plant physiology, the materiality of the paint and paper and its organic relation to plant pigment and tissue. They are sensuous, resplendent, incandescent, surreal, elegant, and visibly mortal. They are more than a beautiful compliment to the texts; they are an integral part of the field guide.

Observing flowers in the field, studying their Latin and common names, learning about their uses, and seeking their impressions in literature, has been one of the great unexpected joys of my life. As Elaine Scarry wrote, beauty "comes to us, with no work of our own; then leaves us prepared to undergo a giant labor."[18] This compendium is the evidence of the abundance of American wildflower writing, the labors of those who were witnesses to wild beauty, and who wished to pass their experience on to others, as I do now, to you.

---

18   Scarry, 53.

Daisy
Chrysanthemum leucanthemum

A NOTE ON THE ILLUSTRATIONS

When I was approached by the poet Susan Barba and the Oak Spring Garden Foundation to make the illustrations for this book, I leapt, like a lizard. Painting flowers is a habit and a joy—a deep pleasure. What a gift to stare at flowers—these ephemeral miracles of color and synthesis and botany. I figured, early on, that my paintings should refer to pressed specimens rather than studies in the wild. The flowers would sit still for their portraits, and I could look at them for months. This attempt to stop time, to dry and preserve, felt in keeping with the work of the writers Susan has selected for this book. Naming to elevate and intensify life, I think Thomas Mann said. Or, in the case of my assignment, flattening, to keep and to hold. I hope that the readers of this book might pick and press their own flowers between these pages, the pollen and anthocyanins marking the printed colors and words.

—*Leanne Shapton*

LIST OF ILLUSTRATED SPECIES

Aster .... *Asteraceae spp.* 8, 94, 97
Daisy .... *Chrysanthemum leucanthemum* 19, 114
Snowdrop .... *Galanthus nivalis*............................ 30
Queen Anne's lace .... *Daucus carota* 37, 40, 45
Milkweed .... *Asclepias syriaca* 46, 50
Yucca bell .... *Yucca arkansana* 55
Solomon's seal .... *Polygonatum biflorum* 60, 63
Sunflower .... *Helianthus spp.* 64, 69
Dandelion .... *Taraxacum officinale* 80, 84, 89, 90
Goldenrod .... *Solidago spp.* 98, 105
Chicory .... *Cichorium intybus* 110, 113
Black-eyed Susan .... *Rudbeckia hirta* 117
Mayapple .... *Podophyllum peltatum* 122, 125
Forget-me-not .... *Myosotis sylvatica* 127
Draba .... *Draba verna* 128
Night-blooming cereus .... *Peniocereus greggii* 133
Cardinal flower .... *Lobelia cardinalis* 134
Golden canna .... *Canna flaccida* 137
Spiderwort .... *Tradescantia ohiensis* 138
Acony bell, Oconee bells .... *Shortia galacifolia* 144
Rhodora .... *Rhododendron canadense* 147
Mayflower, trailing arbutus ... *Epigaea repens* 149, 150, 153
Indian pipe .... *Monotropa uniflora* 154, 321
Red clover .... *Trifolium pratense* 157, 161
Milkvetch .... *Astragalus spp.* 169
Closed gentian .... *Gentiana rubricaulis* 170, 173
Iris, blue flag .... *Iris versicolor* 174, 177
Hibiscus .... *Hibiscus furcellatus* 180
Cotton flower .... *Gossypium hirsutum* 183
Red trillium, red wake robin .. *Trillium erectum* 184, 340
'Ōhi'a .... *Metrosideros polymorpha* 193
Fragrant water lily .... *Nymphaea odorata* 197
Lilac .... *Syringa vulgaris* 206, 215
Fireweed .... *Chamaenerion angustifolium* 220
Evening primrose .... *Oenothera biennis* 225, 284, 289
Lady's slipper orchid .... *Cypripedium parviflorum* 229
Indian paintbrush .... *Castilleja spp.* 233
Mimulus, monkeyflower .... *Mimulus guttatus* 236, 239
Water hyacinth .... *Eichhornia crassipes* 240, 243
Wolfsbane .... *Aconitum delphiniifolium* 246
Wild rose .... *Rosa acicularis* 249
Violet, field pansy .... *Viola bicolor* 252, 255, 259
Yellow pitcherplant .... *Sarracenia flava* 265, 268
Fragrant bedstraw .... *Galium triflorum* 273
Cranesbill .... *Geranium spp.* 277
Coneflower .... *Echinacea angustifolia* 293
California poppy .... *Eschscholzia californica* 302
Bloodroot .... *Sanguinaria canadensis* 305
Dogtooth violet .... *Erythronium americanum* 309
Toadflax .... *Linaria vulgaris* 313
Narcissus .... *Narcissus pseudonarcissus* 318

LIST OF TEXTS, ARRANGED BY SPECIES

AMARYLLIDACEAE / ONION FAMILY

Snowdrop *Galanthus nivalis**
SANDRA LIM, Snowdrops   31

Narcissus *Narcissus pseudonarcissus**
YUSEF KOMUNYAKAA, Work   32

APIACEAE / CARROT FAMILY

Queen Anne's lace *Daucus carota*
LYDIA DAVIS, Cohabitating with Beautiful Weeds   34
JUNE JORDAN, Queen Anne's Lace   39

Wild carrot *Daucus pusillus*
WILLIAM CARLOS WILLIAMS, Spring and All (Part I)   41
WALT WHITMAN, Wild Flowers   43

APOCYNACEAE / PERIWINKLE FAMILY

Milkweed *Asclepias syriaca*
DEBORAH DIGGES, what woman   47

Butterfly weed *Asclepias tuberosa*
A. R. AMMONS, Butterflyweed   48

Honeyvine milkweed *Cynanchum laeve*
DEVIN JOHNSTON, Domestic Scenes   49

ASPARAGACEAE / HYACINTH FAMILY

Lechuguilla *Agave lechuguilla*
JEFFREY YANG, Lechuguilla   52

Yucca bell *Yucca arkansana*
NATALIE DIAZ, If I Should Come Upon Your House
    Lonely in the West Texas Desert   53

Blue camas *Camassia quamash*
MERIWETHER LEWIS, Wednesday June 11th, 1806   56

Solomon's seal *Polygonatum biflorum*
LINDA GREGG, Too Bright to See   61

False Solomon's seal *Maianthemum racemosum*
RICHARD WILBUR, Signatures   62

ASTERACEAE / DAISY FAMILY

Sunflower *Helianthus spp.*
ALLEN GINSBERG, Sunflower Sutra   65
HENRI COLE, Sunflower   67

JILL BIALOSKY, Oh Giant Flowers   **68**

GARY PAUL NABHAN, The Exile and the Holy
    Anomaly: Wild American Sunflowers   **70**

Dandelion *Taraxacum officinale**
MARY SIISIP GENIUSZ, The South Wind and the
    Maiden of the Golden Hair   **81**

MARY SIISIP GENIUSZ, Doodooshaaboojiibik   **83**

EMILY DICKINSON, The Dandelion's pallid tube   **92**

Aster *Asteraceae* spp.
JERICHO BROWN, The Tradition   **93**

LESLIE MARMON SILKO, The purple asters are growing   **95**

Goldenrod *Solidago* spp.
STEPHANIE BURT, Wildflower Meadow, Medawisla   **96**

ROBIN WALL KIMMERER, Asters and Goldenrod   **99**

HERMAN MELVILLE, A Way-side Weed   **108**

Chicory *Cichorium intybus**
WILLIAM CARLOS WILLIAMS, Chicory and Daisies   **109**

D. A. POWELL, Tender Mercies   **111**

Daisy *Chrysanthemum leucanthemum**
A. R. AMMONS, Loss   **115**

Black-eyed Susan *Rudbeckia hirta*
WILLIAM MEREDITH, An Assent to Wildflowers   **116**

Compass plant *Silphium laciniatum*
ALDO LEOPOLD, Prairie Birthday   **118**

Cornflower *Centaurea cyanus**
BEN LERNER, Also Known as Hurtsickle, Cyani Flower,
    and Bachelor's Button   **120**

BERBERIDACEAE / BARBERRY FAMILY

Mayapple *Podophyllum peltatum*
EUELL GIBBONS, May Apple, or American Mandrake
    (*Podophyllum peltatum*)   **123**

BORAGINACEAE / FORGET-ME-NOT FAMILY

Forget-me-not *Myosotis sylvatica**
DENISE LEVERTOV, The Message   **126**

BRASSICACEAE / CABBAGE FAMILY

Draba *Draba verna*
ALDO LEOPOLD, Draba   **129**

CACTACEAE / CACTUS FAMILY

Night-blooming cereus *Peniocereus greggii*
ROBERT HAYDEN, The Night-Blooming Cereus   **130**

CAMPANULACEAE / BELLFLOWER FAMILY

Cardinal flower *Lobelia cardinalis*
ROSS GAY, Ending the Estrangement   **135**

CANNACEAE / CANNA FAMILY

Golden canna *Canna flaccida*
WALLACE STEVENS, Anecdote of Canna   **136**

COMMELINACEAE / SPIDERWORT FAMILY

Spiderwort *Tradescantia ohiensis*
MARIANNE MOORE, The Steeple-Jack   **139**

DIAPENSIACEAE / PINCUSHION FAMILY

Acony bell, Oconee bells *Shortia galacifolia*
ALICE LOUNSBERRY, *Shortia galacifolia*   **142**

ERICACEAE / HEATHER FAMILY

Rhodora *Rhododendron canadense*
RALPH WALDO EMERSON, The Rhodora   **146**

Mayflower, trailing arbutus *Epigaea repens*
JOHN GREENLEAF WHITTIER, The Mayflowers   **148**
NELTJE BLANCHAN, The Trailing Arbutus   **152**

Indian pipe *Monotropa uniflora*
EMILY DICKINSON, 'Tis whiter than an Indian Pipe   **155**

FABACEAE / PEA FAMILY

Red clover *Trifolium pratense**
EMILY DICKINSON, There is a flower that Bees prefer   **156**
The Clover's simple Fame   **158**
To make a prairie   **158**
HERMAN MELVILLE, To Winnefred   **159**

Wild indigo *Baptisia australis*
CYRUS CASSELLS, A Siren Patch of Indigo   **162**

Touch-me-not *Mimosa pudica**
AIMEE NEZHUKUMATATHIL, Touch-Me-Nots
(*Mimosa pudica*)   **164**

Texas bluebonnets *Lupinus texensis*
GARY SNYDER, Brighter Yellow   166

Milkvetch *Astragalus* spp.
ENRIQUE SALMÓN, Milkvetch   167

GENTIANACEAE / GENTIAN FAMILY

Closed gentian *Gentiana rubricaulis*
JAMES SCHUYLER, Closed Gentian Distances   171

Fringed gentian *Gentiana crinita*
WILLIAM CULLEN BRYANT, To the Fringed Gentian   172

IRIDACEAE / IRIS FAMILY

Iris, blue flag *Iris versicolor*
LOUISE GLÜCK, The Wild Iris   175
LI-YOUNG LEE, Irises   176

LILIACEAE / LILY FAMILY

Wild red lily *Lilium* spp.
WILLIAM CARLOS WILLIAMS, The Red Lily   178

MALVACEAE / MALLOW FAMILY

Hibiscus *Hibiscus furcellatus*
W. S. MERWIN, The Rose Beetle   181

Cotton flower *Gossypium hirsutum*
JEAN TOOMER, November Cotton Flower   182

MELANTHIACEAE / WAKE ROBIN FAMILY

Red trillium, red wake robin *Trillium erectum*
DAVID BAKER, The Spring Ephemerals   185

MONTIACEAE / BLINKS FAMILY

Bitterroot *Lewisia rediviva*
JOSEPH BRUCHAC, The Bitterroot   187

MYRTACEAE / MYRTLE FAMILY

'Ōhi'a *Metrosideros polymorpha*
MARY KAWENA PUKUI, Kūka'ōhi'aakalaka   189

NYMPHAEACEAE / WATER LILY FAMILY

Spatterdock, yellow pond lily *Nuphar lutea*
HENRY DAVID THOREAU, Oct. 18, 1860   194

ROBIN WALL KIMMERER, The Consolation of
Water Lilies   195

Fragrant water lily *Nymphaea odorata*
KATHARINE S. WHITE, Green Thoughts in a
Green Shade   202

OLEACEAE / OLIVE FAMILY

Lilac *Syringa vulgaris**
WALT WHITMAN, When Lilacs Last in the
Dooryard Bloom'd   207
T. S. ELIOT, The Waste Land (Part I)   216

ONAGRACEAE / FUSCHIA FAMILY

Fireweed *Chamaenerion angustifolium*
GALWAY KINNELL, Farewell   219
JAMES WRIGHT, A Flower Passage   222

Evening primrose *Oenothera caespitosa*
RITA DOVE, Evening Primrose   224

ORCHIDACEAE / ORCHID FAMILY

Calypso orchid *Calypso bulbosa*
ROBERT FROST, An Encounter   226

Lady's slipper orchid *Cypripedium parviflorum*
SUSAN BARBA, Second Nature   227

OROBANCHACEAE / BROOMRAPE FAMILY

Indian paintbrush *Castilleja* spp.
PATRICIA SPEARS JONES, What Beauty Does   231

PHRYMACEAE / LOPSEED FAMILY

Mimulus, monkeyflower *Mimulus guttatus*
GARY SNYDER, Mimulus on the Road to Town   235
FORREST GANDER, Rexroth's Cabin   237

PONTEDERIACEAE / WATER HYACINTH FAMILY

Water hyacinth *Eichhornia crassipes**
JAMES MERRILL, The Water Hyacinth   241

RANUNCULACEAE / BUTTERCUP FAMILY

Columbine *Aquilegia coerulea*
JORIE GRAHAM, Of Forced Sightes and Trusty
Ferefulness   244

Wolfsbane *Aconitum delphiniifolium*
JOAN NAVIYUK KANE, Hyperboreal 247

ROSACEAE / ROSE FAMILY

Wild rose *Rosa acicularis*
JUNE JORDAN, Letter to the Local Police 248
ANN TOWNSEND, The Enclosure Act 251

VIOLACEAE / VIOLET FAMILY

Violet, field pansy *Viola bicolor*
AMY CLAMPITT, The Field Pansy 253
ALICE DUNBAR-NELSON, Violets 256
WILLIAM CARLOS WILLIAMS, The Flowers Alone 257

WILDFLOWERS: VARIOUS, ANONYMOUS, GENERAL
FRANCISCO X. ALARCÓN, *In Xochitl In Cuicatl* 260
WILLIAM BARTRAM, Introduction to *Travels Through
    North and South Carolina* ... 261
ELIZABETH BISHOP, North Haven 274
JOHN BURROUGHS, To the Lapland Longspur 276
GEORGE WASHINGTON CARVER, Nature's Garden
    for Victory and Peace 279
LUCILLE CLIFTON, flowers 290
ROBERT CREELEY, The Flower 291
CAMILLE DUNGY, Letter to America: Diversity, a Garden
    Allegory with Suggestions for Direct Action 292
MEGAN FERNANDES, Quentin Compson at the
    Natural History Museum, Harvard University 298
PAUL GOODMAN, Pagan Rites 299
ROBERT HASS, Spring Rain 303
BERNADETTE MAYER, Renaming Things 304
ELEANOR PERÉNYI, Wild Flowers 306
MICHAEL HOFMANN, Idyll 310
KATIE PETERSON, The Government 311
STANLEY PLUMLY, Wildflower 312
JAKE SKEETS, Tácheeh 315
GARY SNYDER, For the Children 319

(*Asterisks denote non-native species*)

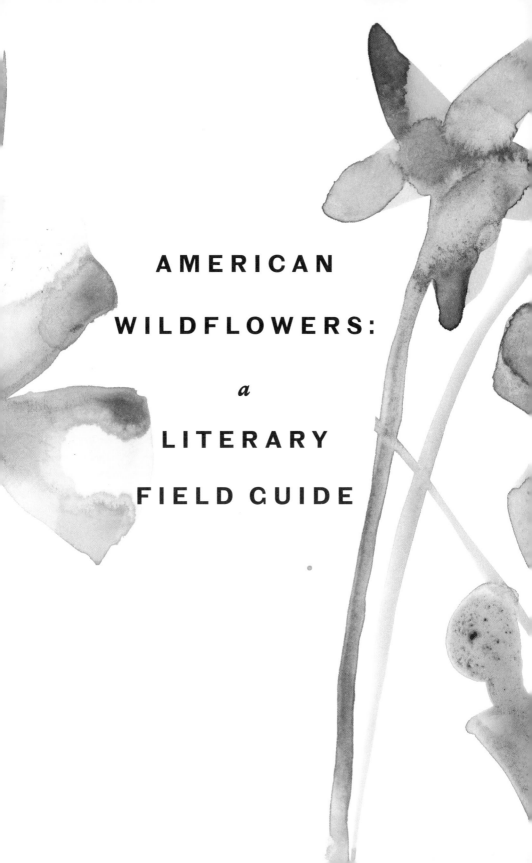

AMERICAN
WILDFLOWERS:

a

LITERARY
FIELD GUIDE

Snowdrop
Galanthus nivalis

Snowdrops

Spring comes forward as a late-winter confection, and I cannot decide
if it advances a philosophy of meekness or daring.

This year's snowdrops: is it that they are spare, and have a slightly
fraught lucidity, or are they proof that pain, too, can be ornate?

Even a propped skull is human nature. And its humor is monstrous,
rich with an existence that owes nothing to anyone.

Fat little pearls against the ice, battering softly, try even fewer
qualities—

To say that you love someone or something *to death* is to hover around
the draw of irrevocability.

More faith is asked of us, a trained imagination against the ice-white.

Work

I won't look at her.
My body's been one
Solid motion from sunrise,
Leaning into the lawnmower's
Roar through pine needles
& crabgrass. Tiger-colored
Bumblebees nudge pale blossoms
But I won't look.
Her husband's outside Oxford,
Mississippi, bidding on miles
Of timber. I wonder if he's buying
Faulkner's ghost, if he might run
Into Colonel Sartoris
Along some dusty road.
Their teenage daughter & son sped off
An hour ago in a red Corvette
For the tennis courts,
& the cook, Roberta,
Only works a half day
Saturdays. This antebellum house
Looms behind oak & pine
Like a secret, as quail
Flash through branches.
I won't look at her. Nude
On a hammock among elephant ears
& ferns, a pitcher of lemonade
Sweating like our skin.
Afternoon burns on the pool
Till everything's blue,
Till I hear Johnny Mathis
Beside her like a whisper.
I work all the quick hooks

Of light, the same unbroken
Rhythm my father taught me
Years ago: Always give
A man a good day's labor.
I won't look. The engine
Pulls me like a dare.
Scent of honeysuckle
Sings black sap through mystery,
Taboo, law, creed, what kills
A fire that is its own heart
Burning open the mouth.
But I won't look
At the insinuation of buds
Tipped with cinnabar.
I'm here, as if I never left,
Stopped in this garden,
Drawn to some Lotus-eater. Pollen
Explodes, but I only smell
Gasoline & oil on my hands,
& can't say why there's this bed
Of crushed narcissus
As if gods wrestled here.

LYDIA DAVIS

Cohabitating with Beautiful Weeds

Searching a bookstore, in late spring, for yet another book about the art and science of permaculture gardening, a new but tenacious obsession that had begun some weeks earlier and continues still, I found among the small collection of garden and plant books not what I was looking for, but three I was happy to have. One thenceforth became an unexpected but constant companion as the seasons unfolded, and that was a collection of Henry David Thoreau's wild plant observations, excerpted from his journals and accompanied by helpful line drawings. The entries are arranged chronologically by the day of the year.

My interest in permaculture and, more generally, what the small parcel of earth that makes up my yard and gardens might yield, both on its own and with some ambitiously coordinated planting, had awoken in me a fresh interest in the wild plants that were already at home here. In tandem with my busy planning and acquiring of nursery stock, I had begun identifying each wild plant as it came up, consulting, usually, all eight of the rather motley guides stacked by my end of the sofa. I had never paid as much attention to these plants as I did this year: how they kept coming, in overlapping relays, in all their variety of forms, and remained usually for weeks, sometimes months. I admired their independence, their decisiveness; how each one, as Thoreau says, "waited a whole year and then blossomed the instant it was ready and the earth was ready for it." And the fact that the modest white sweet clover or melilot, for instance, aka honey lotus, also bloomed in Europe and Asia – that a plant so local, preferring just this patch of soil, here and now, in my yard, and there and then in Thoreau's neighborhood, is yet so widespread, coming up just as deliberately thousands of miles away.

Thoreau would walk through his native Concord landscape (150 miles east of where I am, on more or less the same latitude) with a small diary in his breast pocket, which he often consulted, and with perhaps a sprig of pennyroyal in another pocket for its scent, covering as much as 20 to 30 miles in a day and carrying home specimens in his straw hat to put in water on his writing desk. He had long taken an interest in botany, and he grew so thoroughly knowledgeable over the decade or so before his death in 1862 that he came to be regarded as the town botanist. The diary excerpts cover most of these years.

What emerges from his entries, besides his close observations of wild flowers, trees, grasses, sedges, and shrubs, is the features of the landscape where he walked – the rivers and ponds, the railroad causeway, powder mill, churchyard, almshouse, cattle that stood in the shallows under the bridge, one man's swamp, another's orchard; the Wheeler meadow, Tuttle's sluice, Lee's cliff, Anthony's corner, Hubbard's grove, Sted Buttrick's field, Mrs. Hoar's garden, Tarbell's watering place, Emerson's muck heap.

What also emerge are the differences between Thoreau's Concord and our own rural neighborhoods nowadays: habitats for wild flowers and creatures were far more intact then. Swamps were not as often drained, roads not paved – offering puddles wet and dry – grassy road margins and orchards not mowed; there were cracked foundations and old outbuildings, smaller lawns, less tidiness in general. And masses of blooms were loud with insects, not mostly silent as they often are now. One May, Thoreau reports that the sugar maple blossoms on the common "resound with bees." In a favorite bass tree, they and the other insects are so loud, it is, at a distance, "like the sound of a waterfall," and, close up, "like a factory full of looms."

There are few plants in my garden crowded enough with bees for even a modest "susurrus": this year, in the herb garden, a small flowering onion with its little globes of bluish white; and, last year, when I let it spring up all over the vegetable rows, the slender sprawling arugula (rocket). Thoreau was not fearful of deer ticks, as we are with good reason here, now, as he pushed his way through a field "yellowed with a Xerxean army of *Solidago nemoralis*" (gray goldenrod); he did not hesitate to lie down under a shrub or tree.

There was a more somber reason for my interest in wild plants this year. I felt more acutely now, as increasingly grim news came in every day, that the generosity of the earth and the seasons, even in one yard, should not be ignored or carelessly dismissed, but consciously valued and noted. Thoreau lamented that so few people noticed the wildflowers. It is hard to miss the beauty that flashes by the car window: the pastel phlox, the wild roses with their sweet fragrance, the dark orange day lilies and blue chicory, the white dogwoods in the woods. But in my own yard I had ignored the more humble volunteers in the waste places, had uprooted pretty intruders from the flowerbeds, and trampled, in the lawn, the drifts of ghostly white *Antennaria* (called pussy-toes in my books and admired by Thoreau as mouse-ears).

This year, I observed the first sign of a new arrival and watched for the flowering that would help me learn the plant's name – not always easy. I would find out its properties and uses, record all this in my notebook, and then usually leave the plant undisturbed where it stood, in that particular spot of its own choosing – dry or moist, shady or part-shady or sunny, in just the kind of soil it preferred.

Now, I was as moved as Thoreau was by these "cohabitants," as he calls them, "of this part of the planet"; moved "that this weed should have withheld itself so long, biding its appointed time, and now without fail be coming up all over the land."

Every wild flower, or almost every one that I found in my books, has a useful function for humans, insects, or birds. The Queen Anne's lace is a good insectary, and its root is edible; the monarch butterfly likes the goldenrod for protein before migrating south; the seed-head of the dandelion is said to be eaten by the wren and I have seen three goldfinches at once feeding from the fleabane's spent flower heads; the leaves of the New Jersey tea shrub can be brewed.

The pokeweed (*Phytolacca americana*) that unexpectedly reappeared in a corner of my vegetable garden this year also came up on Ebenezer Hubbard's hillside, where it "quite dazzled" Thoreau with its "purple stems gracefully drooping," with its vigor, its brilliant color, its eccentric habit of displaying all stages – blossoms, green fruit, and ripe fruit – at once. I thought I had dug it out last year.

A gardening friend said, Get rid of it – remember how large it grows. But I hesitated, given my new interest in the potentials of these volunteers. I turned to my books, and to Thoreau. It is poisonous to humans in parts, though early in the season the emerging shoots can be cooked and eaten like asparagus. It is a host plant for the giant leopard moth, and its spikes of sweet-smelling white blossoms provide nectar for other insects, as well as for the ruby-throated hummingbird. What Thoreau describes as its "great drooping cylindrical racemes of *blackish* purple berries" are a rich food for the birds before their fall migration; for those birds that do not leave, the berries remain until late winter.

And so I left it in place. It grew to be about ten feet high and five or six feet wide, but still looked handsome as summer turned to fall, and did no harm even to the Swiss chard that grew deep in shadow by its feet.

In mid-June appeared the ox-eye daisy, the daisy fleabane, and the birdfoot trefoil. In July appeared the modest, spindly enchanter's nightshade (*Circaea lutetiana* or *C. quadrisorleata* or *C. canadensis*), also mentioned by Thoreau: such a romantic common name, and so much nomenclature, I thought, for an inconspicuous flower. It came up tightly massed under the crab-apple tree and I let it be: I was hoping to recreate the dense toad habitat that I had, last year, over-enthusiastically weeded away. By September, however, I realized that it was the same bothersome plant that every fall produced small burrs the size of peppercorns that stuck tenaciously to any fabric and were so tiresome to pick off.

Most of the plants I identified remained for a surprisingly long time – the hawkweed is gone, but the fleabane is still standing tall; the wide-faced ox-eye daisy did not stay long, but the yellow-blossomed celandine, with its deeply, prettily indented leaves – the same that Thoreau observed growing along Deacon Brown's fence – lasted many weeks by the east wall of the house before its leaves yellowed.

With Thoreau, I saw signs, even in July, of autumn coming, in the sunflowers, the crickets, the enlarged apples, and the goldenrod beginning. "The fall," he says, "begins with the first heat of July." And, he goes on, evoking the constant procession of the seasons (as well as introducing me to two prized new words), "It is one long acclivity from winter to midsummer – and another long declivity from midsummer to winter."

In mid-September, one year, Thoreau thought nature "had about wound up her affairs." But then he saw the small white aster (*Aster tradescanti*) crowding the ditches "with millions of little stars," as I, too, saw a host of it in the herb garden near the rugosas and flowering quince, and a few more under the white pines.

The evenings and mornings are cold now. The end of summer took me by surprise, absorbed as I was in the unreeling of the plant succession. Thoreau chose to believe (he said one September 24) that as long as the milkweed matured its seed, preparing for the following spring, the world could not come to an end. It would be nice to imagine, as he did, that "Summer clenches hands with summer under the snow."

Queen Anne's Lace

Unseemly as a marvelous an astral renegade
now luminous and startling (rakish)
at the top of its thin/ordinary stem
the flower overpowers or outstares me
as I walk by thinking *weeds* and *poison*
ivy, bush and *fern* or *runaway grass:*
You (where are you, really?) never leave me
to my boredom: numb as I might like to be.
Repeatedly
you do revive
arouse alive

a suffering.

Queen Anne's lace
Daucus carota

WILLIAM CARLOS WILLIAMS

from "Spring and All"

I
By the road to the contagious hospital
under the surge of the blue
mottled clouds driven from the
northeast—a cold wind. Beyond, the
waste of broad, muddy fields
brown with dried weeds, standing and fallen

patches of standing water
the scattering of tall trees

All along the road the reddish
purplish, forked, upstanding, twiggy
stuff of bushes and small trees
with dead, brown leaves under them
leafless vines—

Lifeless in appearance, sluggish
dazed spring approaches—

They enter the new world naked,
cold, uncertain of all
save that they enter. All about them
the cold, familiar wind—

Now the grass, tomorrow
the stiff curl of wildcarrot leaf

One by one objects are defined—
It quickens: clarity, outline of a leaf

One by one objects are defined—
It quickens: clarity, outline of a leaf

But now the stark dignity of
entrance—Still, the profound change
has come upon them: rooted, they
grip down and begin to awaken

Wild Flowers

This has been and is yet a great season for wild flowers; oceans of them
line the roads through the woods, border the edges of the water-runlets,
grow all along the old fences, and are scatter'd in profusion over the fields.
An eight-petal'd blossom of gold-yellow clear and bright, with a brown
tuft in the middle, nearly as large as a silver half-dollar, is very common;
yesterday on a long drive I noticed it thickly lining the borders of the
brooks everywhere. Then there is a beautiful weed cover'd with blue
flowers, (the blue of the old Chinese teacups treasur'd by our grand-aunts,)
I am continually stopping to admire—a little larger than a dime, and very
plentiful. White, however, is the prevailing color. The wild carrot I have
spoken of; also the fragrant life-everlasting. But there are all hues and
beauties, especially on the frequent tracts of half-open scrub-oak and
dwarf-cedar hereabout—wild asters of all colors. Notwithstanding the
frost-touch the hardy little chaps maintain themselves in all their bloom.
The tree-leaves, too, some of them are beginning to turn yellow or drab or
dull green. The deep wine-color of the sumachs and gum-trees is already
visible, and the straw-color of the dog-wood and beech. Let me give the
names of some of these perennial blossoms and friendly weeds I have
made acquaintance with hereabout one season or another in my walks:

> wild azalea,
> dandelions,
> wild honeysuckle,
> yarrow,
> wild roses,
> coreopsis,
> golden rod,
> wild pea,
> larkspur,
> woodbine,
> early crocus,
> elderberry,

sweet flag, (great patches of it,)
poke-weed,
creeper, trumpet-flower,
sun-flower,
scented marjoram,
chamomile,
snakeroot,
violets,
Solomon's seal,
clematis,
sweet balm,
bloodroot,
mint, (great plenty,)
swamp magnolia,
wild geranium,
milk-weed,
wild heliotrope,
wild daisy, (plenty,)
burdock,
wild chrysanthemum.

Milkweed
Asclepias syriaca

what woman

What woman talks to weeds,
who walks the gardens
like a jailer.
It's nearly fall. The few flowers,
summer-ridden, want only to die back,
go home, the earth flat as a grave,
the snows stalked windless.
Fields. Light are the dead, and careless.
There thistle, milkweed, goldenrod crushed under boot
or in my glove
smelled almost of days
the hard walks across that which would not lie down,
such bitter walks, such bitter sadness.
A widow talks to weeds
whose feet I knelt before and wept last spring,
oh anything grown green,
and picked fistfuls of dandelions,
this side the veil the great betrayers,
and spent my purse on seeds,
too early sewn, too early planted, dead
by June. And then the feast!
Armfuls of light, the season first and wildly blossoming.
What was it for?
A cemetery lot mindless of absence,
as wrenched as it's glorious.

Butterflyweed

The butterfly that
named the weed
drank there, Monarch,
scrolled, medallioned—
his wings lifted close
in pale underwing salute

occasionally would
with tense evenness
open down

hinged coffers
lawned against the sun:
anchored in
dream, I could hardly
fall when earth
dropped and looped away.

DEVIN JOHNSTON

Domestic Scenes

A spray of toothbrushes,
stems in a mug:
a family portrait.

*

In dirty light, disordered pairs
of snow boots and galoshes
line the welcome mat:

the stragglers have come home
and passed inward on stocking feet
to the apartment's hidden core.

*

With eyes shut, the child
twirls on the kitchen tile,
a whirling dervish
turning continuously
toward herself
like the spindle
on a phonograph
until she wobbles,
drunk with vertigo;
another song
about a baby
and a bottle
ends with a crash.

*

Alone in his room
the youngest one
dreams of whatever
takes place while
he sleeps—the flutter
of a distant storm,

Milkweed
Asclepias syriaca

the clink of cups,
a midnight visitor—
and wakes to tell
what we already know.

*

Nothing that we plant thrives here.
Dead wood advances down
our rose stems year by year.
And yet the honeyvine, a weed,
curls around the base
and climbs with mindless mastery
to reach a waving height
free of thorns and shade.
There, it hangs an anglepod
to feed on the morning light.

JEFFREY YANG

Lechuguilla

It can take twenty years
for the agave lechuguilla
to bloom and seed, maize-
yellow anthers, perched
like commas atop crimson
filaments, hang ten in the air
around the lone
panicle
stalk, giant
hummingbird tongue
bends to sky
from the mouth of a spiny
star body, rooted to earth, wildly
suckering rosettes, fruit sets once
a lifetime, the lechuguilla
flowers for maybe four days
before it dies
only to be
reborn
as a clone
off-
shoots choice toxic juice
for javelinas

If I Should Come Upon Your House Lonely in the West Texas Desert

I will swing my lasso of headlights
across your front porch,

let it drop like a rope of knotted light
at your feet.

While I put the car in park,
you will tie and tighten the loop

of light around your waist—
and I will be there with the other end

wrapped three times
around my hips horned with loneliness.

Reel me in across the glow-throbbing sea
of greenthread, bluestem prickly poppy,

the white inflorescence of yucca bells,
up the dust-lit stairs into your arms.

If you say to me, *This is not your new house
but I am your new home,*

I will enter the door of your throat,
hang my last lariat in the hallway,

build my altar of best books on your bedside table,
turn the lamp on and off, on and off, on and off.

I will lie down in you.
Eat my meals at the red table of your heart.

Each steaming bowl will be, *Just right.*
I will eat it all up,

break all your chairs to pieces.
If I try running off into the deep-purpling scrub brush,

you will remind me,
There is nowhere to go if you are already here,

and pat your hand on your lap lighted
by the topazion lux of the moon through the window,

say, *Here, Love, sit here*—when I do,
I will say, *And here I still am.*

Until then, Where are you? What is your address?
I am hurting. I am riding the night

on a full tank of gas and my headlights
are reaching out for something.

Yucca bell
Yucca arkansana

Wednesday June 11th, 1806

All our hunters were out this morning by daylight; <u>Labuish</u> and <u>Gibson</u> only proved successful, the former killed a black bear of the brown speceis and a very large buck, the latter also killed a fine fat buck.   five of the Indians also turned out and hunted untill noon, when they returned without having killed anything; at three P. M. the left us on their return to ther villages.   previous to their departure one of our men exchanged an indifferent horse with one of them for a very good one.   in the evening our hunters resumed the chase; as game has become scarce and shye near our camp they were directed to hunt at a greater distance and therefore set our prepared to remain <out> all night and make a mornings hunt in grounds not recently frequented. Whitehouse returned this morning to our camp on the Kooskooske in surch of his horse.—   As I have had frequent occasion to mention the plant which the Choppunish call quawmash I shall here give a more particular discription of that plant and the mode of preparing it for food as practiced by the Chopunnish and others in the vicinity of the Rocky Mountains with whom it forms much the greatest portion of their subsistence.   we have never met with this plant but in or adjacent to a piny or fir timbered country, and there always in the open grounds and glades; in the Columbian vally and near the coast it is to be found in small quantities and inferior in size to that found in this neighbourhood and in the high rich flatts and vallees within the rocky mountains.   it delights in a black rich moist soil, and even grows most luxuriantly where the land remains from 6 to nine inches under water untill the seed are nearly perfect which in this neighbourhood or on these flats is about the last of this month. neare the river where I had an opportunity of observing it the seed were begining to ripen on the 9th inst. and the soil was nearly dry.   it seems devoted to it's particular soil and situation, and you will seldom find it more than a few feet from the inundated soil tho' within it's limits it grows very closely in short almost as much so as the bulbs will permit; the radix is a tunicated bulb, much the consistence shape and appearance of the onion, glutanous or somewhat <slymy> when chewed and almost tasteless and without smell in it's unprepared state; it is white except the thin or outer tunicated scales which are few black and not succulent; this bulb is from the size of a nutmeg to that of a hens egg and most commonly of an intermediate size or about as large as an onion of one years growth from the seed. the radicles are numerous, reather large, white, flexable, succulent and diverging. the foliage consists of from one to four seldom five radicale, linear sessile and revolute pointed leaves; they are from 12 to 18 inches in length and from 1 to ¾ of an inch in widest part which is near the middle; the uper disk is somewhat groved of a pale green and marked it's whole length with a number of small longitudinal channels; the under disk is a deep glossy green and smooth. the leaves sheath the peduncle and each other as high as the surface of the earth or about 2 inches; they are more succulent than the grasses and less so than most of the lillies hyesinths &c.— the peduncle is soletary, proceeds from the root, is columner, smooth leafless and rises to the hight of 2 or 2½ feet. it supports from 10 to forty flowers which are each supported by seperate footstalk of ½ an inch in length scattered without order on the upper portion of the peduncle. the calix is a partial involucret situated at the base of the footstalk of each flower on the peduncle; it is long thin and begins to decline as soon as the corolla expands. the corolla consists of six long oval, obtusly pointed skye blue or water coloured petals, each about 1 inch in length; the corolla is regular as to the form and size of the petals but irregular as to their position, five of them are placed near ech other pointing upward while one stands horizantally or pointing downwards, they are inserted with a short claw on the extremity of the footstalk at the base of the germ; the corolla is of course inferior; it is also shriveling, and continues untill the seeds are perfect. The stamens are perfect, six in number; the filaments each elivate an anther, near their base are flat on the inside and rounded on the outer terminate in a subulate point, are bowed or bent upwards, inserted on the inner side and on the base of the claws of the petals, below the germ, are equal both with rispect to themselves and the corolla, smooth & membraneous. the Anther is oblong, obtusely pointed, 2 horned or forked at one end and furrowed longitudinally with four channels, the upper and lower of which seem almost to divide it into two loabs, incumbent patent, membranous, very short, naked, two valved and fertile with pollen, which last is of a yellow colour—. the anther in a few hours after the corolla unfoalds, bursts, discharges it's pollen and becomes very minute and shrivled; the above discription of the anther is therefore to be understood of it at the moment of it's first appearance. the pistillum is only one, of which, the germ is triangular reather swolen on the sides, smooth superior, sessile, pedicelled, short in proportion to the corolla atho' wide or bulky; the style is very long or longer than the stamens, simple, cilindrical, bowed or bent upwards, placed on the top of the germ, membranous shrivels and falls off when the pericarp has obtained its full size. the stigma is three cleft very minute, & pubescent. the pericarp is a capsule, triangular, oblong, obtuse, and trilocular with three longitudinal valves. the seed so far as I could judge are numerous not very minute and globelar.— soon after the seeds are mature the peduncle and foliage of this plant perishes, the grownd becomes dry or nearly so and the root encreases in size and shortly becomes fit for use; this happens about the middle of July when the natives begin to collect it for use which they continue untill the leaves of the plant attain some size in the spring of the year. when they have collected a considerable quantity of these roots or 20 30 bushels which they readily do by means of stick sharpened at one end, they dig away the surface of the earth forming a circular concavity of 2½ feet in the center and 10 feet in diameter; they next collect a parsel of split dry wood with which they cover this bason in the grown perhaps a foot thick, they next collect a large parsel of stones of about 4 or 6 lbs. weight which are placed on the dry wood; fire is then set to the wood which birning heats the stones; when the fire has subsided and the stones are sufficiently heated which are nearly a red heat, they are adjusted in such manner in the whole as to form as level a surface as pissible, a small quantity of earth is sprinkled over the stones and a layer of grass about an inch thick is put over the stones; the roots, which have been previously devested of the black or outer coat and radicles which rub off easily with the fingers, are now laid on in a conical pile, are then covered with a layer of grass about 2 or 3 inches thick; water is now thrown on the summit of the pile and passes through the roots and to the hot stones at bottom; some water is allso poared arround the edges of the hole and also finds its way to the hot stones; as soon as they discover from the quantity of steem which issues that the water has found its way generally to the hot stones, they cover the roots and grass over with earth to the debth of four inches and then build a fire of dry wood all over the coninical mound which they continue to renew through the course of the night or for ten or 12 hours after which it is suffered to cool two or three hours when the earth and grass are removed and the roots thus sweated and cooked with steam are taken out, and most commonly exposed to the sun on scaffoalds untill they become dry, when they are black and of a sweet agreeable flavor. these roots are fit for use when first taken from the pitt, are soft of a sweetish tast and much the consistency of a roasted onion; but if they are suffered to remain in bulk 24 hour after being cooked they spoil. if the design is to make bread or cakes of these roots they undergo a second process of baking being previously pounded after the fist baking between two stones untill they are reduced to the consistency of dough and then rolled in grass in cakes of eight or ten lbs are returned to the sweat intermixed with fresh roots in order that the steam may get freely to these loaves of bread. when taken out the second time the women make up this dough into cakes of various shapes and sizes usually from ½ to ¾ of an inch thick and expose it on sticks to dry in the sun, or place it over the smoke of their fires.— the bread this prepared if kept free from moisture will keep sound for a great length of time. this bread or the dryed roots are frequently eaten alone by the natives without further preparation, and when they have them in abundance they form an ingredient in almost every dish they prepared. this root is palateable but disagrees with me in every shape I have ever used it.—

Solomon's seal
Polygonatum biflorum

Too Bright to See

Just before dark the light gets dark. Violet
where my hands pull weeds around the Solomon's seals.
I see with difficulty what before was easy.
Perceive what I saw before
but with more tight effort. I am moon
to what I am doing and what I was.
It is a real beauty that I lived
and dreamed would be, now know
but never then. Can tell by looking hard,
feeling which is weed and what is form.
My hands are intermediary. Neither lover
nor liar. Sweet being, if you are anywhere that hears,
come quickly. I weep, face set, no tears, mouth open.

RICHARD WILBUR

Signatures

False Solomon's Seal –
So called because it lacks a
Star-scar on the heel,

And ends its arched stem
In a spray of white florets,
Later changing them

To a red, not blue,
Spatter of berries – is no
Falser than the true.

Solomon, who raised
The temple and wrote the song,
Wouldn't have dispraised

This bowed, graceful plant
So like an aspergillum,
Nor its variant

With root duly scarred,
Whose bloom-hung stem is like the
Bell-branch of a bard.

Liking best to live
In the deep woods whose light is
Most contemplative,

Both are often found
Where mandrake, wintergreen, and
Dry leaves strew the ground,

Their heads inclining
Toward the dark earth, one blessing
And one divining.

Solomon's seal
Polygonatum biflorum

Sunflower
Helianthus spp.

ALLEN GINSBERG

Sunflower Sutra

I walked on the banks of the tincan banana dock and sat down under
the huge shade of a Southern Pacific locomotive to look at the sunset over the box house hills and cry.

Jack Kerouac sat beside me on a busted rusty iron pole, companion, we
thought the same thoughts of the soul, bleak and blue and sad-eyed,
surrounded by the gnarled steel roots of trees of machinery.

The oily water on the river mirrored the red sky, sun sank on top of final Frisco peaks, no fish in that stream, no hermit in those mounts,
just ourselves rheumy-eyed and hung-over like old bums on the
riverbank, tired and wily.

Look at the Sunflower, he said, there was a dead gray shadow against
the sky, big as a man, sitting dry on top of a pile of ancient sawdust—

—I rushed up enchanted—it was my first sunflower, memories of
Blake—my visions—Harlem

and Hells of the Eastern rivers, bridges clanking Joes Greasy Sand-
wiches, dead baby carriages, black treadless tires forgotten and un-
retreaded, the poem of the riverbank, condoms & pots, steel knives,
nothing stainless, only the dank muck and the razor-sharp artifacts
passing into the past—

and the gray Sunflower poised against the sunset, crackly bleak and
dusty with the smut and smog and smoke of olden locomotives in
its eye—

corolla of bleary spikes pushed down and broken like a battered
crown, seeds fallen out of its face, soon-to-be-toothless mouth of
sunny air, sunrays obliterated on its hairy head like a dried wire
spiderweb,

leaves stuck out like arms out of the stem, gestures from the sawdust
root, broke pieces of plaster fallen out of the black twigs, a dead fly
in its ear,

Unholy battered old thing you were, my sunflower O my soul, I loved
you then!

The grime was no man's grime but death and human locomotives,
all that dress of dust, that veil of darkened railroad skin, that smog of
    cheek, that eyelid of black mis'ry, that sooty hand or phallus or pro-
    tuberance of artificial worse-than-dirt—industrial—modern—all
    that civilization spotting your crazy golden crown—
and those blear thoughts of death and dusty loveless eyes and ends
    and withered roots below, in the home-pile of sand and sawdust,
    rubber dollar bills, skin of machinery, the guts and innards of the
    weeping coughing car, the empty lonely tincans with their rusty
    tongues alack, what more could I name, the smoked ashes of some
    cock cigar, the cunts of wheelbarrows and the milky breasts of cars,
    wornout asses out of chairs & sphincters of dynamos—all these
entangled in your mummied roots—and you there standing before me
    in the sunset, all your glory in your form!
A perfect beauty of a sunflower! a perfect excellent lovely sunflower
    existence! a sweet natural eye to the new hip moon, woke up alive
    and excited grasping in the sunset shadow sunrise golden monthly
    breeze!
How many flies buzzed round you innocent of your grime, while you
    cursed the heavens of the railroad and your flower soul?
Poor dead flower? when did you forget you were a flower? when did
    you look at your skin and decide you were an impotent dirty old
    locomotive? the ghost of a locomotive? the specter and shade of a
    once powerful mad American locomotive?
You were never no locomotive, Sunflower, you were a sunflower!
And you Locomotive, you are a locomotive, forget me not!
So I grabbed up the skeleton thick sunflower and stuck it at my side
    like a scepter,
and deliver my sermon to my soul, and Jack's soul too, and anyone
    who'll listen,
—We're not our skin of grime, we're not dread bleak dusty imageless
    locomotives, we're golden sunflowers inside, blessed by our own
    seed & hairy naked accomplishment-bodies growing into mad black
    formal sunflowers in the sunset, spied on by our own eyes under the
    shadow of the mad locomotive riverbank sunset Frisco hilly tincan
    evening sitdown vision.
                                                —Berkeley, 1955

Sunflower

When Mother and I first had the do-not-
resuscitate conversation, she lifted her head,
like a drooped sunflower, and said,
"Those dying always want to stay."
Months later, on the kitchen table,
Mars red gladiolus sang *Ode to Joy*,
and we listened. House flies swooped and veered
around us, like the Holy Spirit. "Nature
is always expressing something human,"
Mother commented, her mouth twisting,
as I plucked whiskers from around it.
"Yes, no, please." Tenderness was not yet dust.
Mother sat up, rubbed her eyes drowsily, her breaths
like breakers, the living man the beach.

Oh Giant Flowers

Every day I walk past the house
with the blue morning glories
covering the walls and the four sunflowers

growing in front, their tall stalks
bent over, and have to stop
and touch the dark centers

almost the size of a face.
It began the morning I awoke before you.
The blanket was wrapped tightly around you

and the sun came through the window
on your face. I couldn't stand
to see you that way. I looked outside.

The leaves red, yellow, and finishing.
A squirrel was in the yard rummaging for food
in the grass, the apple tree letting go

its bruised fruit; preparations had to be made.
How could you sleep with so much sun on your face?
When I left I didn't know where I was going.

There was so much color it seemed as if the whole
sky would ignite. The light loves the earth so much
it has to burn to prove it. Oh giant flowers,

when I came across you I wanted to bury my face
in your huge petals, I wanted to lie down
in the grass beneath you.

GARY PAUL NABHAN

The Exile and the Holy Anomaly:
Wild American Sunflowers

I.

Most people go to Napa County, California, for the wine, not for the oil
that can be pressed from one of the world's more obscure wild sunflowers.
Going north from the fertile viticultural valleys, the wine-tasting traffic
gradually thins out as narrow roads wind into the Inner Coast Range.
I was surprised to find it so unpopulated and so little of it cultivated.
It struck me that northern Napa County's dwarf chaparral had its own
backwoods charm. I sensed that this charm is geological as much as it
is botanical.

Because of the glistening, soapy serpentine rocks that form chunks
of this range, plants face mineral problems here—too much magnesium
relative to calcium, too much nickel, chromium, and cobalt. This serpentine stretch of coastal mountain range is relatively stark, with stunted
shrubs and exposed, thin soils. The trees and shrubs that take to these
slopes are a peculiar mix: the leather oak whose leaves curl under at the
edges, the gangly Digger pine, Sargent cypress, chamise, and a rather
localized manzanita. Many of the plants are "edaphic endemics," or specialists that have come upon ways to deal with the problems peculiar to
being rooted in a serpentine setting.

While serpentine soils and outcrops cover less than one percent
of California, geobotanist Arthur Kruckeberg has counted over 180
kinds of plants supported solely by these substrates, notwithstanding
the difficulty of their getting a balanced ration of minerals. It is this kind
of stimulus that drives the divergence of plants into new forms, which,
when isolated in time and space, develop into distinct species. But alas,
as Kruckeberg vigorously reminds us, serpentine also attracts miners of
gold, quicksilver, nickel, asbestos, and magnesite. Mining operations may
have a disastrous impact on rare plants, because these plants target such
a limited environmental type as their turf.

Within one such mining zone along the Inner Coast Range, I found
wild annual sunflowers growing below remnant serpentine outcrops and

on the edges of eroded, mineral-stained gullies. As I looked closely at these sunflowers, I could see features distinct from those of their more common roadside relatives. I knew in advance that if I found sunflowers with narrow leaves and bracts, plus tiny achenes on smallish flowers with few petal-like rays, I could be sure I had stumbled upon a special serpentine form. While a few botanists in the past have considered these serpentine-loving sunflowers to be merely stunted variants of a common California weed, *Helianthus bolanderi*, Loren Rieseberg has recently estimated from chloroplast DNA studies that the weed may have diverged from the serpentine sunflowers as much as three million years ago. Because it has so many unique genetic characteristics, the serpentine-adapted form is considered by many botanists and geneticists to be a fully distinct species, *Helianthus exilis*.

Exiles they are, for gold mining operations have already extirpated thirteen of the sixty-six sunflower populations known previously in this area. Seeds were collected from at least four of these populations before recent land clearing. The mining company itself has helped to fence two of the remaining sunflower stands and has agreed to avoid damaging certain additional places where this plant and other serpentine endemics grow.

Despite the intensity of mining activity, there may be no immediate danger that the exiled sunflower species will become extinct. Though the species may survive, some biologists nevertheless lament the loss of several of its populations. Rick Kesseli of the University of California at Davis devoted a good part of a year to studying the genetic variation of seed populations taken near the mines. "*Helianthus exilis* is very variable, both within and between populations," Kesseli said. He added that "some populations of it have unique alleles," referring to the alternate forms of genes that are responsible for the passing on of particular traits to a plant's progeny.

Kesseli's mentor, world-famous geneticist Subodh Jain, also underscores the importance of each exiled sunflower population. Dr. Jain's decade-long interest in this species is due in part to the unusually valuable genetic traits found within the populations in the vicinity of the mines.

"There is unique fatty acid stability in *exilis* that we can transfer into cultivated sunflowers to improve their oilseed quality," Jain says. Whereas the percentage of linoleic acid in the seed of most sunflowers varies greatly in response to night temperatures during growth, the percentage in the seed of *exilis* hardly varies. And in 1977, Jain and his students also discovered that *exilis* seeds contain a high percentage of linoleic acid in exiled sunflower's seed. Since then, more than twenty other kinds of wild sunflowers have been screened for this characteristic. None has surpassed *exilis* in linoleic fatty acid scores.

At first glance, this may seem to be a fact of interest only to a biochemist with a penchant for greasy subjects. But a superior linoleic content gives a vegetable oil a high ratio of polyunsaturated to saturated fats. Diets in which polyunsaturated oils prevail over saturated fats with high cholesterol may prevent heart disease, the greatest single cause of death in Western societies. Since the early 1970s, crop geneticists have been attempting to breed edible oilseeds higher in polyunsaturates in order to reduce atherosclerosis and coronary complications in consumers.

Of all the genetic materials now available to sunflower breeders that could decrease saturated fats in their products, the exiled sunflower is the most outstanding. A former student member of Jain's team, A. M. Olivieri, has recently accomplished the necessary first steps for exiled sunflower gene transfer, using seed stocks he took with him to Padua, Italy. There, he crossed the exiled sunflower with the closely related but distinct species, *Helianthus bolanderi*, a plant widespread in California.

This hybrid shows a few abnormalities, further indicating some evolutionary distance between the two California sunflowers. Nevertheless, fertile seeds were obtained. Olivieri then used progeny from this cross in hand pollinations of cultivated sunflowers, and must now work with their hybrid offspring to assure that the fatty acid stability and high linoleic content have been transferred. Because oil-type sunflowers are grown on over two million acres in the United States today, Olivieri's work will be of great value to farmers as soon as the exiled sunflower genes are fitted into the right commercial cultivar.

II.

As California gold miners drive home from work each day, they pass the remaining stands of the exiled sunflower. Charlie Rogers, a specialist on sunflowers and their associated insects, recalled to me the time he was collecting seeds of *exilis* along the roadside not far from the mine. A truck drove up and a miner stuck his head out of the window.

"Hey man, tell me where I can get a license."

"A license for what?" asked Charlie, continuing his business.

"Are you high or something? Doves! A hunting license. It's dove season! What are you doing there?"

"I'm collecting sunflower seeds," Charlie replied, still moving along through the stand.

"I can't believe my ears! It's dove season, and this guy is hunting sunflowers. You must be high and out of it!" The driver roared off.

If you told these gold miners that the genes from these plants might be more valuable than the precious metal in the ground beneath them, few would immediately believe you. The limp golden rays of the exiled sunflower simply do not provoke the same response in a man as a handful of gold ore. Not many people realize that the sunflower crop, highly dependent upon genes from wild species native to North America, is valued at more than a billion dollars annually.

Nevertheless, the justifications for conserving these sunflowers are not all economic. Joe Callizo, a Napa Valley nurseryman and amateur botanist, loves them because they are unpredictable waifs.

"I have a hunch," Joe muses, "that their seeds are very long-lived in the soil." The exiled sunflowers surprised him one year when they appeared in a spot recently bladed for pipeline construction. Robust, multiheaded annual sunflowers suddenly covered the wounded earth, adding new hues to a landscape long familiar to Joe. "I had been by there all my life. . . . It hadn't been growing all those years, or I would have known it. The color was outstanding."

As a teenager, Joe was impressed by a neighboring farmer's curiosity about the wild plants that volunteered in his fields. Joe recalls how this farmer "would even stop the harvester to climb down to see some odd plant that happened to catch his eye. Later, in college, I learned that the plants which I had seen this farmer examine all had names. What a revelation!"

It was years after his college days that Joe first put name and plant together for *Helianthus exilis*. Since 1983, Joe and his friend Glenn Clifton have been monitoring the status of the exiled sunflower and twenty-five other species of rare plants in close proximity to the gold mining activity. Much of this work has been done voluntarily through a chapter of the California Native Plant Society, which Joe has led. Fearful that the original mining plans would have extirpated over 125 of the 400 populations of the rare plants endemic to serpentine soils of the area, Joe and Glenn offered suggestions for reducing the number destroyed. They tagged plants and flagged the perimeters of populations so that bulldozers could avoid rolling over them when other routes were available. Twice a year, they revisit the sites to assess impending dangers from mining, related erosion, or other factors.

"We have played a chess game with the mining company," Joe admits, as he recalls how certain rare plant stands had to be sacrificed to allow others to be spared. Serpentine seeps where seven or eight rare species grow together have been fenced, and thirty-nine sites continue to be monitored. They have saved nearly fifty populations that would have been obliterated by the original mining scheme. Several of the sunflower stands have survived thanks to their good work.

Joe and Glenn believe that the twenty-five other rare species have just as much right to exist as the more economically valuable *Helianthus exilis*. Their protection efforts do not favor the sunflower over the others, some of which are threatened to a much greater degree. But until the time comes when the general public shares the concerns of Joe Callizo and Glenn Clifton, the potential economic value of this oilseed resource may be a way of deflating one-sided arguments in favor of gold over plants. According to Christine and Robert Prescott-Allen, gene transfer from other wild sunflower species has already resulted in an 88-million-dollar-a-year contribution to the U.S. sunflower industry. There is reason to believe that the work begun with *exilis* by Olivieri and Jain will result in significant benefits in due time.

If such arguments can provide additional incentives for protecting exiled sunflower populations, other rare plants on the same serpentine soils will he saved too. As long as people remain in power who are swayed only by economic arguments, Joe and Glenn cannot afford to dispense with the parable of the sunflower.

Nevertheless, *Helianthus exilis* and other wild sunflowers are not merely economic resources; they are also lifeforms with an intrinsic right to exist. Two wildlife conservationists, Robert and Christine Prescott-Allen have argued that there is no need to deny either the intrinsic or the extrinsic (economic) values of a species. In their book *The First Resource*, they note that "Many aboriginal peoples live with this dichotomy well enough, expressing strong spiritual bonds with the species that feed, clothe, and cure them as well as with those that make no identifiable contribution to their lives. Improving our understanding of how people benefit from wild plants and animals should not impede the development of a sense of companionship with them. Rather, it should increase our sense of obligation to them."

Where the winding roads of the Inner Coast Range weave past a sprinkle of golden-rayed sunflowers amid the tough-leaved chaparral, I hope that the human sense of obligation will grow. If it does, the exiled sunflower may return to survive and thrive in its homeland once more.

III.

If pressed to name where such a sense of cultural responsibility for wild sunflowers is already in place, I can only reply, "Qa'qa wungu."

Below one of the Hopi Mesas, there's a valley called that—in English, "Place of Many Sunflowers." The sunflower referred to has seeds and heads unusually large for a wild species, hence the name *Helianthus anomalus*. Documented as growing around the Mesas for no less than a century, it is known from fewer than twenty-five Utah and Arizona locations, two of them in this valley.

The anomalous sunflower also grows above, on the mesa, in a special place—around the lip of a kiva, the underground ceremonial chamber of the Hopi. Whether it was planted there on purpose, or sprouted there by chance, this rare sunflower has persisted in the midst of the Hopi fields and villages, despite all that has happened with the passage of time. The Hopi relationship with sunflowers here is not merely a passing association, since certain of these Hopi pueblos are among the oldest continuously inhabited villages in North America.

Within these villages, Hopi maidens customarily dance in the Lagon and Oaqol ceremonies during October and November. To prepare for these dances, they gather wild sunflower petals, dry, and then grind them into a yellow powder. They then wet their faces, and the powder is applied to their skin prior to dressing in elaborate costumes for the dance. Their faces glisten like gold. This Hopi gold is gleaned from the anomalous sunflower.

I first saw this sunflower while collecting Indian strains of cultivated sunflowers for the U.S. Department of Agriculture. I had been given a gift of a few seeds of the Hopi blue dye sunflower earlier in the day at one of the villages. Winding down the road on the side of one of the mesas, I decided to pull off and look at the fields below. But between them and where I parked my pickup, I noticed some wild sunflowers growing in a blowout in the sand dunes. I scrambled down to them, picked off a small side branch, and placed it in my plant press. Assuming it was the common weedy *Helianthus annus*, I forgot about it for nearly a year. I was supposed to be collecting seeds of Indian crops, not weeds, although I would occasionally throw a few weedy associates of crops into my press. At that time, despite its affinity to the domesticated sunflowers that I was after, I did not assign any more significance to this wildling than I would have to any other.

During the following year, I received a message from the team of sunflower researchers based at Bushland, Texas. They had been successful in obtaining seed of most sunflower species on the continent, but had unfortunately failed to collect seed of *Helianthus anomalus* in the vicinity of the Hopi Indian Reservation. Charlie Rogers wrote me that he had seen "only a single glistening plant from the highway below the big mesas." Aware that I had collected domesticated sunflowers there, he asked if I was willing to go up and search for seeds of this rare wild species. Before I followed through on the request, I checked the herbarium specimen I had made the season before and discovered that I had collected the anomalous sunflower without realizing it. Remembering the location, I agreed to return for seed.

My next trip up to the mesas was during the fall harvest time. Fortunately, a Hopi farmer happened to be out in the field closest to the few sunflowers I had seen the year before. As l walked toward him to ask if it was all right to collect some seed there, I noticed that there were even more wild sunflowers growing on the field edges.

I explained what I had hoped to do, and asked who worked the fields. The man explained that most of the sunflowers were on the edge of his cousin's fields this year, but that it seemed all right for me to take a few seeds from each of the plants around there. He recalled that they formerly grew above the fields, on the snakeweed-covered slopes of the mesa. There, the sunflowers had been so abundant when he was young that he and other Hopi children would regularly scramble through the "tunnels" between their overhanging branches. Whenever they came up around his field, he let them be.

This was curious to me, since his annual crops and his orchard in the sand dunes were relatively weed-free. "Why do you hoe out most weeds, but not this one?" I asked him.

"The place is really named after those sunflowers, so that's why I leave them there," the Hopi farmer answered.

"I'm glad you do," I replied. "There are people in other parts of the world who are interested in that sunflower."

Perhaps because he sometimes grew domesticated dye sunflowers, or because he was generally interested in plants, the farmer tolerated my seed collection and measurement of various sunflower volunteers in his fields. Over the following four years, we would see each other seasonally, as I came up to the mesas to bring native crop seeds to friends, and to keep an eye on this and other sunflower stands. Whenever we sat down for coffee, piki, or a slice of watermelon, the farmer and I would talk of many things: his katsina carvings, our gardens, old paperback novels, and travels. And when the wild sunflower cropped up in our conversations, I would always try to express my gratitude not only for the chance to see it, but for its continued presence.

Over those years, I watched the number of anomalous sunflowers in his field grow from eighteen to over three hundred individual plants. He would leave patches of them out among his crops if they happened to sprout there, while others volunteered on the field margins, or between his peach trees and grapevine hummocks.

These plants tended to be taller and to have more flowerheads than ones from specimens collected earlier in the century from northern Arizona and adjacent Utah. Curiously, the anomalous sunflowers from Hopi fields also have longer ray flowers. These are the golden "petals" that were used in Hopi ceremonies.

Long petals won't make them any more valuable to plant breeders, but their chemical and physiological qualities may be important. *Helianthus anomalus* appears to be a good source of genes for tolerance to drought, heat, and alkalinity, for resistance to lodging, and for high polyunsaturated oil quality. Its potential has not, as yet, been investigated as much as that of other wild sunflowers. However rare, this species is clearly not as threatened as other wild sunflower taxa under observation by the Office of Endangered Species. The protection afforded to the anomalous sunflower by several Hopi farmers is possibly enough to keep it from being officially listed as endangered—even if other populations were to be devastated by livestock, mining, or land clearing. However, if Hopi agriculture ever switched over to pre-emergent herbicides and frequent, deep plowing with tractors, this plant could easily disappear.

There may be no immediate need to worry about the rare anomalous sunflower, thanks to the continuity between generations of Hopi farmers. Still, a dozen other rare taxa urgently require our concern. They constitute nearly a quarter of the species in the genus *Helianthus* in the United States. One distinctive subspecies, the Los Angeles sunflower, already has been extirpated by suburban sprawl and marsh draining. Another species, from the dry lands of New Mexico, has not been relocated for decades, and is presumed to be extinct. The remaining rare species receive little protection in habitat; at best, a few seeds are stuffed into an envelope and considered "saved."

I felt sad when I first realized that so many wild species are threatened. They are so often used as the classic examples of wild plants that contribute to crop improvement. To date, wild *Helianthus* species have been used for powdery mildew and rust resistance, for recessive branching, and for cytoplasmic male sterility, a trait necessary for producing hybrid sunflowers. Resistance to rots, wilts, broomrapes, aphids, sunflower moths, and leafhoppers has been found in wild *Helianthus*, and is being transferred to cultivated sunflowers or to their relatives, the Jerusalem artichokes.

Nonetheless, a number of the rarer species have never been screened for any of their useful features, because of the difficulty of obtaining their seldom collected seeds. And for the species that have been collected for frozen seed storage banks, the populations that remain in the wild may be destroyed without regard to their value. However, it is true that the U.S. Department of Agriculture's collection of wild sunflower species is its best effort so far for *in situ* conservation of a suite of genetic resources native to this continent. The National Plant Genetic Resources Board advisory to the USDA claims that high-tech gene banks are entirely adequate for conserving wild sunflowers and other crop relatives. For some reason, it has shied away from advocating *in situ* conservation of plant genetic resources, even though the USDA administers many lands that harbor species needed by breeders. USDA publications even claim that *in situ* conservation is too unstable and lacking in long-term continuity to be a worthwhile investment.

However risky *in situ* conservation may appear in a time of rapid acculturation and economic upheaval, the USDA could learn a bit about stability from Joe Callizo or a Hopi farmer. Much of the USDA wild sunflower collection assembled at Bushland, Texas, is now being moved, since several of its key caretakers have been reassigned to other research areas. Another wild sunflower project, based for years at the University of California, has been largely dismantled although part of its work continues at Fargo, North Dakota. The brightest students from that program were retrained to work with rice and lettuce when sunflower money dried up on the Davis campus. They cannot obtain jobs with commercial sunflower-breeding firms, for these shy away from long-term, slow-payoff projects. USDA-funded wild sunflower work has been gutted to the point that it can hardly tout its own stability.

Despite the changes that have occurred in their universities and USDA laboratories, sunflower researchers such as Charlie Heiser, Charlie Rogers, Gerald Seiler, John Chandler, Tommy Thompson, and C. C. Jan have given conservationists many reasons to work for better protection of sunflowers and their habitats. Even though some of these men were "reassigned" or forced to move on from their *Helianthus* studies, they have still retained a wonder over sunflowers, in all their diverse forms. If allowed to pursue this fascination in one place for more time, they would be the kind of men who would further the conservation of, as well as the knowledge about, particular sunflowers.

IV.

On a sunny October day in Fargo, North Dakota, I had the pleasure of wandering through C. C. Jan's greenhouses of perennial and annual sunflowers. Whatever awareness I have had of sunflower diversity beforehand was overwhelmed and humbled within a minute of putting my foot in the door. I stood among nine-foot-tall monsters that had not yet reached their flowering stage, and foot-tall dwarfs already spent. Some species had flower heads the size of the palm of my hand, others, heads the size of my thumbnail. Leaf sizes and shapes ranged from arrow-shaped miniatures to wide, fanlike giants.

I stood there for a few minutes, awed, hidden between the rows of perennial species, breathing in warm, humid air with them. Hidden from me that moment were the landscapes that shaped this diversity of forms—the serpentine outcrops of the Inner Coast Range, the windswept Hopi Mesas, the alkaline flood plain of the Rio Pecos, the shores of the Florida Keys, and sand dunes surrounding the Colorado River delta. I closed my eyes for a moment, trying to root myself within those habitats. The sun above warmed me as I faced it. I opened my eyes again, and the world flashed green.

Dandelion
Taraxacum officinale

The South Wind and the Maiden of the Golden Hair

Gichi-mewinzha, gii-oshki-niiging akiing, a very long time ago, when the earth was new, ten Anishinaabeg warrior brothers fought a great battle with a famous, huge, monstrous and dangerous bear who wore a marvelous necklace of shells. Mudjekewis and his nine brothers overcame the great Manidoo Mishi-makwa with the help of their Guardians and with cunning and bravery. They succeeded in killing the monstrous bear who had threatened their people, and, in so doing, they obtained the wondrous necklace that he wore. As reward for their bravery in obtaining the necklace that brought great happiness to the Anishinaabeg, the ten brothers became Manidoog themselves. The nine eldest went off to the Spirit World to undertake their new duties, and the youngest Mudjekewis was given control of the winds of the Earth. To acknowledge his new responsibilities he was given the name of Kabeyun, Father of the Winds.

Kabeyun himself undertook the job of directing Ningaabii'an, the West Wind, the wind that blows from the Gates of Espingishmuk, the place of our Landing, the blood-red land of the Ancestral Spirits. To his son Giiwedin he gave the North Wind and instructed him to blow winter down on the land of dreams and healing, the black of night, the dark of the year. The East Wind he gave to his son Waaban, that he might blow from the white land of the rising sun, bringing the spring of infancy and new beginnings, inspiration and light to the earth. To his son Shaawondasee he gave the South Wind, on which the warm breezes of the South Land blow summer's warmth and the green of new growth, adult life, and creativity onto the earth.

Kabeyan's son Naanabozho was given nothing until, after a long journey and great struggle, Naanabozho found and fought his father the West Wind, to avenge the death of his mother the Anishinaabekwe. Once reconciled to his father, Naanabozho was given the Northwest Wind to manage jointly with his elder brother Giiwedin. Naanabozho's nephews, the Anishinaabeg, say that when the Northwest Wind is playful and pleasant their Great Uncle Naanabozho is controlling it, but when it turns colder and harsher it is being controlled by Giiwedin. All of these things happened in the beginning of our world when all things were put to right and assigned their proper places in the order and balance of life.

Shaawondasee was a mild fellow. He grew fat and happy lying in the warm and gentle South Lands. He lay with his face ever toward the north, that he might watch his brothers and how they blew upon Anishinaabewaki. One day as he lay watching his family, Shaawondasee saw a beautiful maiden standing alone in a grassy meadow. The maiden was tall and straight, slim and graceful. Her hair was as golden as the light of the sun, so he called her Wezaawaaskwaneg, "Golden Light." Shaawondasee sighed when he saw her, and his sigh caused the maiden to dance. Each day the South Wind looked for his new *Niinimoshenh*, little cousin, little sweetheart, as he lay in the South Land with his face toward the north. Each morning as the sun arose, Shaawondasee would look for his beautiful, golden-haired maiden, for watching her filled his heart with love. One morning, as he looked for her eagerly, Shaawondasee saw that overnight she had grown old. Her beautiful golden hair was now a mass of white.

Shaawondasee was shocked and grieved. He thought, "A Mindimooyenh, an old lady! Oh, my beautiful maiden! My brother Giiwedin the North Wind, the Cold Blower, must have touched Niinimoshenh, my beloved, with his breath and made her old."

In his sorrow Shaawondasee sighed a great sigh that blew the white hair of the maiden up and off in a swirl of white. As he watched his beloved's hair blowing away, Shaawondasee laughed a great laugh for he realized his Wezaawaaskwaneg, "Golden Light," who in her age is called Mindimooyenh, "Old Lady," was a meadow flower, the dandelion (*Taraxacum officinale*).

Doodooshaaboojiibik

Mindimooyenh
Wezaawaaskwaneg
"Little Suns"
Dandelion
Taraxacum officinale

Dandelions have always been my favorite flower. It is the one flower I personally want on my grave. I have asked my children to visit my grave after the dandelions have gone to seed and to kick a few of the white seed heads if they want to plant flowers in my memory. I really am not kidding. I just love dandelions. I know of no prettier flower. The sight of a full field or lawn covered with gold in the bright sunlight is as aesthetically pleasing as any sight I have ever seen.

People say, "Ya, but they go to seed." Well, that is true, dandelions do go to seed, but so do tulips and daffodils. They look just as scraggy after their flowering. I truly believe that the hatred of dandelions is just the hatred of the natural world. People spend fortunes and pollute a lot of ground water all in an attempt to kill this beautiful little plant. Then they plant exotic bulbs in the spot and struggle to get them to grow. Perhaps the dandelion is despised because it is free.

The scientific name for the dandelion is *Taraxacum officinale*. The genus, the first part of the name, comes from the Greek word *taraxos*, meaning "disorder," and *akos*, meaning "remedy." The species name, the second part, means that at one time it was on the official lists from which a physician can write prescriptions. So the scientific name for this plant means the "Official Remedy of Disorders," and that is a very good name for this plant because it has been a strong medicinal for the Anishinaabeg and for many, many other peoples as well, all over the world, all across the Northern temperate zones of the planet, across Turtle Island and Europe and Asia, too.

The English common name "dandelion" is a corruption of the French "dent-de-lion" meaning "the teeth of the lion," because someone thought the leaves of the plant look like the canine teeth of a lion. The old medieval herbals sometimes really intensified this supposed similarity by

Dandelion
Taraxacum officinale

drawing vicious-looking illustrations of the leaves and of open-mouthed lions. But it cannot be denied that this little plant really does "put the bite" on many of the problems that beset the People.

In the times of the Gete-Anishinaabeg, the end of winter was a time of hardship. Since so much of the People's diet in winter consisted of dried foods and whatever game was still available, diseases that we now know are caused by vitamin deficiencies were very prevalent. For such disorders, the dandelion has very effective medicine. The green-growing parts of the plant are rich in vitamins A, E, B1-thiamine, and C. The roots store a lot of calcium, protein, phosphorus, iron, riboflavin, niacin, and potassium, but Kee[1] taught that the chief virtue that the dandelion has to share with Anishinaabeg is the fact that it is the only natural source of body-assimilatable copper. The human body does not need very much copper. It is one of the trace elements that, although we do not need much, we cannot entirely do without, either. And dandelion has it for us. If a person just ate three or four helpings of dandelion greens or flowers in a whole year's time, they would get enough of the mineral to keep them healthy. Kee told me to dry either the flower petals of the dandelion or the leaves and to pulverize them and sprinkle them across a stew or soup for my family a few times a year to be sure that they received all of the copper that they needed.

When using dandelion flowers for cooking be very, very sure to take all of the greens off of the heads when picking the flowers. One has to use one's thumbnail to scoop out the part of the stem that is at the bottom, where the stem goes into the green leaves at the base of the flower. If even a tiny bit of stem gets into the plant material, the resulting food will be bitter.

In the old days, if a person was suffering from lack of vitamins come *Onaabani-giizis*, "The Hard Crust on the Snow Moon," or in *Iskigamizige-giizis*, "The Maple Sap Boiling Moon," at the end of a hard winter, the mashkikiiwikwe would dig up dandelion roots and pulverize them and pour just-boiled and slightly cooled water over the roots. The plant material was allowed to steep, covered, for 10 minutes or so; then it was filtered and given to the patient as a tea, three or four times a day. This treatment was sure to act as a "spring tonic" on a person suffering from poor diet and get them back to feeling chipper in a very short time.

The spring tonic approach to curing vitamin deficiency is not as tasty as utilizing dandelions as a food source early in the year. One can

---

1   Keewaydinoquay Peschel, an Anishinaabe teacher and ethnobotanist, to whom the author was apprenticed.

get all of the vitamins and minerals in the plants by just adjusting one's cooking habits to include a good dose of dandelions as soon as they start to grow in the spring. Nowadays we have fresh fruits and vegetables available to us year-round, but who knows whether we always will be so privileged. It pays to keep the knowledge against the time when we or our descendants may need it.

Dandelions have a food to share with Anishinaabeg at any time of the year. In the early spring, when the leaves are first up and before the flowers form, one can eat the leaves of dandelions raw. They have a pleasant, if slightly nippy, bitter taste that will enliven a "blah" lettuce salad, rather the way radishes do. If the leaves are a little too bitter for one's taste (and they do get more bitter as the season progresses, until they are all but inedible once the flower develops), one can cook them in one or two changes of boiling water to remove the bitter taste. The resulting potherb is both a healthy and a tasty addition to the diet and really very good with a dab of butter or salad dressing or a few shakes of parmesan cheese. One can extend the time in which leaves are edible by covering them and allowing the plant to blanch, the way celery is blanched, to make it white and bland-tasting. One can cut off the top of an older plant or just cover the older leaves with mulch or a piece of black plastic or with an overturned bucket to keep the sun off of the leaves. Since dandelions have a good, strong taproot, the plants will just put up more and tenderer leaves even if they are denied the sun for a week or more. Some people even dig roots up in the fall and put them in sand in a basement to harvest the blanched, mild-tasting, but nutritious leaves all winter long.

The flowers that follow so readily in the spring and continue into the summer (and may even come back again in the cool of the fall) are really good, too. My family likes dandelion flowers dipped in egg and cornmeal and fried in butter. The complete recipe is offered in the Recipes section under the name "Little Suns," which was Kee's title for dandelions cooked this way.[2] One can pick the yellow petals off of the bitter stems and green leaves and scatter them over a mixed salad or over a bowl of mashed potatoes or cooked rice or over the top of a soup or stew to create an interesting and pretty dish. One can extend the time in which dandelion flowers are available by picking the flowers when they are in full bloom and spreading them to dry on a cookie sheet or a cooking rack. Once the flowers are dry, one then pulls the yellow petals

---

2   See Mary Siisip Geniusz, *Plants Have So Much to Give Us, All We Have to Do Is Ask*, 307.

off of the green part of the flower and stores the petals in a jar for later use. I have included recipes for using either the fresh or the dried petals in baking dishes in the Recipes section, too.

Once the flowering is over for the season, the roots of the dandelion are ready for harvesting. If one wants the biggest roots, dig the plants that had the biggest flowers. It is easiest to dig the long taproot after a rain or when one is weeding a flower or vegetable garden that has had its soil tilled recently. Kee always hated using the roots of any plant, probably because as the child of gardeners and the apprentice of a medicine woman she had spent too many hours scrubbing and cleaning roots of various food and medicinal plants. But she was rather fond of dandelion and chicory root coffees, and so she did teach about the process of turning dandelion roots into a coffee-like drink. One digs and cleans all of the dirt off of dandelion roots. One scrubs the roots with a good, stiff vegetable brush or one uses a potato peeler to get off the skin. Then one dries the roots very well in a very slow oven overnight or in the hot sun for several days or on rocks beside a fire. It is the key to making a palatable coffee to dry the roots very slowly. Roots dried too quickly are much too bitter to make a tasty drink. One knows when the roots are properly dry when one breaks one in half: it will snap when it is really dry, and it will be dark brown all of the way through. The roots can be cooled and put in sealed jars for later use, or brewed into a coffee-like drink immediately. One breaks the roots into pieces and grinds them in a coffee grinder, then perks them in a percolator the same way one makes coffee, but, because dandelion roots are strong, only about 1 teaspoon of the root is necessary to make one cup of the dandelion-root coffee. I have never been a coffee drinker, but Kee, who was, assured me that one could easily get used to dandelion coffee if one had no access to coffee beans. She actually preferred a drink made by mixing dandelion roots with similarly processed and dried chicory roots to the one made with dandelion roots alone.

There is another use of dandelion root that Kee taught me about but that I have not yet tried. She said one could make a pretty magenta, purplish-pink, dye from the crushed roots of mature dandelion roots. One digs the roots, washes them well, cuts them up very fine, smashes them with a rock, or grinds them in a meat grinder. Then one covers the crushed roots with water. Rain water works well, as it is softer than tap water. Then one simmers the plant material for several hours and allows it to sit in the pot at the back of the stove until morning. One filters out the liquid, then one puts pre-wetted wool in the bath to simmer gently for one half hour or longer. The resulting color is said to be rather pretty and can be made more permanent by soaking the material to be dyed in alum before adding to the dye bath.

Keewaydinoquay taught me several medicinal virtues dandelion has to share with the People. She said it was helpful as a blood purifier and was often given after a long illness or in cases of severe acne and eczema. In such cases a person was usually given a dried-leaf infusion, 1 teaspoon dried leaf to 1 cup boiling water, covered and steeped for 10 to 15 minutes with cover on pot. The resulting tea would be filtered and sweetened with honey and given once or twice or three times a day, depending on the severity of the case and on how well the patient took it. Dandelions can be a laxative, and they also increase the flow of urine, which helps in some cases where the system has to be cleaned out.

Dandelions are a powerful liver treatment as well. They were traditionally used to treat jaundice. A tea of the dried leaf, rather weaker than the tea described above made from roots, is used for small children. A decoction of the root is used in an older person with jaundice if they do not respond to the tea of the leaf.

Dandelions are also used to treat arthritis. A leaf tea of the kind described above, 1 teaspoon dried leaf to 1 cup boiling water, sweetened with honey or maple sugar to make it palatable, is given to a person with arthritis to reduce the swelling of joints. The affected joints are wrapped in a poultice of chopped dandelion leaves and flowers covered with boiling water and simmered to break down the plant material until it is very soft. The material is slightly cooled and applied to the swollen joints warm and covered with cloth. This kind of poultice helps to reduce the swelling if applied several times daily while the patient is sipping dandelion tea.

Another of the virtues that the dandelion has to share with the People, and a virtue that should not be disregarded just because the plant also gives us so much for our physical comfort both as a food and as physical medicine, is the fact that dandelion are just so much fun. They are a beautiful flower in all stages of their growth. The perfectly formed, little, golden flowers soon give way to an equally beautiful, delicate white seed head that when blown upon by wind or child explodes into a cloud of tiny, fairy-winged parachutes. As children we used to

Dandelion
Taraxacum officinale

Dandelion
Taraxacum officinale

pick the mindimooyenyag, the "old ladies," and blow upon their hair. Some of the kids said that one should count how many puffs it took to completely blow all of the seeds off of the head, and that would tell one what time it was. If one had to blow twice it was two o'clock, three times and it was three o'clock. Some said if one blew on a seed head and there were any seeds left on the plant that was the number of children one could expect in later years. We also believed that a wish made on a dandelion would be granted if one could blow off all of the seeds with one breath. We used to say that if one whispered a secret one wanted another person to know, but instead of telling the person one whispered it to a dandelion, then blew off all of the seeds with one blow, the other person would hear one's words. We picked the stems, and nipped off the flowers, and pushed the small upper part of the stalk into the wider lower part to form a circle. This circle became a link in a chain when we pushed another stem through the first circle and continued to make a chain long enough for a necklace. This project always got our fingers wonderfully stained with juice, and for some reason that was part of the fun of the game. I went through the summers of my childhood with wonderfully grimy fingers. And dandelions were always a flower that no one scolded a child for picking, even out of a neighbor's garden or lawn. A person could bring a big handful to his or her mom and make her smile. To this day I always pick a big handful of the first dandelions of the season. I bring them into the house and put them in the finest crystal vase that I own, and I put them on my dining-room table.

EMILY DICKINSON

The Dandelion's pallid tube
Astonishes the Grass
And Winter instantly becomes
An infinite Alas —

The tube uplifts a signal Bud
And then a shouting Flower, —
The Proclamation of the Suns
That sepulture is o'er.

JERICHO BROWN

The Tradition

Aster. Nasturtium. Delphinium. We thought
Fingers in dirt meant it was our dirt, learning
Names in heat, in elements classical
Philosophers said could change us. *Stargazer.*
Foxglove. Summer seemed to bloom against the will
Of the sun, which news reports claimed flamed hotter
On this planet than when our dead fathers
Wiped sweat from their necks. *Cosmos. Baby's Breath.*
Men like me and my brothers filmed what we
Planted for proof we existed before
Too late, sped the video to see blossoms
Brought in seconds, colors you expect in poems
Where the world ends, everything cut down.
John Crawford. Eric Garner. Mike Brown.

Aster
Asteraceae spp.

LESLIE MARMON SILKO

"The purple asters are growing"

The purple asters are growing in wide fields around the red rocks past Mesita clear to the Sedillo Grant. This year there has been more rain here than I have ever seen. Yesterday at Dripping Springs I saw a blue flower I had never seen before, something like an orchid, growing from a succulent leafless bulb. So many of these plants had never bloomed in my lifetime and so I had assumed these plants did not bloom; now I find that through all these years they were only waiting for enough rain. I remember the stories they used to tell us about places that were meadows full of flowers or about canyons that had wide clear streams. I remember our amazement at these stories of lush grass and running water because the places they spoke of had all changed; the places they spoke of were dry and covered with tumbleweeds and all that was left of the streams were deep arroyos. But I understand now. I will remember this September like they remembered the meadows and streams; I will talk about the yellow beeweed solid on all the hills, and maybe my grandchildren will also be amazed and wonder what has become of the fields of wild asters and all the little toads that sang in the evening. Maybe after they listen to me talking about this rainy lush September they will walk over the sandrock at the old house at Dripping Springs trying to imagine the pools of rainwater and the pollywogs of this year.

—from a letter to Lawson F. Inada,
September 1975

STEPHANIE BURT

Wildflower Meadow, Medawisla

The many-
oared asters
are coracles;
the goldenrod
pods, triremes.
They do not
plan their
voyages
to please us.
The tangle
of brambles
and drupes shifts
only slightly
when the wind
attempts to
part the knee-
or waist-high stalks
and thorns. What will
you do or
be in that state
you fear and look
forward to,
when none of
them needs
us, after
the last
seeds leave?

Aster
Asteraceae spp.

Goldenrod
Solidago spp.

ROBIN WALL KIMMERER

Asters and Goldenrod

The girl in the picture holds a slate with her name and "class of '75" chalked in, a girl the color of deerskin with long dark hair and inky unreadable eyes that meet yours and won't look away. I remember that day. I was wearing the new plaid shirt that my parents had given me, an outfit I thought to be the hallmark of all foresters. When I looked back at the photo later in life, it was a puzzle to me. I recall being elated to be going to college, but there is no trace of that in the girl's face.

Even before I arrived at school, I had all of my answers prepared for the freshman intake interview. I wanted to make a good first impression. There were hardly any women at the forestry school in those days and certainly none who looked like me. The adviser peered at me over his glasses and said, "So, why do you want to major in botany?" His pencil was poised over the registrar's form.

How could I answer, how could I tell him that I was born a botanist, that I had shoeboxes of seeds and piles of pressed leaves under my bed, that I'd stop my bike along the road to identify a new species, that plants colored my dreams, that the plants had chosen me? So I told him the truth. I was proud of my well-planned answer, its freshman sophistication apparent to anyone, the way it showed that I already knew some plants and their habitats, that I had thought deeply about their nature and was clearly well prepared for college work. I told him that I chose botany because I wanted to learn about why asters and goldenrod looked so beautiful together. I'm sure I was smiling then, in my red plaid shirt.

But he was not. He laid down his pencil as if there was no need to record what I had said. "Miss Wall," he said, fixing me with a disappointed smile, "I must tell you that *that* is not science. That is not at all the sort of thing with which botanists concern themselves." But he promised to put me right. "I'll enroll you in General Botany so you can learn what it is." And so it began.

I like to imagine that they were the first flowers I saw, over my mother's shoulder, as the pink blanket slipped away from my face and their colors flooded my consciousness. I've heard that early experience can attune the brain to certain stimuli, so that they are processed with greater speed and certainty, so that they can be used again and again, so that we remember. Love at first sight. Through cloudy newborn eyes their radiance formed the first botanical synapses in my wide-awake, newborn brain, which until then had encountered only the blurry gentleness of pink faces. I'm guessing all eyes were on me, a little round baby all swaddled in bunting, but mine were on Goldenrod and Asters. I was born to these flowers and they came back for my birthday every year, weaving me into our mutual celebration.

People flock to our hills for the fiery suite of October but they often miss the sublime prelude of September fields. As if harvest time were not enough—peaches, grapes, sweet corn, squash—the fields are also embroidered with drifts of golden yellow and pools of deepest purple, a masterpiece.

If a fountain could jet bouquets of chrome yellow in dazzling arches of chrysanthemum fireworks, that would be Canada Goldenrod. Each three-foot stem is a geyser of tiny gold daisies, ladylike in miniature, exuberant en masse. Where the soil is damp enough, they stand side by side with their perfect counterpart, New England Asters. Not the pale domesticates of the perennial border, the weak sauce of lavender or sky blue, but full-on royal purple that would make a violet shrink. The daisylike fringe of purple petals surrounds a disc as bright as the sun at high noon, a golden-orange pool, just a tantalizing shade darker than the surrounding goldenrod. Alone, each is a botanical superlative. Together, the visual effect is stunning. Purple and gold, the heraldic colors of the king and queen of the meadow, a regal procession in complementary colors. I just wanted to know why.

Why do they stand beside each other when they could grow alone? Why this particular pair? There are plenty of pinks and whites and blues dotting the fields, so is it only happenstance that the magnificence of purple and gold end up side by side? Einstein himself said that "God doesn't play dice with the universe." What is the source of this pattern? Why is the world so beautiful? It could so easily be otherwise: flowers could be ugly to us and still fulfill their own purpose. But they're not. It seemed like a good question to me.

But my adviser said, "It's not science," not what botany was about. I wanted to know why certain stems bent easily for baskets and some would break, why the biggest berries grew in the shade and why they made us medicines, which plants are edible, why those little pink orchids only grow under pines. "Not science," he said, and he ought to know, sitting in his laboratory, a learned professor of botany. "And if you want to study beauty, you should go to art school." He reminded me of my deliberations over choosing a college, when I had vacillated between training as a botanist or as a poet. Since everyone told me I couldn't do both, I'd chosen plants. He told me that science was not about beauty, not about the embrace between plants and humans.

I had no rejoinder; I had made a mistake. There was no fight in me, only embarrassment at my error. I did not have the words for resistance. He signed me up for my classes and I was dismissed to go get my photo taken for registration. I didn't think about it at the time, but it was happening all over again, an echo of my grandfather's first day at school, when he was ordered to leave everything—language, culture, family—behind. The professor made me doubt where I came from, what I knew, and claimed that his was the *right* way to think. Only he didn't cut my hair off.

In moving from a childhood in the woods to the university I had unknowingly shifted between worldviews, from a natural history of experience, in which I knew plants as teachers and companions to whom I was linked with mutual responsibility, into the realm of science. The questions scientists raised were not "Who are you?" but "What is it?" No one asked plants, "What can you tell us?" The primary question was "How does it work?" The botany I was taught was reductionist, mechanistic, and strictly objective. Plants were reduced to objects; they were not subjects. The way botany was conceived and taught didn't seem to leave much room for a person who thought the way I did. The only way I could make sense of it was to conclude that the things I had always believed about plants must not be true after all.

That first plant science class was a disaster. I barely scraped by with a C and could not muster much enthusiasm for memorizing the concentrations of essential plant nutrients. There were times when I wanted to quit, but the more I learned, the more fascinated I became with the intricate structures that made up a leaf and the alchemy of photosynthesis. Companionship between asters and goldenrod was never mentioned, but

I memorized botanical Latin as if it was poetry, eagerly tossing aside the name "goldenrod" for *Solidago canadensis*. I was mesmerized by plant ecology, evolution, taxonomy, physiology, soils, and fungi. All around me were my good teachers, the plants. I found good mentors, too, warm and kind professors who were doing heart-driven science, whether they could admit it or not. They too were my teachers. And yet there was always something tapping at my shoulder, willing me to turn around. When I did, I did not know how to recognize what stood behind me.

My natural inclination was to see relationships, to seek the threads that connect the world, to join instead of divide. But science is rigorous in separating the observer from the observed, and the observed from the observer. Why two flowers are beautiful together would violate the division necessary for objectivity.

I scarcely doubted the primacy of scientific thought. Following the path of science trained me to separate, to distinguish perception from physical reality, to atomize complexity into its smallest components, to honor the chain of evidence and logic, to discern one thing from another, to savor the pleasure of precision. The more I did this, the better I got at it, and I was accepted to do graduate work in one of the world's finest botany programs, no doubt on the strength of the letter of recommendation from my adviser, which read, "She's done remarkably well for an Indian girl."

A master's degree, a PhD, and a faculty position followed. I am grateful for the knowledge that was shared with me and deeply privileged to carry the powerful tools of science as a way of engaging the world. It took me to other plant communities, far from the asters and goldenrod. I remember feeling, as a new faculty member, as if I finally understood plants. I too began to teach the mechanics of botany, emulating the approach that I had been taught.

It reminds me of a story told by my friend Holly Youngbear Tibbetts. A plant scientist, armed with his notebooks and equipment, is exploring the rainforests for new botanical discoveries, and he has hired an indigenous guide to lead him. Knowing the scientist's interests, the young guide takes care to point out the interesting species. The botanist looks at him appraisingly, surprised by his capacity. "Well, well, young man, you certainly know the names of a lot of these plants." The guide nods and replies with downcast eyes. "Yes, I have learned the names of all the bushes, but I have yet to learn their songs."

I was teaching the names and ignoring the songs.

When I was in graduate school in Wisconsin, my then husband and I had the good fortune to land jobs as caretakers at the university arboretum. In return for a little house at the edge of the prairie, we had only to make the nighttime rounds, checking that doors and gates were secure before we left the darkness to the crickets. There was just one time that a light was left burning, a door left ajar, in the horticulture garage. There was no mischief, but as my husband checked around, I stood and idly scanned the bulletin board. There was a news clipping there with a photo of a magnificent American elm, which had just been named the champion for its species, the largest of its kind. It had a name: The Louis Vieux Elm.

My heart began to pound and I knew my world was about to change, for I'd known the name Louis Vieux all my life and here was his face looking at me from a news clipping. He was our Potawatomi grandfather, one who had walked all the way from the Wisconsin forests to the Kansas prairie with my grandma Sha-note. He was a leader, one who took care of the people in their hardship. That garage door was left ajar, that light was left burning, and it shone on the path back home for me. It was the beginning of a long, slow journey back to my people, called out to me by the tree that stood above their bones.

To walk the science path I had stepped off the path of indigenous knowledge. But the world has a way of guiding your steps. Seemingly out of the blue came an invitation to a small gathering of Native elders, to talk about traditional knowledge of plants. One I will never forget—a Navajo woman without a day of university botany training in her life—spoke for hours and I hung on every word. One by one, name by name, she told of the plants in her valley. Where each one lived, when it bloomed, who it liked to live near and all its relationships, who ate it, who lined their nests with its fibers, what kind of medicine it offered. She also shared the stories held by those plants, their origin myths, how they got their names, and what they have to tell us. She spoke of beauty.

Her words were like smelling salts waking me to what I had known back when I was picking strawberries. I realized how shallow my under-standing was. Her knowledge was so much deeper and wider and engaged all the human ways of understanding. She could have explained asters and goldenrod. To a new PhD, this was humbling. It was the beginning of my reclaiming that other way of knowing that I had helplessly let science supplant. I felt like a malnourished refugee invited to a feast, the dishes scented with the herbs of home.

I circled right back to where I had begun, to the question of beauty. Back to the questions that science does not ask, not because they aren't important, but because science as a way of knowing is too narrow for the task. Had my adviser been a better scholar, he would have celebrated my questions, not dismissed them. He offered me only the cliché that beauty is in the eye of the beholder, and since science separates the observer and the observed, by definition beauty could not be a valid scientific question. I should have been told that my questions were bigger than science could touch.

He *was* right about beauty being in the eye of the beholder, especially when it comes to purple and yellow. Color perception in humans relies on banks of specialized receptor cells, the rods and cones in the retina. The job of the cone cells is to absorb light of different wavelengths and pass it on to the brain's visual cortex, where it can be interpreted. The visible light spectrum, the rainbow of colors, is broad, so the most effective means of discerning color is not one generalized jack-of-all-trades cone cell, but rather an array of specialists, each perfectly tuned to absorb certain wavelengths. The human eye has three kinds. One type excels at detecting red and associated wavelengths. One is tuned to blue. The other optimally perceives light of two colors: purple and yellow.

The human eye is superbly equipped to detect these colors and send a signal pulsing to the brain. This doesn't explain why I perceive them as beautiful, but it does explain why that combination gets my undivided attention. I asked my artist buddies about the power of purple and gold, and they sent me right to the color wheel: these two are complementary colors, as different in nature as could be. In composing a palette, putting them together makes each more vivid; just a touch of one will bring out the other. In an 1890 treatise on color perception, Goethe, who was both a scientist and a poet, wrote that "the colors diametrically opposed to each other . . . are those which *reciprocally* evoke each other in the eye." Purple and yellow are a reciprocal pair.

Our eyes are so sensitive to these wavelengths that the cones can get oversaturated and the stimulus pours over onto the other cells. A printmaker I know showed me that if you stare for a long time at a block of yellow and then shift your gaze to a white sheet of paper, you will see

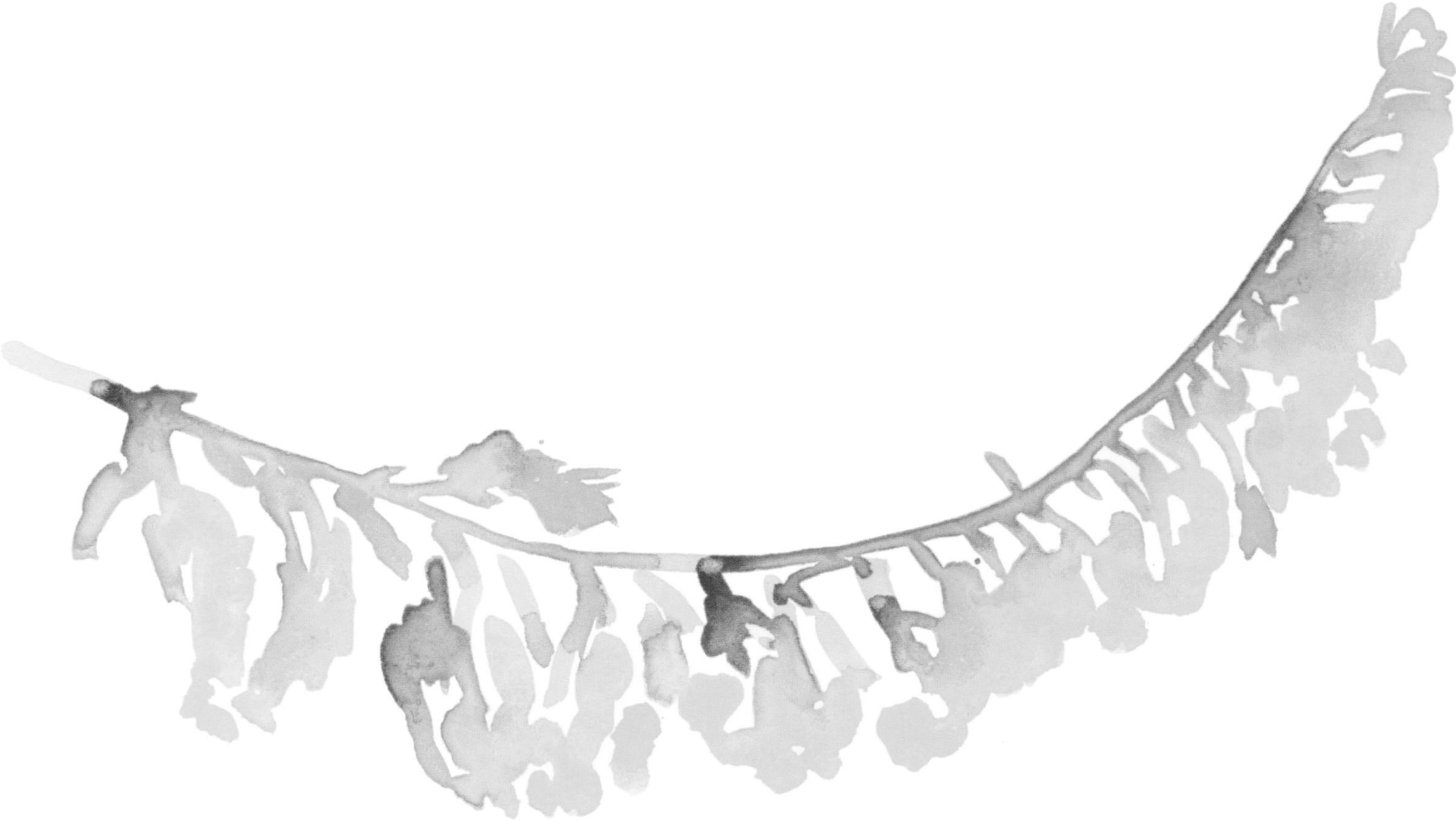

Goldenrod
Solidago spp.

it, for a moment, as violet. This phenomenon—the colored afterimage—occurs because there is energetic reciprocity between purple and yellow pigments, which goldenrod and asters knew well before we did.

If my adviser was correct, the visual effect that so delights a human like me may be irrelevant to the flowers. The real beholder whose eye they hope to catch is a bee bent on pollination. Bees perceive many flowers differently than humans do due to their perception of additional spectra such as ultraviolet radiation. As it turns out, though, goldenrod and asters appear very similarly to bee eyes and human eyes. We both think they're beautiful. Their striking contrast when they grow together makes them the most attractive target in the whole meadow, a beacon for bees. Growing together, both receive more pollinator visits than they would if they were growing alone. It's a testable hypothesis; it's a question of science, a question of art, and a question of beauty.

Why are they beautiful together? It is a phenomenon simultaneously material and spiritual, for which we need all wavelengths, for which we need depth perception. When I stare too long at the world with science eyes, I see an afterimage of traditional knowledge. Might science and traditional knowledge be purple and yellow to one another, might they be goldenrod and asters? We see the world more fully when we use both.

The question of goldenrod and asters was of course just emblematic of what I really wanted to know. It was an architecture of relationships, of connections that I yearned to understand. I wanted to see the shimmering threads that hold it all together. And I wanted to know why we love the world, why the most ordinary scrap of meadow can rock us back on our heels in awe.

When botanists go walking the forests and fields looking for plants, we say we are going on a *foray*. When writers do the same, we should call it a *metaphoray*, and the land is rich in both. We need them both; scientist and poet Jeffrey Burton Russell writes that "as the sign of a deeper truth, metaphor was close to sacrament. Because the vastness and richness of reality cannot be expressed by the overt sense of a statement alone."

Native scholar Greg Cajete has written that in indigenous ways of knowing, we understand a thing only when we understand it with all four aspects of our being: mind, body, emotion, and spirit. I came to understand quite sharply when I began my training as a scientist that science privileges only one, possibly two, of those ways of knowing:

mind and body. As a young person wanting to know everything about plants, I did not question this. But it is a whole human being who finds the beautiful path.

There was a time when I teetered precariously with an awkward foot in each of two worlds—the scientific and the indigenous. But then I learned to fly. Or at least try. It was the bees that showed me how to move between different flowers—to drink the nectar and gather pollen from both. It is this dance of cross-pollination that can produce a new species of knowledge, a new way of being in the world. After all, there aren't two worlds, there is just this one good green earth.

That September pairing of purple and gold is lived reciprocity; its wisdom is that the beauty of one is illuminated by the radiance of the other. Science and art, matter and spirit, indigenous knowledge and Western science—can they be goldenrod and asters for each other? When I am in their presence, their beauty asks me for reciprocity, to be the complementary color, to make something beautiful in response.

HERMAN MELVILLE

A Way-side Weed

By orchards red he whisks along,
    A charioteer from villa fine;
With passing lash o' the whip he cuts
    A way-side Weed divine.

But knows he what it is he does?
    He flouts October's god
Whose sceptre is this Way-side Weed,
    This swaying Golden Rod?

WILLIAM CARLOS WILLIAMS

Chicory and Daisies

I
Lift your flowers
on bitter stems
chicory!
Lift them up
out of the scorched ground!
Bear no foliage
but give yourself
wholly to that!
Strain under them
you bitter stems
that no beast eats—
and scorn greyness!
Into the heat with them:
cool!
luxuriant! sky-blue!
The earth cracks and
is shriveled up;
the wind moans piteously;
the sky goes out
if you should fail.

II
I saw a child with daisies
for weaving into the hair
tear the stems
with her teeth!

Chicory
Cichorium intybus

D. A. POWELL

Tender Mercies

The dandelions, ditch-blown brood,
       the evening snow and dew-soaked phlox,
the Brewer's pea, the Jepson's pea
(these, the bright eyes of the viridian fields)
in chaparral, the hillside pea and angled pea,
          intensities of light and pomp
       that distress the easy upswept grass.
The smack the rain plants as it smudges past
         and penetrates the canvas.

The smattering on field and railroad tracks,
       both hardy blooms and dainty flowers,
the judge's house, the chicken farm,
a migratory camp, a flesh motel,
        a stucco digs
where all that mitigates the August swelter
       is the swamp cooler's immutable burr,
       a straggling house that draws its water
from a hard-water well and flushes out
       with the help of a crude sump pump.

        Before the flatland is occluded
by the staunch of light at end of day,
I wanted to be content with all its surfaces:
        weed, barb, crack, rill, rise . . .
But every candid shoot and fulgent branch
       depends upon the arteries beneath.
The houses have their siphons
        and their circuit vents.
The heart—I mean the literal heart—
must rely upon its own plaqued valves;
the duodenal canal, its unremitting grumble.

The brain upon its stem,
and underneath,
a network, vast, of nerves that rationalize.

The earth's a little harder than it was.
But I expect that it will soften soon,
            voluptuous in some age hence,
because we captured it as art
                        the moment it was most itself:
fragile, flecked with nimbleweed,
                              and so alone,
it almost welcomed its own ravishment.

I was a maiden in this versicolor plain.
            I watched it change.
Withstood that change, the infidelities
of light, the solar interval, the shift of time,
                  the shift from farm to town.
I had a man that pressed me down
into the soil. I was that man. I was that town.

They call the chicory "ragged sailors" here:
            sojourners who have finally returned
and are content to see the summer to its end.
            Be unafraid of what the future brings.
I will not use this particular blue again.

—for Betty Buckley

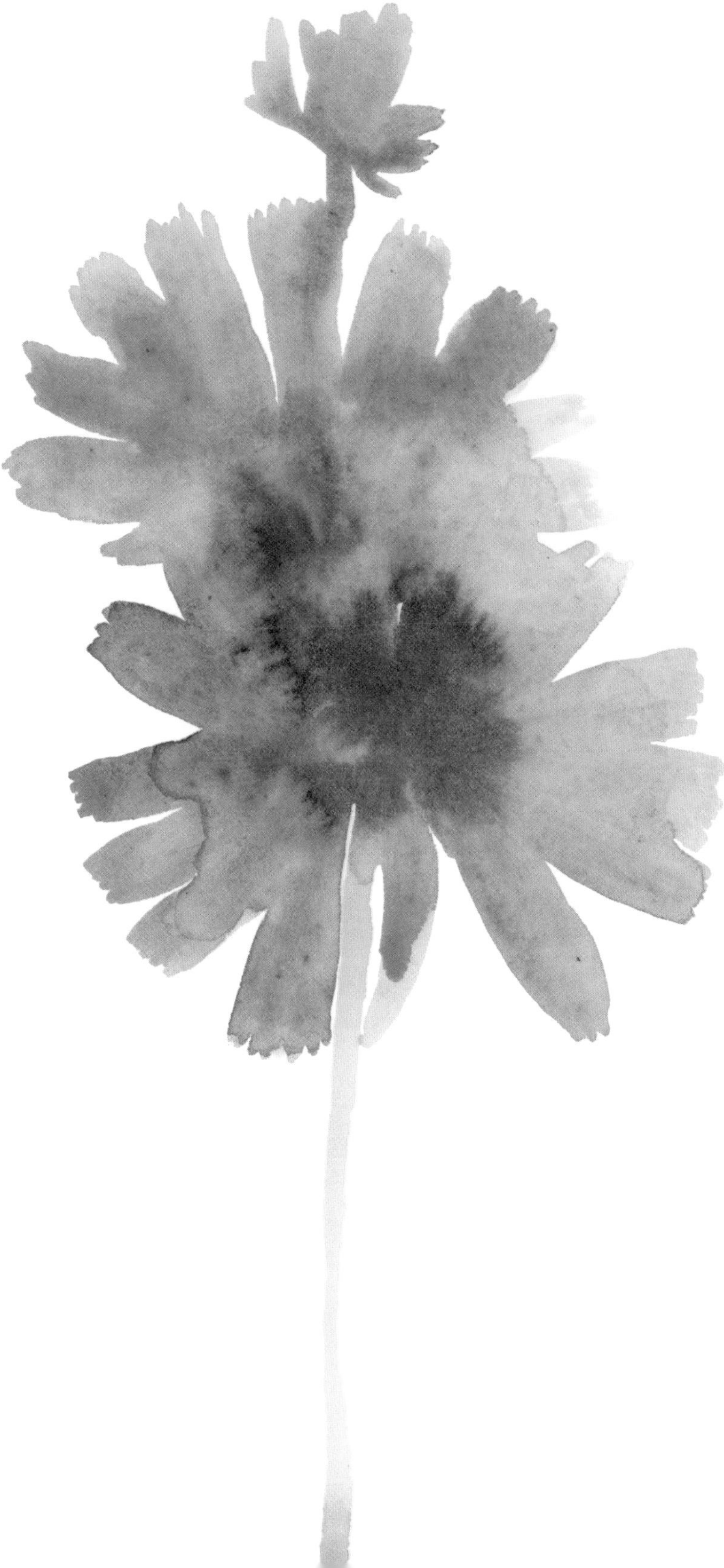

Chicory
Cichorium intybus

Daisy
Chrysanthemum leucanthemum

A. R. AMMONS

Loss

When the sun
falls behind the sumac
thicket the
wild
yellow daisies
in diffuse evening shade
lose their
rigorous attention
and
half-wild with loss
turn
any way the wind does
and lift their
petals up
to float
off their stems
and go

WILLIAM MEREDITH

An Assent to Wildflowers

" 'Ay' and 'no' too was no good divinity."
—*King Lear*

Plucked from their sockets like eyes that gave offense,
Dozens of black-eyed Susans gaze
Into the room—a composite lens
Like a fly's, staring out of a bronze vase.

Gloucestered out of the meadow by the hands
I love, they ask me do I know
What they mean by this bold flower-glance?
Do I know who made the room glow?

And the answer of course is love, but before I say
Love, I see the other question they raise,
Like anything blind that gapes at you that way.
A man may see how this world goes with no eyes.

The luster of the room goes blear for a minute,
Then, like Gloucester, I begin to guess;
I imagine the world, I imagine the world and you in it:
There's flowering, there's a dark question answered yes.

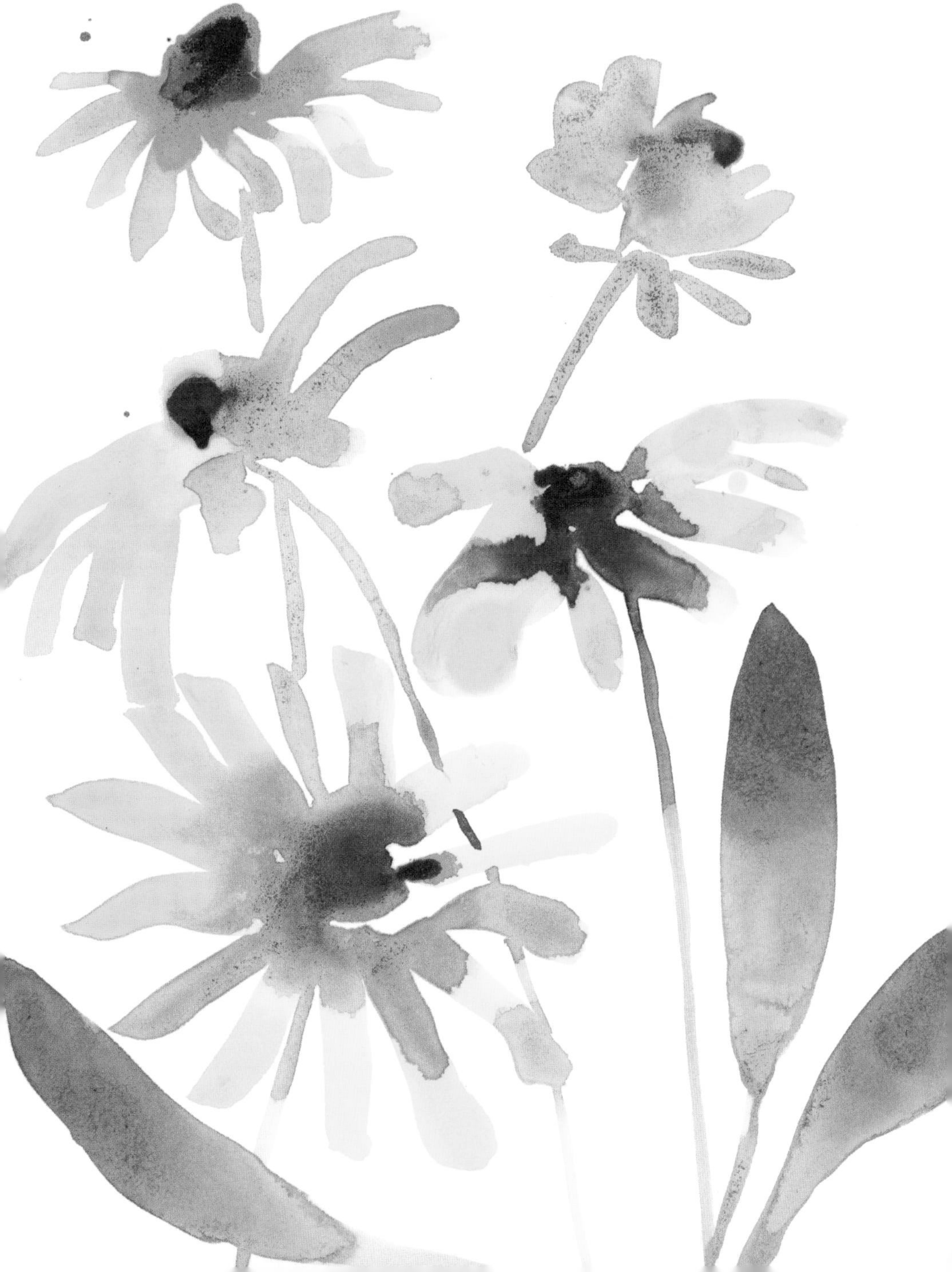

Black-eyed Susan
Rudbeckia hirta

Prairie Birthday

Every July I watch eagerly a certain country graveyard that I pass in driving to and from my farm. It is time for a prairie birthday, and in one corner of this graveyard lives a surviving celebrant of that once important event.

It is an ordinary graveyard, bordered by the usual spruces, and studded with the usual pink granite or white marble headstones, each with the usual Sunday bouquet of red or pink geraniums. It is extraordinary only in being triangular instead of square, and in harboring, within the sharp angle of its fence, a pin-point remnant of the native prairie on which the graveyard was established in the 1840's. Heretofore unreachable by scythe or mower, this yard-square relic of original Wisconsin gives birth, each July, to a man-high stalk of compass plant or cutleaf Silphium, spangled with saucer-sized yellow blooms resembling sunflowers. It is the sole remnant of this plant along this highway, and perhaps the sole remnant in the western half of our county. What a thousand acres of Silphiums looked like when they tickled the bellies of the buffalo is a question never again to be answered, and perhaps not even asked.

This year I found the Silphium in first bloom on 24 July, a week later than usual; during the last six years the average date was 15 July.

When I passed the graveyard again on 3 August, the fence had been removed by a road crew, and the Silphium cut. It is easy now to predict the future; for a few years my Silphium will try in vain to rise above the mowing machine, and then it will die. With it will die the prairie epoch.

The Highway Department says that 100,000 cars pass yearly over this route during the three summer months when the Silphium is in bloom. In them must ride at least 100,000 people who have "taken" what is called history, and perhaps 25,000 who have "taken" what is called botany. Yet I doubt whether a dozen have seen the Silphium, and of these hardly one will notice its demise. If I were to tell a preacher of the adjoining church that the road crew has been burning history books in his cemetery, under the guise of mowing weeds, he would be amazed and uncomprehending. How could a weed be a book?

This is one little episode in the funeral of the native flora which in turn is one episode in the funeral of the floras of the world. Mechanized man, oblivious of floras, is proud of his progress in cleaning up the landscape on which, willynilly, he must live out his days. It might be wise to prohibit at once all teaching of real botany and real history, lest some future citizen suffer qualms about the floristic price of his good life.

BEN LERNER

Also Known as Hurtsickle, Cyani Flower, and Bachelor's Button

Light snow falling in the listening
area, something has to keep me from
the radio and other forms of incidental
contact like *The current time is*
or *I see silver plunging in the days ahead.*
Why not poetry? AM clouds give way
to PM sun. I wish I'd written that
and did, and publish it on air
the way a match publishes in my hand

before I hold it to the cigarette I took
from my first teacher's son in light
snow at her improvised wake, contract
pneumonia there, let it bloom
in the left lung for a while, then postpone
Berlin. *I discourage you from flying*
is the nicest thing anyone has ever
except maybe the command to *look*
alive when I was a boy undead among

small purple flowers in the outfield.
The plan was to wander around Kreuzberg
mourning, but this will do: overheard
forecasts, adjustments to internal
flora, light snow that turns to rain in time,
just not *for* anything. If you turn
literally inward, touch the breastbone
with radiation, locate a shadow, then
the tech will print you out an image, freeing

up the elegy for other things, like wandering
beyond the field of play while bases
empty. (They're talking about *the off-season*,
beautiful phrase that's mine and now
it's gone.) Cornflower, bluebottle,
the involucre is urn-shaped and the margins
irregularly cleft. Thrives on roadsides,
thrives on waste sites, is sometimes
toothed or lobed.

Mayapple
Podophyllum peltatum

May Apple, or American Mandrake
(*Podophyllum peltatum*)

> Go and catch a falling star
> Get with child a mandrake root.
> —from "Song" by John Donne

The original Mandrake (*Mandragora officinarum*) was easily the most famous and most revered of all the ancient medicinal herbs, and became surrounded with an unbelievable amount of superstition and folklore. It is a native of Mediterranean countries and during medieval times mandrake roots, trimmed to look like tiny human figures, were sold all over Europe, including England, where it was much used in medicine and magic—not necessarily two separate pursuits in those days.

When early settlers in America learned from the Indians that the plant we now call May Apple had a root, which, like that of the Mediterranean plant, was at once a valuable medicine and, in overdoses, a drastic poison, they transferred the name and much of the lore of the mandrake to this unrelated American plant. It was by the name of mandrake that I knew this plant as a child. When the fruit was thoroughly ripe, we ate it freely, but we regarded the rest of the plant, and especially the root, with considerable awe.

May apple roots owe their medicinal properties to their content of podophyllin. The roots were not only used by herb doctors and in home remedies, but also became an ingredient in many patent medicines and achieved a respectable place in medicine. In *The Herbalist* Joseph E. Meyer, the author, says of May apple:

> The Indians were well acquainted with the virtues of this plant. The proper time for collecting the root is in the latter part of October or early part of November, soon after the fruit has ripened. Its active principle is podophyllin, which acts upon the liver in the same manner

but far superior to mercury, and with intelligent physicians it has dethroned that noxious mineral as a cholagogue.

Properties and Uses—May apple is cathartic, emetic, alternative, anthelmintic, hydrogogue and sialagogue. It is an active and certain cathartic. It can also be used as an alternative. In constipation it acts upon the bowels without disposing them to subsequent costiveness.

Dose—A teaspoonful of the root, cut fine to a pint of boiling water. Take one teaspoonful at a time as required....

The *Encyclopaedia Britannica* gives this warning about podophyllin: "In toxic doses podophyllin causes intense enteritis which may end in death." It is my opinion that amateurs would do well to go slow on home dosage with this powerful drug.

Besides mandrake the May apple is also known as Raccoon Berry, Hog Apple and Wild Lemon in various parts of its range. Found from Quebec to Florida and west to Minnesota, Kansas and Texas, this is one of the most familiar of the wild flowers which beautify low, rich woods in the spring. Its horizontal roots persist in the ground year after year, and in the first warm days they send up a one- or two-leaved plant, the new leaves unfolding like tiny umbrellas. They shoot up very quickly and soon reach twelve to eighteen inches in height, growing in dense clusters that often hide the ground. If the plant has but one leaf, the stem is attached to the center. These single-leaved plants do not produce blossoms or fruit, but the yellowish-green leaves, a foot or more in diameter, with seven to nine lobes, drooping around the stem like an open umbrella, are very decorative.

The fruiting stems fork near the top and make a pair of similar but somewhat smaller leaves with the stems attached near the inner edge. The single flower, a beautiful, waxy-white blossom nearly two inches across, appears in the fork of the stem. It is seldom seen by those who only look at May apples from the windows of their speeding cars, for it tends to hide itself under the ample leaves. The flower is followed by a single fruit the size and shape of an egg, with a smooth, yellow skin when ripe, in August or early September in the latitude of Philadelphia. At this time the parent plants have mostly fallen down, and one picks up the ripe luscious fruit where it has fallen to the ground.

Most people consider the flowers ill-smelling, but I love the sweet scent of the ripe fruit with its hint of mysterious muskiness. I have often "smelled out" a patch of ripe May apples while walking through the woods

Mayapple
Podophyllum peltatum

The Message

Cross-country, out of sea fog
comes a letter in dream: a Bard
claims from me "on whose land they grow,"
seeds of the forget-me-not.

"I ask you
to gather them for me," says
the Spirit of Poetry.
                            The varied blue
in small compass. In multitude
a cloud of blue, a river
beside the brown river.

Not flowers but
their seeds, I am to send him.
And he bids me
remember my nature, speaking of it
as of a power.
And gather
the flowers, and the flowers
of "labor" (pink in the dream,
a bright centaury with more petals.
Or the form changes to a sea-pink.)

Ripple of blue in which are
distinct blues. Bold
centaur-seahorse-salt-carnation
flower of work and transition.
Out of sea fog, from a hermitage,
at break of day.

Shall I find them, then—
here on my own land, recalled
to my nature?
                O, great Spirit!

Draba
Draba verna

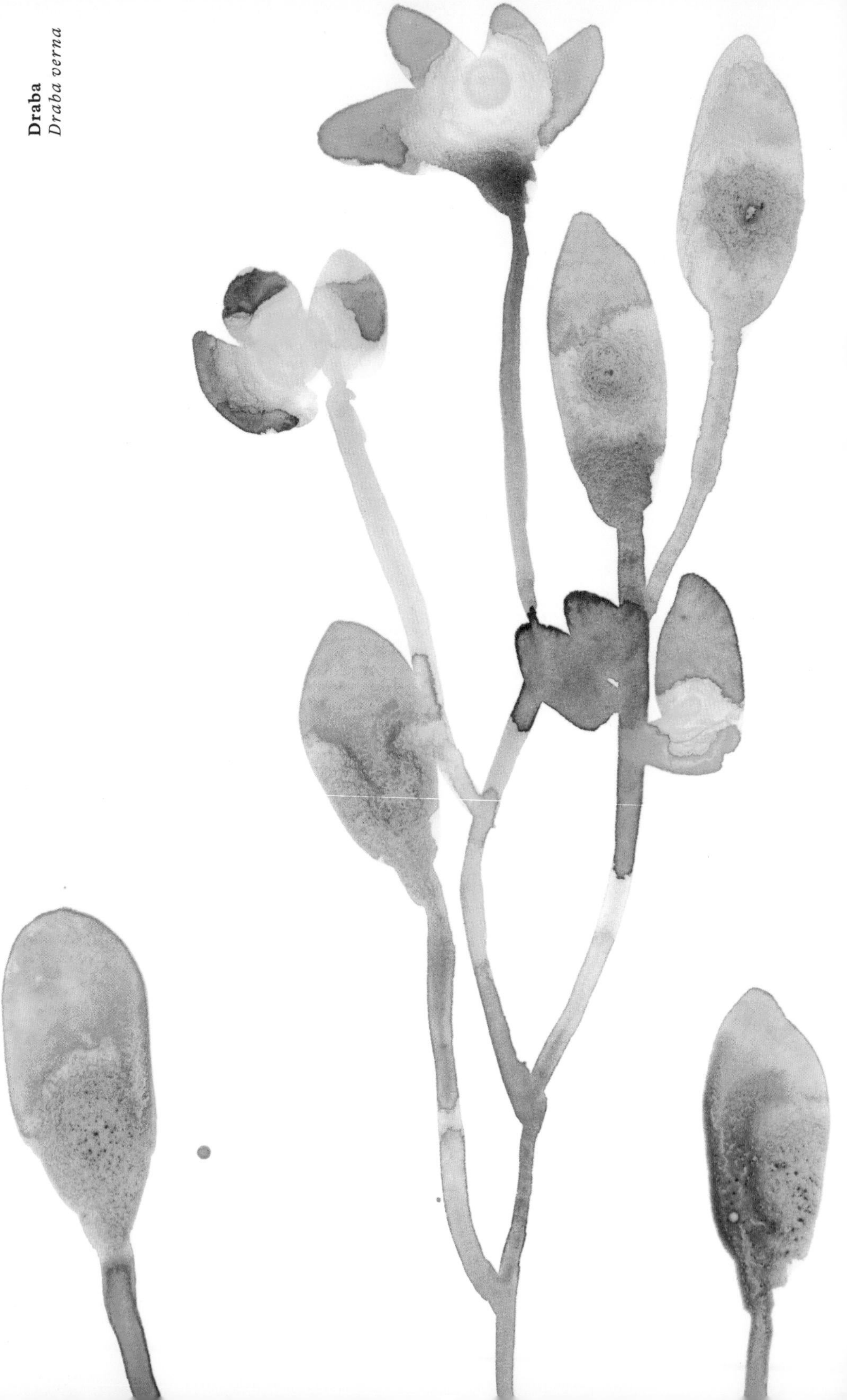

ALDO LEOPOLD

Draba

Within a few weeks now Draba, the smallest flower that blows, will sprinkle every sandy place with small blooms.

He who hopes for spring with upturned eye never sees so small a thing as Draba. He who despairs of spring with downcast eye steps on it, unknowing. He who searches for spring with his knees in the mud finds it, in abundance.

Draba asks, and gets, but scant allowance of warmth and comfort; it subsists on the leavings of unwanted time and space. Botany books give it two or three lines, but never a plate or portrait. Sand too poor and sun too weak for bigger, better blooms are good enough for Draba. After all it is no spring flower, but only a postscript to a hope.

Draba plucks no heartstrings. Its perfume, if there is any, is lost in the gusty winds. Its color is plain white. Its leaves wear a sensible woolly coat. Nothing eats it; it is too small. No poets sing of it. Some botanist once gave it a Latin name, and then forgot it. Altogether it is of no importance—just a small creature that does a small job quickly and well.

ROBERT HAYDEN

The Night-Blooming Cereus

And so for nights
we waited, hoping to see
the heavy bud
        break into flower.

        On its neck-like tube
hooking down from the edge
of the leaf-branch
        nearly to the floor,

        the bud packed
tight with its miracle swayed
stiffly on breaths
        of air, moved

        as though impelled
by stirrings within itself.
It repelled as much
        as it fascinated me

        sometimes–snake,
eyeless bird head,
beak that would gape
        with grotesque life-squawk.

        But you, my dear,
conceded less to the bizarre
than to the imminence
        of bloom. Yet we agreed

we ought
to celebrate the blossom,
paint ourselves, dance
      in honor of

      archaic mysteries
when it appeared. Meanwhile
we waited, aware
      of rigorous design.

      Backster's
polygraph, I thought,
would have shown
      (as clearly as it had

      a philodendron's
fear) tribal sentience
in the cactus, focused
      energy of will.

      The belling of
tropic perfume–that
signaling
      not meant for us;

      the darkness
cloying with summoning
fragrance. We dropped
      trivial tasks

      and marveling
beheld at last the achieved
flower. Its moonlight
      petals were

still unfold-
ing, the spike fringe of the outer
perianth recessing
        as we watched.

        Lunar presence,
foredoomed, already dying,
it charged the room
        with plangency

        older than human
cries, ancient as prayers
invoking Osiris, Krishna,
        Tezcatlipoca.

        We spoke
in whispers when
we spoke
        at all ...

Night-blooming cereus
Peniocereus greggii

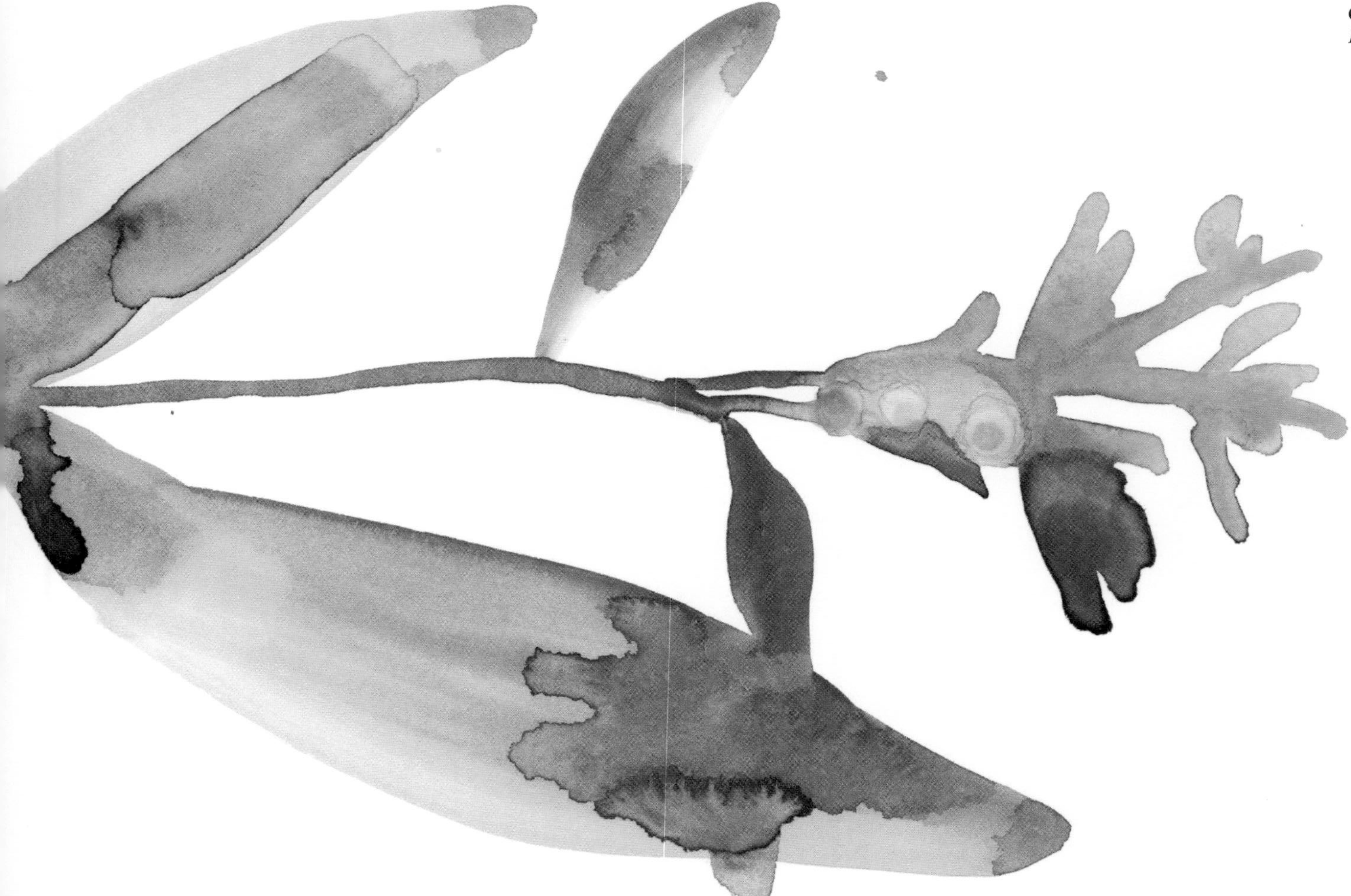

Cardinal flower
Lobelia cardinalis

ROSS GAY

Ending the Estrangement

from my mother's sadness, which was,
to me, unbearable, until,
it felt to me
not like what I thought it felt like
to her, and so felt inside myself—like death,
like dying, which I would almost
have rather done, though adding to her sadness
would rather die than do—
but, by sitting still, like what, in fact, it was—
a form of gratitude
which when last it came
drifted like a meadow lit by torches
of cardinal flower, one of whose crimson blooms,
when a hummingbird hovered nearby,
I slipped into my mouth
thereby coaxing the bird
to scrawl on my tongue
its heart's frenzy, its fleet
nectar-questing song,
with whom, with you, dear mother,
I now sing along.

Anecdote of Canna

Huge are the canna in the dreams of
X, the mighty thought, the mighty man.
They fill the terrace of his capitol.

His thought sleeps not. Yet the thought that wakes
In sleep may never meet another thought
Or thing.... Now day-break comes....

X promenades the dewy stones,
Observes the canna with a clinging eye,
Observes and then continues to observe.

Spiderwort
Tradescantia ohiensis

The Steeple-Jack

Dürer would have seen a reason for living
    in a town like this, with eight stranded whales
to look at; with the sweet sea air coming into your house
on a fine day, from water etched
    with waves as formal as the scales
on a fish.

One by one in two's and three's, the seagulls keep
    flying back and forth over the town clock,
or sailing around the lighthouse without moving their wings—
rising steadily with a slight
    quiver of the body—or flock
mewing where

a sea the purple of the peacock's neck is
    paled to greenish azure as Dürer changed
the pine green of the Tyrol to peacock blue and guinea
gray. You can see a twenty-five-
    pound lobster; and fish nets arranged
to dry. The

whirlwind fife-and-drum of the storm bends the salt
    marsh grass, disturbs stars in the sky and the
star on the steeple; it is a privilege to see so
much confusion. Disguised by what
    might seem the opposite, the sea-
side flowers and

trees are favored by the fog so that you have
    the tropics at first hand: the trumpet-vine,
fox-glove, giant snap-dragon, a salpiglossis that has

COMMELINACEAE / SPIDERWORT FAMILY   **139**

spots and stripes; morning-glories, gourds,
        or moon-vines trained on fishing-twine
at the back door;

cat-tails, flags, blueberries and spiderwort,
        striped grass, lichens, sunflowers, asters, daisies—
yellow and crab-claw ragged sailors with green bracts—toad-plant,
petunias, ferns; pink lilies, blue
        ones, tigers; poppies; black sweet-peas.
The climate

is not right for the banyan, frangipani, or
        jack-fruit trees; or for exotic serpent
life. Ring lizard and snake-skin for the foot, if you see fit;
but here they've cats, not cobras, to
        keep down the rats. The diffident
little newt

with white pin-dots on black horizontal spaced-
        out bands lives here; yet there is nothing that
ambition can buy or take away. The college student
named Ambrose sits on the hillside
        with his not-native books and hat
and sees boats

at sea progress white and rigid as if in
        a groove. Liking an elegance of which
the source is not bravado, he knows by heart the antique
sugar-bowl shaped summer-house of
        interlacing slats, and the pitch
of the church

spire, not true, from which a man in scarlet lets
        down a rope as a spider spins a thread;
he might be part of a novel, but on the sidewalk a
sign says C. J. Poole, Steeple-Jack,

in black and white; and one in red
and white says

Danger. The church portico has four fluted
    columns, each a single piece of stone, made
modester by white-wash. This would be a fit haven for
waifs, children, animals, prisoners,
    and presidents who have repaid
sin-driven

senators by not thinking about them. The
    place has a school-house, a post-office in a
store, fish-houses, hen-houses, a three-masted
    schooner on
the stocks. The hero, the student,
    the steeple-jack, each in his way,
is at home.

It could not be dangerous to be living
    in a town like this, of simple people,
who have a steeple-jack placing danger-signs by the church
while he is gilding the solid-
    pointed star, which on a steeple
stands for hope.

Shortia galacifolia

About the sprightly form of shortia there clings a strange story. It is the plant that has interested great men who searched for it until its haunts were revealed and its beauty universally acknowledged. It was the much desired of Dr. Asa Gray, and is as indelibly associated with his memory as is the Catawba rhododendron with that of Michaux.

When Dr. Gray was in Paris in 1839 he observed in the herbarium of the elder Michaux an unnamed specimen of a plant. The leaves and a single fruit were all that was preserved of it, and its label stated simply that it had been collected in "les hautes montagnes de Carolinie." Its power to arouse Dr. Gray's curiosity was so great that on his return to America he hunted assiduously for the plant in the mountains of North Carolina, but wholly without success. In fact, in an account he gave after his return from these mountains, he said: "We were likewise unsuccessful in our search for a remarkable undescribed plant with the habit of pyrola and the foliage of galax which was obtained by Michaux in the high mountains of Carolina. The only specimen extant is among the Plantæ incognitæ of the Michauxian herbarium, in fruit; and we were anxious to obtain flowering specimens that we might complete its history: as I have long wished to dedicate the plant to Professor Short of Kentucky whose attainments and eminent services in North American botany are well known and appreciated both at home and abroad."

Two years after this, however, Dr. Gray ventured to describe the plant and dedicated it, as he had wished, to Dr. C. W. Short. In this way it received its first public recognition. Henceforth no botanist ever visited the region without searching for shortia. It was courted almost as faithfully as was the philosopher's stone. In the meantime, Dr. Gray had found among a collection of Japanese plants a specimen almost identical with the well-remembered one of Michaux, a coincidence which strengthened his faith in the existence of the American species. It was not, however, until 1877 that it was found, and then quite accidentally, by G. M. Hyams, a boy who knew little about the good luck that had befallen him. He had picked it up on the banks of the Catawba River near the town of Marion in McDowell County, North Carolina. Fortunately the father of this boy was a professed herbalist and through a correspondent finally learned the true nature of the plant. It had been collected when in flower. With its aid, therefore, Dr. Gray was enabled to substantiate his original ideas of the genus and to perfect its description. But as for its natural habitat he still maintained that Michaux could not have been so mistaken; that the true home of shortia must be in "les hautes montagnes de Carolinie." It was quite possible, he argued, that the point on the Catawba where it had been found was an outlying haven to which it might have been washed. So with renewed energy it was searched for through the mountains until discouragement lagged the footsteps of the seekers.

In the autumn of the year 1886 Professor Sargent visited the mountainous region of North Carolina about the head waters of the Keowee River, the great eastern fork of the Savannah, with the object in view of rediscovering Magnolia cordata. At Hog Back, a place now called Sapphire, he was met by Mr. Frank Boynton. One evening after dark Professor Sargent came in with his portfolio and took from it, among other things that he had gathered, a leaf. "What is it?" he asked. Mr. Boynton was about to answer, "It is galax"; but on looking at the leaf more closely, he said he didn't know. During that evening the Professor's mail was brought in, among the letters being one from Dr. Gray, which read as follows:

September 17, 1886

My dear Sargent:
Would I were with you! I can only say crown yourself with glory by discovering a habitat—the original habitat of shortia—which we will believe Michaux found near where the Magnolia cordata came from—or in that first expedition.

Yours ever,
Asa Gray

Mr. Stiles the editor of *Garden and Forest* who also was present on this eventful evening then said, in a joking way: "That's shortia you have in your hand." This proved to be true. The leaf was shortia. Professor Sargent had found it, just ninety-eighty years after Michaux's discovery, probably near the same spot.

About two weeks later, when this astonishing fact had been fully ascertained by Professor Sargent, he sent word to Mr. Boynton who, with

Acony bell,
Oconee bells
Shortia galacifolia

his brother, then went back definitely to locate the plant. They found it growing near Bear Camp Creek in a rather limited quantity, but still enough for them to carry away a bag full of specimens for distribution.

In the following spring Mr. Harbison started out in quest of it. He went beyond Bear Creek to the forks of the rivers. There he saw it growing in great masses, acres, in fact, which were as thickly covered as clover fields. Wagon-loads of it were eventually taken away and still there appeared to be no diminution of its abundance.

So ended the search for shortia, once deemed so rare. Through the further efforts of Mr. Harbison the plant is now well known, and a common one in nursery catalogues. In its wild state it grows best under the shade of kalmias and rhododendrons.

RALPH WALDO EMERSON

The Rhodora

On being asked, whence is the flower.

In May, when sea-winds pierced our solitudes,
I found the fresh Rhodora in the woods,
Spreading its leafless blooms in a damp nook,
To please the desert and the sluggish brook.
The purple petals fallen in the pool
Made the black water with their beauty gay;
Here might the red-bird come his plumes to cool,
And court the flower that cheapens his array.
Rhodora! if the sages ask thee why
This charm is wasted on the earth and sky,
Tell them, dear, that, if eyes were made for seeing,
Then beauty is its own excuse for Being;
Why thou wert there, O rival of the rose!
I never thought to ask; I never knew;
But in my simple ignorance suppose
The self-same power that brought me there, brought you.

Rhodora
Rhododendron canadense

The Mayflowers

The trailing arbutus, or mayflower, grows abundantly in the vicinity of Plymouth, and was the first flower that greeted the Pilgrims after their fearful winter. The name *mayflower* was familiar in England, as the application of it to the historic vessel shows, but it was applied by the English, and still is, to the hawthorn. Its use in New England in connection with *Epigæa repens* dates from a very early day, some claiming that the first Pilgrims so used it, in affectionate memory of the vessel and its English flower association.

Sad Mayflower! watched by winter stars,
  And nursed by winter gales,
With petals of the sleeted spars,
  And leaves of frozen sails!

What had she in those dreary hours,
  Within her ice-rimmed bay,
In common with the wild-wood flowers,
  The first sweet smiles of May?

Yet, "God be praised!" the Pilgrim said,
  Who saw the blossoms peer
Above the brown leaves, dry and dead,
  "Behold our Mayflower here!"

"God wills it: here our rest shall be,
  Our years of wandering o'er;
For us the Mayflower of the sea
  Shall spread her sails no more."

O sacred flowers of faith and hope,
  As sweetly now as then
Ye bloom on many a birchen slope,
  In many a pine-dark glen.

Mayflower, trailing arbutus
Epigaea repens

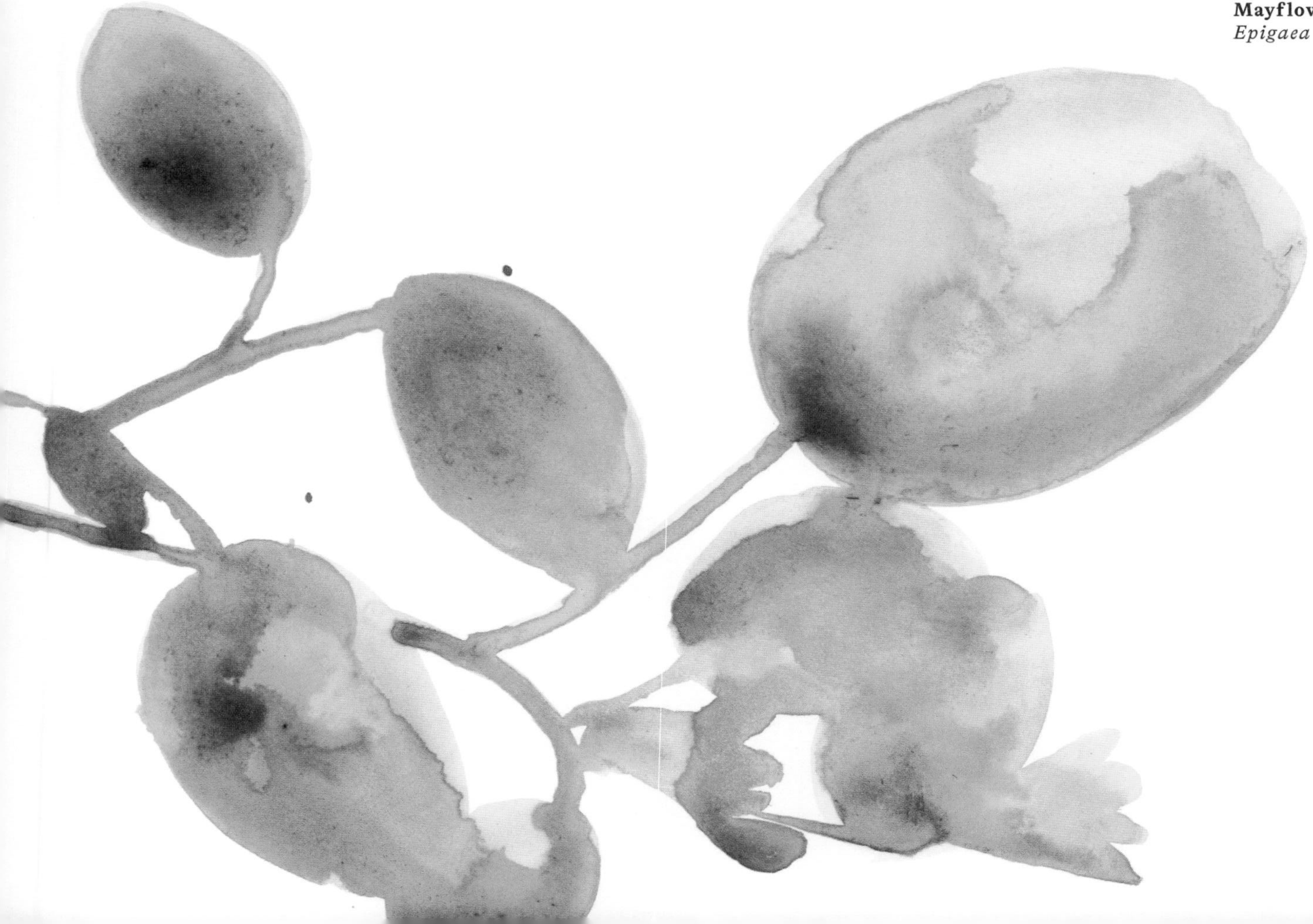

Mayflower, trailing arbutus
Epigaea repens

Behind the sea-wall's rugged length,
  Unchanged, your leaves unfold,
Like love behind the manly strength
  Of the brave hearts of old.

So live the fathers in their sons,
  Their sturdy faith be ours,
And ours the love that overruns
  Its rocky strength with flowers.

The Pilgrim's wild and wintry day
  Its shadow round us draws;
The Mayflower of his stormy bay,
  Our Freedom's struggling cause.

But warmer suns erelong shall bring
  To life the frozen sod;
And through dead leaves of hope shall spring
  Afresh the flowers of God!

The Trailing Arbutus

Can words describe the fragrance of the very breath of spring—that delicious commingling of the perfume of arbutus, the odor of pines, and the snow-soaked soil just warming into life? Those who know the flower only as it is sold in the city streets, tied with wet, dirty string into tight bunches, withered and forlorn, can have little idea of the joy of finding the pink, pearly blossoms freshly opened among the withered leaves of oak and chestnut, moss, and pine needles in which they nestle close to the cold earth in the leafless, windy northern forest. Even in Florida, where broad patches carpet the woods in February, one misses something of the arbutus's accustomed charm simply because there are no slushy remnants of snow drifts, no reminders of winter hardships in the vicinity. There can be no glad surprise at finding dainty spring flowers in a land of perpetual summer. [...]

Certainly the arbutus is not a typical May blossom even in New England. Bryant associates it with the hepatica, our earliest spring flower, in his poem, "The Twenty-seventh of March":

> Within the woods
> Tufts of ground laurel, creeping underneath
> The leaves of the last summer, send their sweets
> Upon the chilly air, and by the oak,
> The squirrel cups, a graceful company
> Hide in their bells a soft aërial blue.

There is little use trying to coax this shyest of sylvan flowers into our gardens where other members of its family, rhododendrons, laurels, and azaleas make themselves delightfully at home. It is wild as a hawk, an untamable creature that slowly pines to death when brought into contact with civilization. Greedy street venders, who ruthlessly tear up the plant by the yard, and others without even the excuse of eking out a paltry income by its sale, have already exterminated it within a wide radius of our Eastern cities. How curious that the majority of people show their appreciation of a flower's beauty only by selfishly, ignorantly picking every specimen they can find!

Indian pipe
Monotropa uniflora

EMILY DICKINSON

'Tis whiter than an Indian Pipe —
'Tis dimmer than a Lace —
No stature has it, like a Fog
When you approach the place —
Not any voice imply it here
Or intimate it there
A spirit — how doth it accost —
What function hath the Air?
This limitless Hyperbole
Each one of us shall be —
'Tis Drama — if Hypothesis
It be not Tragedy —

EMILY DICKINSON

There is a flower that Bees prefer —
And Butterflies — desire —
To gain the Purple Democrat
The Humming Bird — aspire —

And Whatsoever Insect pass —
A Honey bear away
Proportioned to his several dearth
And her — capacity —

Her face be rounder than the Moon
And ruddier than the Gown
Of Orchis in the Pasture—
Or Rhododendron — worn —

She doth not wait for June —
Before the World be Green —
Her sturdy little Countenance
Against the Wind — be seen —

Contending with the Grass —
Near Kinsman to Herself —
For Privilege of Sod and Sun —
Sweet Litigants for Life —

And when the Hills be full —
And newer fashions blow —
Doth not retract a single spice
For pang of jealousy —

Her Public — be the Noon —
Her Providence — the Sun —
Her Progress — by the Bee — proclaimed —
In sovereign — Swerveless Tune —

The Bravest — of the Host —
Surrendering — the last —
Nor even of Defeat — aware —
When cancelled by the Frost —

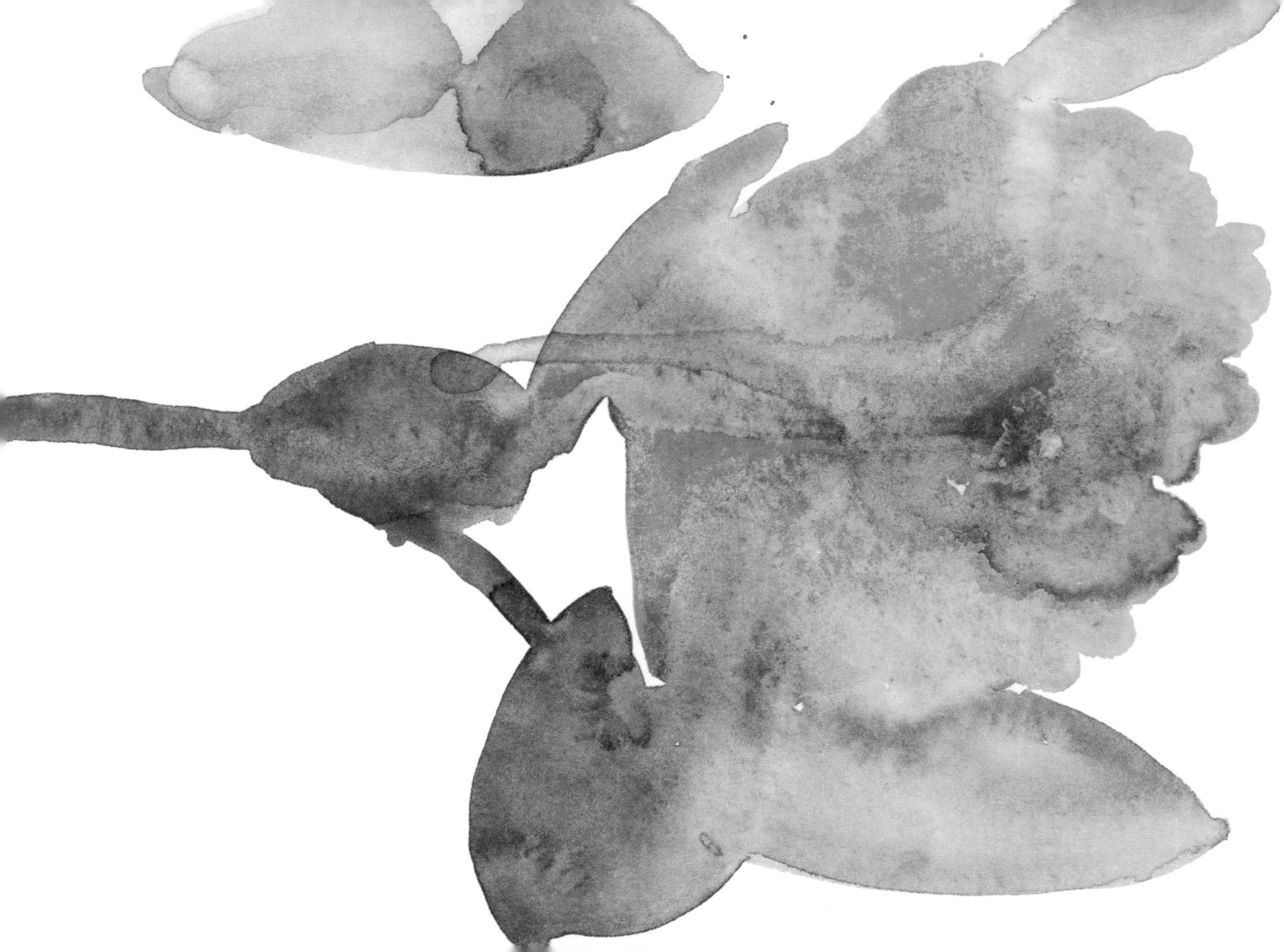

Red clover
Trifolium pratense

EMILY DICKINSON

The Clover's simple Fame
Remembered of the Cow —
Is better than enameled Realms
Of notability.
Renown perceives itself
And that degrades the Flower —
The Daisy that has looked behind
Has compromised its power —

EMILY DICKINSON

To make a prairie it takes a clover and one bee,
One clover, and a bee,
And revery.
The revery alone will do,
If bees are few.

HERMAN MELVILLE

To Winnefred

With you and me, Winnie, Red Clover has always been one of the dearest of the flowers of the field: an avowal—by the way—as you well ween, which implies no undelight as to this ruddy young brother's demure little half-sister, White Clover. Our feeling for both sorts originates in no fanciful associations egotistic in kind. It is not, for example, because in any exceptional way we have verified in experience the aptness of that pleasant figure of speech, *Living in clover*—not for this do we so take to the Ruddy One, for all that we once dwelt annually surrounded by flushed acres of it. Neither have we, jointly or severally, so frequently lighted upon that rare four-leaved variety accounted of happy augury to the finder; though, to be sure, on my part, I yearly remind you of the coincidence in my chancing upon such a specimen by the wayside on the early forenoon of the fourth day of a certain bridal month, now four years more than four times ten years ago.

But, tell, do we not take to this flower—for flower it is, though with the florist hardly ranking with the floral clans—not alone that in itself it is a thing of freshness and beauty, but also that being no delicate foster-child of the nurseryman, but a hardy little creature of out-of-doors accessible and familiar to every one, no one can monopolise its charm. Yes, we are communists here.

Sweet in the mouth of that brindled heifer whose breath you so loved to inhale, and doubtless pleasant to her nostril and eye; sweet as well to the like senses in ourselves; prized by that most practical of men, the farmer, to whom wild amaranths in a pasture, though emblems of immortality, are but weeds and anathema; finding favor even with so peevish a busybody as the bee, is it not the felicitous fortune of our favorite, to incur no creature's displeasure, but to enjoy, and without striving for it, the spontaneous good-will of all? Why it is that this little peasant of the flowers revels in so enviable an immunity and privilege, not in equal degree shared by any of us mortals however gifted and good; that indeed is something the reason whereof may not slumber very deep. But—*In pace*; always leave a sleeper to his repose.

How often at our adopted homestead on the hill-side—now ours no more—the farm-house, long ago shorn by the urbane barbarian succeeding us in the proprietorship—shorn of its gambrel roof and dormer windows, and when I last saw it indolently settling in serene contentment of natural decay; how often, Winnie, did I come in from my ramble, early in the bright summer mornings of old, with a handful of these cheap little cheery roses of the meek, newly purloined from the fields to consecrate them on that bit of a maple-wood mantel—your altar, somebody called it—in the familiar room facing your beloved South! And in October most did I please myself in gathering them from the moist matted aftermath in an enriched little hollow near by, soon to be snowed upon and for consecutive months sheeted from view. And once—you remember it—having culled them in a sunny little flurry of snow, winter's frolic skirmisher in advance, the genial warmth of your chamber melted the fleecy flakes into dew-drops rolling off the ruddiness. "Tears of the happy," you said. Well, and to whom but to thee, Madonna of the Trefoil, should I now dedicate these "Weeds and Wildings," thriftless children of quite another and yet later spontaneous aftergrowth, and bearing indications too apparent it may be, of that terminating season on which the offerer verges. But take them. And for aught suggestive of the "melting mood" that any may possibly betray, call to mind the dissolved snow-flakes on the ruddy oblation of old, and remember your "Tears of the Happy."

Red clover
Trifolium pratense

CYRUS CASSELLS

A Siren Patch of Indigo

Listen: though we swell as rampant
woodland or riverbank blossoms

(*Baptisia australis*)
in your tensile world,

as commonplace beauty
and reachable remedy,

as soothing eyewash for the Osage,
hardy dye for the Cherokee,

quiet as it's kept,
we're more akin to

clearing and hillside way-showers,
offhand griots quietly reminding you

the punishing rows, the grim
nightworld of the Middle Passage

was never your true province;
even in appalling chains,

the light of your integrity,
your inmost wonder

still encircled you,
resolute, inviolate.

Always recall, dear
progeny of Sea Island slaves,

in galling dearth
or in Juneteenth glory,

our deep, annealing, sacramental blue
belongs to you.

Touch-Me-Nots (*Mimosa pudica*)

Of all the approximately 1.5 million plants the Chicago Botanic Garden has on site, the one that scared and delighted me the most when I was a child was *Mimosa pudica*—the touch-me-not plant. (Or, depending on your preference: sensitive plant, shame plant, humble plant, tickle-me plant, and my favorite, sleeping grass.) In Malayalam, my father's language, it's called thottavadi, which—if you are a wily second grader—is an especially fun name to call a shy goldfish or an orphaned bunny you find after school one day, or to simply scream out loud while riding a bike in the suburbs. Why all the fuss and euphoria over some greenery? Well, I still coo over its delightful pinnation, the double-leaf pattern feathering outward then inward from both sides of a single stem, and its spherical lavender-pink flowers, which bloom only in summer, and look as if someone crossed a My Little Pony doll with a tiny firework. But its best and most notable feature is that when you piano your fingers over the leaves of this plant, they give a shudder and a shake and quickly fold shut, like someone doesn't want to spill a secret.

Scientists have learned that when the plant's leaves are touched, potassium ions are released, causing a significant drop in cell pressure and leading the leaves to collapse as if the plant were nodding off to sleep. This elegant movement, called thigmonasty, topples carpenter worms and spider mites to the ground just as they think they'll be getting their bite on.

The touch-me-not is native to Central and South America but can be found along roadsides in Florida and as far north as Maryland. I've seen expensive grow kits for them in hobby and craft stores, which my parents find amusing; in India and the northern Philippines, the plant is often considered a weed. Woe to those who decide to plant it in their yards. The touch-me-not is best considered a whimsical houseplant and that's it, unless you find yourself somehow cavorting with cobras—it can be used as a neutralizer for venom. You don't want to mess with how fast it spreads and drops roots. Dozens of garden and landscaping message boards are filled with urgent pleas for help to remove the plant before it covers up house pets and lawn furniture like a bad imitation of Miss Havisham's garden from *Great Expectations*.

How I wish I could fold inward and shut down and shake off predators with one touch. What a skill, what a thrill that could be: Touch me not on the dance floor, don't you see my wedding ring? Touch me not in the subway; touch me not on the train, on a plane, in a cab or a limo. Touch me not in a funicular going up the side of a mountain, touch me not on the deck of a cruise ship, touch me not in the green room right before I go onstage, touch me not at the bar while I wait for my to-go order, touch me not at a faculty party, touch me not if you are a visiting writer, touch me not at the post office while I'm waiting to send a letter to my grandmother, let me and my children and everyone's children decide who touches them and who touches them not, touch them not, touch them not.

GARY SNYDER

Brighter Yellow

An "Ozark Trucking" bigrig pulls up
by me on the freeway, such a vivid yellow!
a brighter yellow than bulldozers.
This morning James Lee Jobe was talking
          of the wild blue bonnets
and the dark red Indian paintbrush down in Texas.
Said, "from a distance—them growing all together
          makes a field of solid purple."
Hey—keep on the right side
of that yellow line

ENRIQUE SALMÓN

Milkvetch

Astragalus spp.

Family: Fabaceae
Parts Used: leaves, fruit, roots
Season: spring, summer, fall
Region: North America

Toward the end of every fall and during the winter, Navajo people gather at specific places around the large Navajo Nation that is spread across the Four Corners region. They bring food, gifts, and prayers as part of the Night Chant, a nine-day healing ceremony that is performed to restore order and balance in the Navajo universe and to heal not only some of the people in attendance but also the land, the animals, and the plants. The ceremony also presents an opportunity for young Navajos to become initiated into *hózhó*, the Navajo concept of balance and beauty. Yeibichai (Talking Gods) appear and specific chants are performed during four major sections of the ritual. During the ceremony, the singers and participants engage in sweat baths, ritual cleansings, masked dance, and the ingestion of medicinal plants. On the last night of the ninth day, the closing chant is performed. The participants recite after the main singer several lines offered to the thunderbird of pollen. The song lines ask the Yeibichai and the thunderbird of pollen that the people be allowed to walk in balance with all nature. At one point, they recite: "May fair plants of all kinds come with you." The song ends thus:

In beauty I walk,
With beauty before me, I walk,
With beauty behind me, I walk,
With beauty below me, I walk,
With beauty above me, I walk,
With beauty all around me, I walk,
It is finished in beauty,
It is finished in beauty,
It is finished in beauty,
It is finished in beauty.

During this most important of ceremonies, the small purple-flowered *Astragalus allochrous* (*txáa'iiltchóciih* in the Navajo language) plays an important role; its leaves are used as a ceremonial emetic. It too is considered a Navajo life medicine.

USES

An infusion of the leaves can be taken as a laxative or as an emetic. The leaves are ground up by the Cheyenne and applied to poison ivy rash, and a poultice of the leaves can be used externally for back pain. The Acoma eat the young root of *Astragalus lentiginosus*, and the Hopi eat the roots of *A. ceramicus*. An infusion of the root is applied topically to sores and wounds and tired, sore eyes; it can also be taken for stomachaches and coughs and to reduce fevers. A decoction of milkvetch root is applied to bleeding wounds and given to people suffering from convulsions; it is also used to reduce fevers, to relieve menstrual pains, and to treat sore throats and toothaches. The roots are often simply chewed, to relieve toothaches, coughs, and sore throats; as a cathartic; to reduce fevers; and to treat stomachaches, the flu, and cramps. Finally, the seeds are collected and either eaten directly or pounded into a flour and used in other dishes.

IDENTIFICATION AND HARVEST

Astragalus is in the bean family, and one of the identifying characteristics of these little annuals and perennials are the greenish white to cream to purple pea-shaped flowers that often grow at the end of long stalks. Following the flowers are smooth, erect, woody fruit pods that contain several tiny seeds. The leaves of milkvetches are smooth and pinnately compound; the leaflets grow up to 2 inches long. Most plants are small, reaching only about a foot in height; a few species (e.g., *A canadensis*) grow up to 5 feet tall. Around 300 species of milkvetch can be found growing across much of North America, from Vermont to Virginia and west to Washington and California; plants most often occur in open plains and prairie landscapes, and on mesa tops and other open areas of the Southwest.

HEALTH BENEFITS

In general, *Astragalus* species contain galactomannans, saponins, amino acids, flavonoids, isoflavonoids, alkaloids, astragalosides, and terpenes. These phytochemicals demonstrate a variety of pharmacological activities; besides acting as immunoregulators, expectorants, and gastrointestinal protectors, they are antioxidant, diuretic, anti-inflammatory, bactericidal, hypotensive, antidiabetic, hepatoprotective, neuroprotective, and analgesic.

Closed gentian
Gentiana rubricaulis

JAMES SCHUYLER

Closed Gentian Distances

A nothing day full of
wild beauty and the
timer pings. Roll up
the silver off the bay
take down the clouds
sort the spruce and
send to laundry marked,
more starch. Goodbye
golden- and silver-
rod, asters, bayberry
crisp in elegance.
Little fish stream
by, a river in water.

WILLIAM CULLEN BRYANT

To the Fringed Gentian

Thou blossom bright with autumn dew,
And colored with the heaven's own blue,
That openest when the quiet light
Succeeds the keen and frosty night,

Thou comest not when violets lean
O'er wandering brooks and springs unseen,
Or columbines, in purple dressed,
Nod o'er the ground-bird's hidden nest.

Thou waitest late and com'st alone,
When woods are bare and birds are flown,
And frost and shortening days portend
The aged year is near his end.

Then doth thy sweet and quiet eye
Look through its fringes to the sky,
Blue – blue – as if that sky let fall
A flower from its cerulean wall.

I would that thus, when I shall see
The hour of death draw near to me,
Hope, blossoming within my heart,
May look to heaven as I depart.

Iris, blue flag
Iris versicolor

LOUISE GLÜCK

The Wild Iris

At the end of my suffering
there was a door.

Hear me out: that which you call death
I remember.

Overhead, noises, branches of the pine shifting.
Then nothing. The weak sun
flickered over the dry surface.

It is terrible to survive
as consciousness
buried in the dark earth.

Then it was over: that which you fear, being
a soul and unable
to speak, ending abruptly, the stiff earth
bending a little. And what I took to be
birds darting in low shrubs.

You who do not remember
passage from the other world
I tell you I could speak again: whatever
returns from oblivion returns
to find a voice:

from the center of my life came
a great fountain, deep blue
shadows on azure seawater.

Irises

1.
In the night, in the wind, at the edge of the rain,
I find five irises, and call them lovely.
As if a woman, once, lay by them awhile,
then woke, rose, went, the memory of hair
lingers on their sweet tongues.

I'd like to tear these petals with my teeth.
I'd like to investigate these hairy selves,
their beauty and indifference. They hold
their breath all their lives
and open, open.

2.
We are not lovers, not brother and sister,
though we drift hand in hand through a hall
thrilling and burning as thought and desire
expire, and, over this dream of life,
this life of sleep, we waken dying—
violet becoming blue, growing
black, black—all that
an iris ever prays,
when it prays,
to be.

WILLIAM CARLOS WILLIAMS

The Red Lily

To the bob-white's call
and drone of reaper

tumbling daisies in the sun—
one by one

about the smutting panels of
white doors

grey shingles slip and fall—
But you, a loveliness

of even lines
curving to the throat, the

crossroads is your home.
You are, upon

your steady stem
one trumpeted wide flower

slightly tilted
above a scale of buds—

Sometimes a farmer's wife
gathers an armful

for her pitcher on the porch—
Topping a stone wall

against the shale-ledge
a field full—

By the road, the river
the edge of the woods

—opening in the sun
closing in the dark—

everywhere
Red Lily

in your common cup
all beauty lies

Hibiscus
Hibiscus furcellatus

W. S. MERWIN

The Rose Beetle

It is said that you came from China
but you never saw China
you eat up the leaves here

your ancestors travelled blind in eggs
you arrive just after dark from underground
with a clicking whir in the first night
knowing by the smell what leaves to eat here
where you have wakened for the first time

the strawberry leaves foreign as you
the beans the orchid tree the eggplant
the old leaves of the heliconia the banana some palms
and the roses from everywhere but here
and the hibiscus from here the abutilons
the royal ilima

in the night you turn them into lace
into an arid net
into sky

like the sky long ago over China

JEAN TOOMER

November Cotton Flower

Boll-weevil's coming, and the winter's cold,
Made cotton-stalks look rusty, seasons old,
And cotton, scarce as any southern snow,
Was vanishing; the branch, so pinched and slow,
Failed in its function as the autumn rake;
Drouth fighting soil had caused the soil to take
All water from the streams; dead birds were found
In wells a hundred feet below the ground—
Such was the season when the flower bloomed.
Old folks were startled, and it soon assumed
Significance. Superstition saw
Something it had never seen before:
Brown eyes that loved without a trace of fear,
Beauty so sudden for that time of year.

Cotton flower
Gossypium hirsutum

Red trillium, red wake robin
Trillium erectum

The Spring Ephemerals

Here she comes with her face to be kissed. Here she comes
lugging two plastic sacks looped over her arms and stuffed

with fresh shoots. It's barely dawn. She's been out
for an hour already, digging up what she can save

before developers raze the day's lot sites and set
woodpiles ablaze. That's their plan for the ninety-plus acres.

She squats in the sun to show me wild phlox
in pink-running-to-blue, rue anemone, masses

of colt's foot, wild ginger, blood root and may-
apples, bracken and fiddlehead fern—ferns being not

spring ephemerals, per se, but imperiled by road-graders
come to shave the shaded slopes where they grow.

Once I held her in a snow cover of sheets. Wind beat
the world, while we listened. Her back was a sail

unfurling. She wanted me to touch stitches there,
little scabs, where doctors had sliced the sick cells

and cauterized her skin for safety's sake.
Now her hands are spotted by briars, bubbles of blood

daubed in brown. She's got burrs in her red hair.
Both sleeves are torn. She kneels as the sunlight

cuts through pine needles above us, casting a grid
like the plats the surveyors use. It's the irony

of every cell: that it divides to multiply.
This way the greedy have bought up the land

behind ours to parcel for resale at fifty-
fold what they paid weeks ago.

It's a race to outrun their gas cans and matches,
to line the path to our creek with transplants

of spice bush, yellow fawn-lily, to set aside space
in the garden for the frail. She adjusts the map

she's drawn of the tumbling woods—where each
flower and fern come from, under what tree, beside

which ridge. *Dysfunctional junctional nevus*:
a name like a bad joke for the growth on her skin,

pigment too pale for much sunlight. *Drooping trillium*,
she says, handing me a cluster of roots, unfolding leaves—

rare around here. How delicate, a trillium,
whose oils are food for ants, whose sessile leaves are

palm-sized, tripartite. They spread a shadow over
each stem's fragile one bloom, white in most cases,

though this one's maroon. This makes it rarer.
It hangs like a red bell safe from the sun. It bends

like our necks bend, not in grief, not prayer,
as we work with our backs to the trees, as they burn.

The Bitterroot

It was the time just after winter in the valley in the mountains. There was no food and the people were starving. The fish had not yet returned to the streams and the game animals had moved far away into the mountains. The men had gone out to seek game and they had been gone a long time. It was not yet time for berries to ripen, and the women had gathered what plants they could find that could be eaten, but the ones that were left from the winter were tough and stringy.

In one of the lodges, an old woman was grieving because there was no food for her grandchildren. She could no longer bear to look at their thin, sad faces, and she went out before sunrise to sing her death song beside the little stream which ran through the valley.

"I am old," she sang, "but my grandchildren are young. It is a hard time that has come, when children must die with their grandmothers."

As she knelt by the stream, singing and weeping, the Sun came over the mountains. It heard her death song and it spoke to that old woman's spirit helper.

"My daughter is crying for her children who are starving," Sun said. "Go now and help her and her people. Give them food."

Then the spirit helper took the form of a redbird and flew down into the valley. It perched on a limb above the old woman's head and began to sing. When she lifted her eyes to look at it, the bird spoke to her.

"My friend," the redbird said, "your tears have gone into Earth. They have formed a new plant there, one which will help you and your people to live. See it come now from Earth, its leaves close to the ground. When its blossoms form, they will have the red color of my wings and the white of your hair."

The old woman looked and it was as the bird said. All around her, in the moist soil, the leaves of a new plant had lifted from Earth. As the sun touched it, a red blossom began to open.

"How can we use this plant?" said the old woman.

"You will dig this plant up by the roots with a digging stick," the redbird said. "Its taste will be bitter, like your tears, but it will be a food to help the people live. Each year it will always come at this time when no other food can be found."

And so it has been to this day. That stream where the old woman wept is called Little Bitterroot and the valley is also named Bitterroot after that plant, which still comes each year after the snows have left the land. Its flowers, which come only when touched by the sun, are as red as the wings of a red spirit bird and as silver as the hair of an old woman. And its taste is still as bitter as the tears of that old woman whose death song turned into a song of survival.

Kūkaʻōhiʻaakalaka

ʻO Kūkaʻōhiʻaakalaka ke kaikunāne a ʻo Kauakuahine ke kaikuahine. Mai Kahiki mai lāua a noho i Hawaiʻi, ʻo Kauakuahine i ʻŌlaʻa me kāna kāne, a ʻo Kūkaʻōhiʻaakalaka i Keaʻau me kāna wahine. ʻAʻohe keiki a Kūkaʻōhiʻaakalaka, a ʻo ke kaikuahine hoʻi, he mau keiki nō. He mahi ʻai ka hana a ke kaikuahine i ʻŌlaʻa a he lawaiʻa kā ke kaikunāne i Keaʻau.

I kēlā a me kēia manawa, ua iho ʻo Kauakuahine me ka ʻai i kahakai na ke kaikunāne a ʻo ka iʻa kāna e hoʻihoʻi mai ai na kona ʻohana. Ua kauoha ʻo Kūkaʻōhiʻaakalaka i kāna wahine e hāʻawi a nui i ka iʻa maloʻo i kona kaikuahine i nā wā a pau āna e iho mai ai me ka ʻai. Ua nānā ihola ka wahine i ka iʻa maloʻo a minamina, a hoʻihoʻi aku nei ma lalo o nā moena e hūnā ai.

I ka iho ʻana mai o Kauakuahine me ka ʻai, ua hala ke kaikunāne i ka lawaiʻa. ʻŌlelo aku nei ke kaikoʻeke, "ʻAʻohe iʻa a māua lā. E nānā aʻe nō ʻoe i kauhale nei, ua nele. ʻO ka paʻakai wale nō kahi mea i loaʻa." Hele nō ʻo Kauakuahine a loaʻa ka līpahapaha, ʻo ko iala hoʻi nō ia. I ka iho hou ʻana mai o Kauakuahine, ʻo ia ana nō, ʻo ka hoʻi nō me ka nele. I ahona nō i kahi līpahapaha.

No ka pī mau o ke kaikoʻeke, ua lilo ia i mea hoʻokaumaha iā Kauakuahine. I kekahi hoʻi ʻana āna me ka līpahapaha, ua manaʻo ʻo ia he mea makehewa ka hoʻoluhi ʻana iā ia iho e lawe mau aku i ka ʻai i Keaʻau a ʻo ka līpahapaha wale nō ka iʻa e hoʻihoʻi aku ai na kāna kāne hoʻomanawanui a me nā keiki a lāua.

I ke kokoke ʻana aku ona i ka hale o lākou ua holo maila ke kāne a me nā keiki e ʻike iā ia. Ua paʻipaʻi pākahi akula ʻo ia iā lākou a lilo lākou i mau ʻiole. ʻO ka ʻiole māhuahua, ka makua kāne ia; ʻo nā ʻiole makaliʻi, ʻo nā keiki nō ia. No Kauakuahine, ua lilo ʻo ia i pūnāwai me ka ua kilihune e heleleʻi ana ma laila.

I ke kaikunāne e lawaiʻa ana, ua hiki akula ka hōʻike a nā akua iā ia i ke pī o ka wahine i ka iʻa a i ka lilo o ke kaikuahine i wai a ʻo ka ʻohana i pua ʻiole. Ua lilo kēia i mea kaumaha i kona noʻonoʻo a hoʻi aku nei i kauhale a nīnau aku i ka wahine, "Ua hāʻawi anei ʻoe i iʻa na nā pōkiʻi o kāua?" "ʻAe, ke hāʻawi mau nei nō au i ka iʻa."

'O ko Kūka'ōhi'aakalaka lālau akula nō ia i nā moena o ka hale o lāua a hāpai a'ela i luna. 'Ike a'ela 'o ia i nā i'a malo'o, ua ho'onoho papa 'ia ma lalo a'e o ka moena, a e hoholo a'e ana nā pu'u. Ua piha loa 'o ia i ka inaina, a 'ī aku nei i ka wahine, "He keu 'oe a ka wahine loko 'ino. Pō'ino ku'u pōki'i iā 'oe." A me kēia mau hua 'ōlelo ua pepehi 'ia kēlā wahine a make loa.

Ua pi'i akula 'o ia i 'Ōla'a i kahi a ke kaikuahine a 'ike aku nei 'o ia i ka hoholo mai o nā 'iole i kauhale a kulu iho nei kona waimaka aloha no ke kaiko'eke a me nā keiki. Hele pololei aku nei 'o ia a ka pūnāwai a iho iho nei ke po'o i lalo i loko o ka wai, a 'o ke kino, ua lilo a'ela i kumu 'ōhi'a.

He 'elua wale nō pua o kēia kumu 'ōhi'a i nā wā a pau, a ke haki ka lālā, kahe mai ke koko mai kona kino mai.

Kūkaʻōhiʻaakalaka

Kūkaʻōhiʻaakalaka, Kū the ʻŌhiʻa of the Forest, was the brother, and Kauakuahine, the Sister Rain, was the sister. They came from Kahiki and lived in Hawaiʻi, the sister in ʻŌlaʻa with her husband, and the brother at Keaʻau with his wife. The brother had no children, the sister had a flock of them. Her husband was a farmer in ʻŌlaʻa, the brother a fisherman in Keaʻau.

The sister often brought vegetables to the shore for her brother and returned with fish for her family. The brother told his wife to give his sister an abundance of dried fish when she came with the vegetables. The wife hated to give up the fish and laid it under the sleeping mats. While the husband was out fishing, the sister came with vegetables and the wife said, "We have no fish, as you can see for yourself; all we have is salt." The sister went and gathered coarse seaweed to take the place of fish. Again she came with vegetables and went back without anything. She was lucky to get the seaweed. This constant stinginess of her sister-in-law vexed the sister. It seemed to her useless to burden herself with carrying vegetables and to return with only seaweed for her patient husband and children. One day when she came close to the house and her husband and children ran out to meet her, she gave them each a slap and changed them into rats, the husband into a large rat and the children into young rats. She herself became a spring of water where fine rain fell.

While the brother was out fishing, the gods showed him how stingy his wife had been and how his sister had become a spring and her family had changed into rats. He was much distressed and returned home and asked his wife, "Did you give fish to our dear sister?"

"Yes, I always give her fish."

He saw the dried fish laid flat beneath the sleeping mats and what a heap of them there were. He was very angry with his wife. "What a cruel woman you are! You have brought misfortune upon our little sister!" And with many words of reproach, he beat his wife to death.

He ascended to his sister's place in ʻŌlaʻa and saw the rats scampering about where the house had stood, and he shed tears of love for his brother-in-law and the children. He went straight to the spring, plunged in headlong, and was changed into an ʻōhiʻa tree.

This tree bears only two blossoms to this day, and when a branch is broken off, blood flows from the body of the tree.

'Ōhi'a
Metrosideros polymorpha

Oct. 18, 1860

I see spatter-dock pads and pontederia in that little pool at south end of Beck Stow's. How did they get there? There is no stream in this case? It was perhaps rather reptiles and birds than fishes, then. Indeed we might as well ask how they got anywhere, for all the pools and fields have been stocked thus, and we are not to suppose as many new creations as pools. This suggests to inquire how any plant came where it is,—how, for instance, the pools which were stocked with lilies before we were born or this town was settled, and ages ago, were so stocked, as well as those which we dug. I think that we are warranted only in supposing that the former was stocked in the same way as the latter, and that there was not a sudden new creation,—at least since the first; yet I have no doubt that peculiarities more or less considerable have thus been gradually produced in the lilies thus planted in various pools, in consequence of their various conditions, though they all came originally from one seed.

We find ourselves in a world that is already planted, but is also still being planted as at first. We say of some plants that they grow in wet places and of others that they grow in desert places. The truth is that their seeds are scattered almost everywhere, but here only do they succeed. Unless you can show me the pool where the lily was created, I shall believe that the oldest fossil lilies which the geologist has detected (if this is found fossil) originated in that locality in a similar manner to these of Beck Stow's. We see thus how the fossil lilies which the geologist has detected are dispersed, as well as these which we carry in our hands to church.

The development theory implies a greater vital force in nature, because it is more flexible and accommodating, and equivalent to a sort of constant *new* creation.

ROBIN WALL KIMMERER

The Consolation of Water Lilies

Before I knew it, and long before the pond was ready for swimming, they were gone. My daughter Linden chose to leave the little pond and put her feet in the ocean at a redwood college far from home. I went to visit her that first semester and we spent a lazy Sunday afternoon admiring the rocks of the agate beach at Patrick's Point.

Walking the shore, I spotted a smooth green pebble threaded with carnelian, just like one I'd passed by a few steps earlier. I walked back, searching the strand until I found it again. I reunited the two pebbles, letting them lie together, shining wet in the sun until the tide came back and pulled them apart, rolling their edges smoother and their bodies smaller. The whole beach was like that for me, a gallery of beautiful pebbles divided from each other and from the shore. Linden's way on the beach was different. She too was rearranging, but her method was to place gray with black basalt and pink beside a spruce green oval. Her eye was finding new pairings; mine was searching out the old.

I had known it would happen from the first time I held her—from that moment on, all her growing would be away from me. It is the fundamental unfairness of parenthood that if we do our jobs well, the deepest bond we are given will walk out the door with a wave over the shoulder. We get good training along the way. We learn to say "Have a great time, sweetie" while we are longing to pull them back to safety. And against all the evolutionary imperatives of protecting our gene pool, we give them car keys. And freedom. It's our job. And I wanted to be a good mother. I was happy for her, of course, poised at the beginning of a new adventure, but I was sad for myself, enduring the agony of missing her. My friends who had already weathered this passage counseled me to remember the parts of having a house full of children that I wouldn't miss a bit. I would be glad to retire from the worried nights when the roads are snowy, waiting for the sound of tires in the driveway exactly one minute before curfew. The half-done chores and the mysteriously emptying refrigerator.

There were days when I'd get up in the morning and the animals had beaten me to the kitchen. The calico cat yelled from her perch: *Feed me!* The longhair stood by his bowl silently with an accusing stare. The dog threw herself against my legs with happiness and looked expectant. *Feed me!* And I did. I dropped handfuls of oatmeal and cranberries into one pot and stirred hot chocolate in another. The girls came downstairs sleepy-eyed and needing that homework paper from last night. *Feed me,* they said. And I did. I tipped the scraps into the compost bucket so when the next summer's tomato seedlings say *feed me,* I can. And when I kiss the girls good-bye at the door, the horses whicker at the fence for their bucket of grain and the chickadees call from their empty seed tray: *Feed me me me. Feed me me me.* The fern on the windowsill droops its fronds in silent request. When I put the key in the ignition of the car it starts to ping: *fill me.* Which I do. I listen to public radio all the way to school and thank goodness it's not pledge week.

I remember my babies at the breast, the *first* feeding, the long deep suck that drew up from my innermost well, which was filled and filled again, by the look that passed between us, the reciprocity of mother and child. I suppose I should welcome the freedom from all that feeding and worrying, but I'll miss it. Maybe not the laundry, but the immediacy of those looks, the presence of our reciprocal love is hard to say good-bye to.

I understood that part of my sadness at Linden's departure was because I did not know who I would be when I was no longer known as "Linden's Mother." But I had a bit of a reprieve from that crisis, as I am also justly famous for being "Larkin's Mother." But this, too, would pass.

Before my younger daughter, Larkin, left, she and I had a last campfire up at the pond and watched the stars come out. "Thank you," she whispered, "for all of this." The next morning she had the car all packed with dorm furnishings and school supplies. The quilt that I made for her before she was born showed through one of the big plastic tubs of essentials. When everything she needed was stuffed in back, then she helped me load mine on the roof.

After we'd unloaded and decorated the dorm room and went out to lunch as if nothing was happening, I knew it was time for my exit. My work was done and hers was beginning.

I saw girls dismiss their parents with a waggle of fingers, but Larkin walked me out to the dorm parking lot where the herds of minivans were still disgorging their cargos. Under the gaze of deliberately cheerful dads and strained-looking moms, we hugged again and shed some smiley tears that we both thought had already been used up. As I opened the car door,

she started to walk away and called out loudly, "Mom, if you break down in uncontrollable sobs on the highway, please pull over!" The entire parking lot erupted in laughter and then we were all released.

I did not need Kleenex or the breakdown lane. After all, I wasn't going home. I could manage leaving her at college, but I did not want to go home to an empty house. Even the horses were gone and the old family dog had died that spring. There would be no welcoming committee.

I had planned for this with my special grief-containment system strapped on top of my car. Spending every weekend at track meets or hosting slumber parties, I rarely found time to go paddling alone. Now I was going to celebrate my freedom rather than mourn my loss. You hear about those shiny, red midlife crisis Corvettes? Well, mine was strapped on top of the car. I drove down the road to Labrador Pond and slipped my new red kayak into the water.

Just remembering the sound of the first bow wave brings back the whole of the day. Late summer afternoon, golden sun and lapis sky between the hills that fold around the pond. Red-winged blackbirds cackling in the cattails. Not a breath of wind disturbed the glassy pond.

Open water sparkled ahead, but first I had to traverse the marshy edges, beds of pickerelweed and water lilies so thick they covered the water. The long petioles of the spatterdock lilies, stretching six feet from the mucky bottom to the surface, tangled around my paddle as if they wanted to keep me from moving forward. Pulling away the weeds that stuck to my hull, I could see inside their broken stalks. They were packed with spongy white cells filled with air, like a pith of Styrofoam, that botanists call *aerenchyma*. These air cells are unique to floating water plants and give the leaves buoyancy, like a built-in life jacket. This characteristic makes them very hard to paddle through but they serve a larger purpose.

Pond lily leaves get their light and air at the surface, but are attached at the bottom of the lake to a living rhizome as thick as your wrist and as long as your arm. The rhizome inhabits the anaerobic depths of the pond, but without oxygen it will perish. So the aerenchyma forms a convoluted chain of air-filled cells, a conduit between the surface and the depths so that oxygen can slowly diffuse to the buried rhizome. If I pushed the leaves aside I could see them resting below.

Mired in the weeds, I rested for a bit surrounded by water shield, fragrant water lily, rushes, wild calla, and the eccentric flowers known variously as yellow pond lily, bullhead lily, *Nuphar luteum*, spatterdock, and brandybottle. That last name, rarely heard, is perhaps most apt, as the yellow flowers sticking up from the dark water emit a sweet alcoholic scent. It made me wish I had brought a bottle of wine.

Once the showy brandybottle flowers have accomplished their goal of attracting pollinators, they bend below the surface for several weeks, suddenly reclusive while their ovaries swell. When the seeds are mature, the stalks straighten again and lift up above the water the fruit—a curiously flask-shaped pod with a brightly colored lid that looks like its namesake, a miniature brandy cask about the size of a shot glass. I've never witnessed it myself, but I'm told that the seeds pop dramatically from the pod onto the surface, earning one of their other names, spatterdock. All around me there were lilies in all stages of rising and sinking and reemerging, a waterscape of change that is hard to move through, but I bent to the task, pushing my red boat through the green.

I paddled hard and strong out to the deep water, pulling against the weight of the restraining vegetation, eventually breaking free. When I had exhausted my shoulders so they were as empty as my heart, I rested on the water, closed my eyes, and let the sadness come, adrift.

Maybe a little breeze came up, maybe a hidden current, or the earth tilting on its axis to slosh the pond, but whatever the invisible hand, my little boat began to rock gently, like a cradle on the water. Held by the hills and rocked by the water, the hand of the breeze against my cheek, I gave myself over to the comfort that came, unbidden.

I don't know how long I floated, but my little red boat drifted the length of the lake. Rustling whispers around my hull drew me from reverie and the first thing I saw upon opening my eyes were polished green leaves of water lilies and spatterdock smiling up at me again, rooted in darkness and floating in the light. I found myself surrounded by hearts on the water, luminous green hearts. The lilies seemed to pulse with light, green hearts beating with my own. There were young heart leaves below the water on their way up and old leaves on the surface, some with edges tattered by a summer of wind and waves and, no doubt, kayak paddles.

Scientists used to think that the movement of oxygen from the surface leaves of lilies to the rhizome was merely the slow process of diffusion, an inefficient drift of molecules from a region of high concentration in the air to low concentration under water. But new inquiries revealed a flow we could have known by intuition if we had remembered the teachings of plants.

The new leaves take up oxygen into the tightly packed air spaces of their young, developing tissues, whose density creates a pressure gradient. The older leaves, with looser air spaces created by the tatters and tears that open the leaf, create a low-pressure region where oxygen can be released into the atmosphere. This gradient exerts a pull on the air taken in by the young leaf. Since they are connected by air-filled capillary networks, the oxygen moves by mass flow from the young leaves to the old, passing through and oxygenating the rhizome in the process. The young and the old are linked in one long breath, an inhalation that calls for reciprocal exhalation, nourishing the common root from which they both arose. New leaf to old, old to new, mother to daughter—mutuality endures. I am consoled by the lesson of lilies.

I paddled more easily back to the shore. Loading the kayak onto the car in the fading light, I was doused with the leftover pond water draining onto my head. I smiled at the illusion of my grief-containment system: there is no such thing. We spill over into the world and the world spills over into us.

The earth, that first among good mothers, gives us the gift that we cannot provide ourselves. I hadn't realized that I had come to the lake and said *feed me*, but my empty heart was fed. I had a good mother. She gives what we need without being asked. I wonder if she gets tired, old Mother Earth. Or if she too is fed by the giving. "Thanks," I whispered, "for all of this."

It was nearly dark when I got home, but my plan had included leaving the porch light on because a dark house would have been one assault too many. I carried my life jacket into the porch and got out my house keys before I noticed a pile of presents, all beautifully wrapped in brightly colored tissue paper, as if a piñata had burst over my door. A bottle of wine with a single glass on the doorsill. There was a going-away party on the porch and Larkin had missed it. "She's one lucky girl," I thought, "showered with love."

I looked through the gifts for tags or a card, but there was nothing to show who had made the late delivery. The wrapping was just tissue paper so I hunted for a clue. I smoothed the purple paper tight on one gift to read the label underneath. It was a jar of Vicks VapoRub! A little note fell from the twisted tissue paper: "Take comfort." I recognized the handwriting immediately as my cousin's, dear enough to be my sister, who lives hours away. My fairy godmother left eighteen notes and presents, one for every year of mothering Larkin. A compass: "To find your new path." A packet of smoked salmon: "Because they always come home." Pens: "Celebrate having time to write."

We are showered every day with gifts, but they are not meant for us to keep. Their life is in their movement, the inhale and the exhale of our shared breath. Our work and our joy is to pass along the gift and to trust that what we put out into the universe will always come back.

KATHARINE S. WHITE

Green Thoughts in a Green Shade

March 11, 1961. I have read somewhere that no Japanese child will instinctively pick a flower, not even a very young child attracted by its bright color, because the sacredness of flowers is so deeply imbued in the culture of Japan that its children understand the blossoms are there to look at, not to pluck. Be that as it may, my observation is that Occidental children do have this instinctive desire, and I feel certain that almost every American must have a favorite childhood memory of picking flowers—dandelions on a lawn, perhaps, or daisies and buttercups in a meadow, trailing arbutus on a cold New England hillside in spring, a bunch of sweet peas in a hot July garden after admonishments from an adult to cut the stems *long*, or, when one had reached the age of discretion and could be trusted to choose the right rose and cut its stem correctly, a rosebud for the breakfast table. All these examples come from my own recollections of the simple pleasure of gathering flowers, but none of them quite equals my memories of the pure happiness of picking water lilies on a New Hampshire lake. The lake was Chocorua, and picking water lilies was not an unusual event for my next-older sister and me. We spent the best summers of our girlhood on, or in, this lake, and we picked the lilies in the early morning, paddling to the head of the lake, where the water was calm at the foot of the mountain and the sun had just begun to open the white stars of the lilies. The stern paddle had to know precisely how to approach a lily, stem first, getting near enough so the girl in the bow could plunge her arm straight down into the cool water and break off the rubbery stem, at least a foot under the surface, without leaning too far overboard. It took judgment to select the three or four freshest flowers and the shapeliest lily pad to go with them, and it took skill not to upset the canoe. Once the dripping blossoms were gathered and placed in the shade of the bow seat, we paddled home while their heavenly fragrance mounted all around us. I know now that their lovely Latin name was *Nymphaea odorata*, but at the time I knew only that they were the common pond lily of northeast America.

It is no wonder, then, that for years I have had designs on the lilyless pond that lies in the center of our pasture, here in Maine, where I live and from where I write. It is a small, heart-shaped pond, deep enough, I calculate, to grow hardy water lilies that will winter under the ice without freezing their roots. The only problem is the cows that drink at the pond and trample its grassy borders, but I doubt that they would wade in far enough to eat a small clump of lilies planted in the center of the pond and contained in a sunken box. The experiment would be worth trying. I could never attempt wild flag or the other shallow-water plants on the margins of the pond, for the cattle would devour them or tread them down, but a clump or two of lilies in the very center of our one small body of fresh water would satisfy me.

This is why I have been studying the catalogues of the water-lily growers. They make fascinating reading, since a water-garden specialist has to have more tricks to his trade than most nurserymen. Water lilies and lotuses are apt to be his primary horticultural crops, but with them he usually offers a list of floating plants, and shallow-water or bog plants to ornament the margins of the pool, and oxygenating plants to aerate it, and goldfish and scavenger snails to keep it clean, and frogs to eat the mosquitoes it will bring. Most growers also provide the pools, made of wood or fibreglass or steel, in which to plant the lilies, and water pumps, and underwater lights to illuminate a pool at night, and food for the goldfish, and remedies for fungus, algae, and goodness knows what else. This all sounds formidable, but I suspect that growing water lilies need not be complex if one's aims are modest. If one has a natural pond or a brook with a pool, the frills are unnecessary. Our own pond is plentifully supplied with bullfrogs, so I don't have to buy them at two to three dollars a pair, or tadpoles at a dollar a dozen. And the instructions for installing small artificial pools are so clear and simple in all the catalogues that even this task does not sound too difficult.

The five catalogues I have before me have taught me that there are day-blooming hardy water lilies—white, yellow, red, pink, blue, purple, and a whole range of colors in between—and tropical lilies, which are both day- and night-blooming, in just as wide a spectrum of color. These exotics are more floriferous and showy but on the whole less fragrant than the hardy varieties, and most of them will not winter over in a cool climate. In the North they had best be regarded as annuals. If I lived in the South or in California I would certainly want to grow a few, though, and even in the North two or three tropicals could be set out each spring for a moderate cost. One need only read the handsome catalogues of the Three Springs Fisheries (Lilypons, Maryland) and of the Van Ness Water Gardens (Upland, California) to be convinced. Three Springs is a father-and-son enterprise that has been in business since 1917. It started out as a farm and fishery, but there are now twenty-five acres of ponds for aquatic plants, set in the midst of more than three hundred rolling acres ten miles south of Frederick. We are told that Miss Lily Pons has adopted the post office as the place from which to mail her Christmas cards. Despite the punning name, which I can't admire, the beautiful black-and-white and color photographs of the catalogue make me long to visit Three Springs Fisheries and see its seventy-five varieties of hardy lilies, its twenty-five varieties of tropicals, and its lotuses and other water plants in bloom. To me the loveliest of the color portraits are of Gladstone, a hardy white lily; of Blue Beauty, a day-blooming tropical; and of the lotus Three Springs calls, not too correctly, *Nelumbo album striatum*. This sort of Nelumbo, the so-called Egyptian lotus, is one of our links with prehistory. A fossil lotus seventy million years old was recently found in eastern Asia, and in Washington, D.C., at the Kenilworth Aquatic Gardens, pink Manchurian lotuses are growing which were raised from seed that was a thousand years old when it was planted. One needs plenty of space for lotuses, which have leaves from two to three feet in diameter and flower stalks that grow to a height of from two to nine feet. (Unlike water lilies, lotuses bloom above the water.) Let go its own way, Nelumbo will create a small jungle, if that happens to be what you want. We have a native American lotus, of course, with yellow blossoms—the water chinquapin—and Three Springs grows and sells it, as well as ten lotuses from China, Japan, and other lands. The Van Ness catalogue offers far fewer varieties of both lilies and lotuses, but with its emphasis on warm-climate plants—small ones like water poppy and water hawthorn (which it spells "hawthorne"), as well as tropical lilies—it will be of special interest to those living in the Deep South or on the West Coast. Its cultural advice and planting diagrams are particularly helpful. Nearer New York City are three other firms: Slocum Water Gardens, of Binghamton, New York; William Tricker, Inc., of Saddle River, New Jersey (and also of Independence, Ohio, near Cleveland); and S. Scherer & Sons, of Northport, Long Island. Slocum has nine acres of display pools in Binghamton as well as ten ponds at Marathon, New York. Perry Slocum, the proprietor, bred the first patented hardy water lily, Pearl of the Pool, which in its picture is a very pretty pale pink. The Slocum catalogue lists four lotuses, which it claims are hardy and easy to grow; it is the only catalogue to lay much emphasis on the lovely scent of the lotus, which it says is the most fragrant of the water lilies. Tricker is one of the biggest growers of aquatics, but it lists fewer varieties of lilies and lotuses than Three Springs, and the catalogue is far from handsome, what with poor photographs, crude color, and unalluring typography. It is, however, comprehensive, and proffers all the aids and gadgets and fish and pools a water gardener could possibly need. It also has a long and interesting list of shallow-water, bog, and rock plants, both hardy and tropical. If one is after something truly gigantic, Tricker has it in an aquatic plant called a victoria (*Victoria trickeri*, to be exact, said to be hardy as far north as Cleveland), which has flowers eighteen inches in diameter and leaf pads six feet broad, strong enough to support a girl—a pretty one, I trust. (I'm surprised that the fashion magazines in their search for exotic backgrounds have yet to photograph a model wearing a high-style sports outfit while standing on the six-foot pad of a victoria in the center of a pond.)

The Scherer catalogue is a more modest affair than the others, but I like it. This Long Island nursery has been in business for fifty years and is the largest grower of aquatic plants on the Island; it is open to visitors weekdays, and is also open Sundays, holidays, and evenings in April, May, and June. This year Scherer has added to its tropical-lily list, it has fibre-glass pools in seven shapes, and with the help of its booklet one could install a pool and a charming water garden.

If a pool and water plants are too much effort, any one of these five catalogues is useful in another way. In each of their listings are all sorts of plants good for naturalizing and reviving a dismal swamp or bog—wildings like cattails, marsh marigolds, the wild irises (yellow and blue), and, for running brooks, watercress.

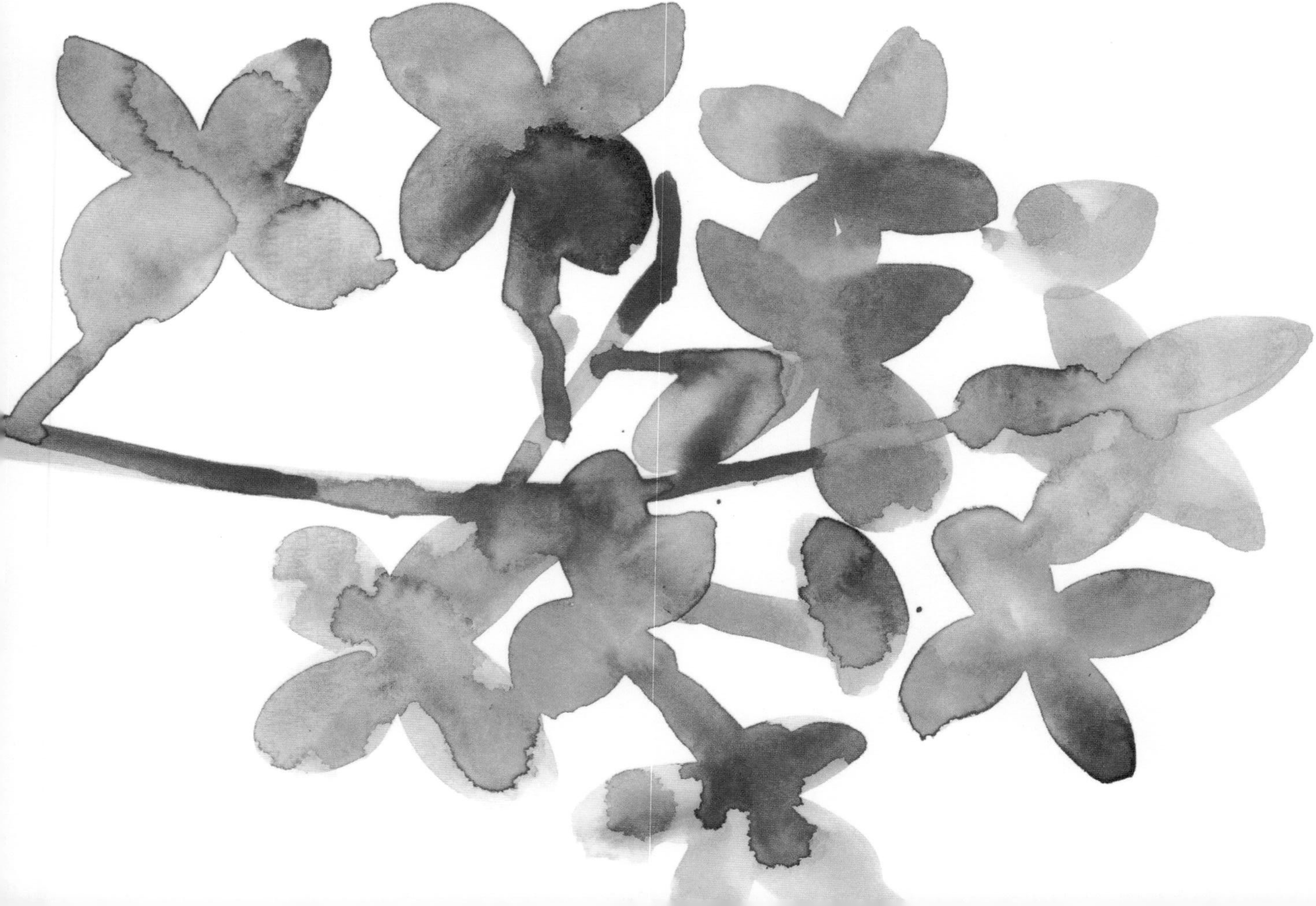

Lilac
Syringa vulgaris

WALT WHITMAN

When Lilacs Last in the Dooryard Bloom'd

1

When lilacs last in the dooryard bloom'd,
And the great star early droop'd in the western sky in the night,
I mourn'd, and yet shall mourn with ever-returning spring.

Ever-returning spring, trinity sure to me you bring,
Lilac blooming perennial and drooping star in the west,
And thought of him I love.

2

O powerful western fallen star!
O shades of night—O moody, tearful night!
O great star disappear'd—O the black murk that hides the star!
O cruel hands that hold me powerless—O helpless soul of me!
O harsh surrounding cloud that will not free my soul.

3

In the dooryard fronting an old farm-house near the white-wash'd
    palings,
Stands the lilac-bush tall-growing with heart-shaped leaves of rich
    green,
With many a pointed blossom rising delicate, with the perfume strong
    I love,
With every leaf a miracle—and from this bush in the dooryard,
With delicate-color'd blossoms and heart-shaped leaves of rich green,
A sprig with its flower I break.

4

In the swamp in secluded recesses,
A shy and hidden bird is warbling a song.

Solitary the thrush,
The hermit withdrawn to himself, avoiding the settlements,
Sings by himself a song.

Song of the bleeding throat,
Death's outlet song of life, (for well dear brother I know,
If thou wast not granted to sing thou would'st surely die.)

5
Over the breast of the spring, the land, amid cities,
Amid lanes and through old woods, where lately the violets peep'd
from the ground, spotting the gray debris,
Amid the grass in the fields each side of the lanes, passing the endless
grass,
Passing the yellow-spear'd wheat, every grain from its shroud in the
dark-brown fields uprisen,
Passing the apple-tree blows of white and pink in the orchards,
Carrying a corpse to where it shall rest in the grave,
Night and day journeys a coffin.

6
Coffin that passes through lanes and streets,
Through day and night with the great cloud darkening the land,
With the pomp of the inloop'd flags with the cities draped in black,
With the show of the States themselves as of crape-veil'd women
standing,
With processions long and winding and the flambeaus of the night,
With the countless torches lit, with the silent sea of faces and the
unbared heads,
With the waiting depot, the arriving coffin, and the sombre faces,
With dirges through the night, with the thousand voices rising strong
and solemn,
With all the mournful voices of the dirges pour'd around the coffin,
The dim-lit churches and the shuddering organs—where amid these
you journey,
With the tolling tolling bells' perpetual clang,
Here, coffin that slowly passes,
I give you my sprig of lilac.

7
(Nor for you, for one alone,
Blossoms and branches green to coffins all I bring,
For fresh as the morning, thus would I chant a song for you O sane and
sacred death.

All over bouquets of roses,
O death, I cover you over with roses and early lilies,
But mostly and now the lilac that blooms the first,
Copious I break, I break the sprigs from the bushes,
With loaded arms I come, pouring for you,
For you and the coffins all of you O death.)

8
O western orb sailing the heaven,
Now I know what you must have meant as a month since I walk'd,
As I walk'd in silence the transparent shadowy night,
As I saw you had something to tell as you bent to me night after night,
As you droop'd from the sky low down as if to my side, (while the
    other stars all look'd on,)
As we wander'd together the solemn night, (for something I know not
    what kept me from sleep,)
As the night advanced, and I saw on the rim of the west how full you
    were of woe,
As I stood on the rising ground in the breeze in the cool transparent
    night,
As I watch'd where you pass'd and was lost in the netherward black of
    the night,
As my soul in its trouble dissatisfied sank, as where you sad orb,
Concluded, dropt in the night, and was gone.

9
Sing on there in the swamp,
O singer bashful and tender, I hear your notes, I hear your call,
I hear, I come presently, I understand you,
But a moment I linger, for the lustrous star has detain'd me,
The star my departing comrade holds and detains me.

10
O how shall I warble myself for the dead one there I loved?
And how shall I deck my song for the large sweet soul that has gone?
And what shall my perfume be for the grave of him I love?

Sea-winds blown from east and west,
Blown from the Eastern sea and blown from the Western sea, till there
    on the prairies meeting,

These and with these and the breath of my chant,
I'll perfume the grave of him I love.

11

O what shall I hang on the chamber walls?
And what shall the pictures be that I hang on the walls,
To adorn the burial-house of him I love?

Pictures of growing spring and farms and homes,
With the Fourth-month eve at sundown, and the gray smoke lucid and
    bright,
With floods of the yellow gold of the gorgeous, indolent, sinking sun,
    burning, expanding the air,
With the fresh sweet herbage under foot, and the pale green leaves of
    the trees prolific,
In the distance the flowing glaze, the breast of the river, with a
    wind-dapple here and there,
With ranging hills on the banks, with many a line against the sky, and
    shadows,
And the city at hand with dwellings so dense, and stacks of chimneys,
And all the scenes of life and the workshops, and the workmen home-
    ward returning.

12

Lo, body and soul—this land,
My own Manhattan with spires, and the sparkling and hurrying tides,
    and the ships,
The varied and ample land, the South and the North in the light,
    Ohio's shores and flashing Missouri,
And ever the far-spreading prairies cover'd with grass and corn.

Lo, the most excellent sun so calm and haughty,
The violet and purple morn with just-felt breezes,
The gentle soft-born measureless light,
The miracle spreading bathing all, the fulfill'd noon,
The coming eve delicious, the welcome night and the stars,
Over my cities shining all, enveloping man and land.

13

Sing on, sing on you gray-brown bird,
Sing from the swamps, the recesses, pour your chant from the bushes,
Limitless out of the dusk, out of the cedars and pines.

Sing on dearest brother, warble your reedy song,
Loud human song, with voice of uttermost woe.

O liquid and free and tender!
O wild and loose to my soul—O wondrous singer!
You only I hear—yet the star holds me, (but will soon depart,)
Yet the lilac with mastering odor holds me.

14

Now while I sat in the day and look'd forth,
In the close of the day with its light and the fields of spring, and the
    farmers preparing their crops,
In the large unconscious scenery of my land with its lakes and forests,
In the heavenly aerial beauty, (after the perturb'd winds and the
    storms,)
Under the arching heavens of the afternoon swift passing, and the
    voices of children and women,
The many-moving sea-tides, and I saw the ships how they sail'd,
And the summer approaching with richness, and the fields all busy
    with labor,
And the infinite separate houses, how they all went on, each with its
    meals and minutia of daily usages,
And the streets how their throbbings throbb'd, and the cities pent—lo,
    then and there,
Falling upon them all and among them all, enveloping me with the
    rest,
Appear'd the cloud, appear'd the long black trail,
And I knew death, its thought, and the sacred knowledge of death.

Then with the knowledge of death as walking one side of me,
And the thought of death close-walking the other side of me,
And I in the middle as with companions, and as holding the hands of
    companions,

I fled forth to the hiding receiving night that talks not,
Down to the shores of the water, the path by the swamp in the
    dimness,
To the solemn shadowy cedars and ghostly pines so still.

And the singer so shy to the rest receiv'd me,
The gray-brown bird I know receiv'd us comrades three,
And he sang the carol of death, and a verse for him I love.

From deep secluded recesses,
From the fragrant cedars and the ghostly pines so still,
Came the carol of the bird.

And the charm of the carol rapt me,
As I held as if by their hands my comrades in the night,
And the voice of my spirit tallied the song of the bird.

Come lovely and soothing death,
Undulate round the world, serenely arriving, arriving,
In the day, in the night, to all, to each,
Sooner or later delicate death.

Prais'd be the fathomless universe,
For life and joy, and for objects and knowledge curious,
And for love, sweet love—but praise! praise! praise!
For the sure-enwinding arms of cool-enfolding death.

Dark mother always gliding near with soft feet,
Have none chanted for thee a chant of fullest welcome?
Then I chant it for thee, I glorify thee above all,
I bring thee a song that when thou must indeed come, come unfalteringly.

Approach strong deliveress,
When it is so, when thou hast taken them I joyously sing the dead,
Lost in the loving floating ocean of thee,
Laved in the flood of thy bliss O death.

From me to thee glad serenades,
Dances for thee I propose saluting thee, adornments and feastings for
  thee,
And the sights of the open landscape and the high-spread sky are fitting,
And life and the fields, and the huge and thoughtful night.

The night in silence under many a star,
The ocean shore and the husky whispering wave whose voice I know,
And the soul turning to thee O vast and well-veil'd death,
And the body gratefully nestling close to thee.

Over the tree-tops I float thee a song,
Over the rising and sinking waves, over the myriad fields and the
  prairies wide,
Over the dense-pack'd cities all and the teeming wharves and ways,
I float this carol with joy, with joy to thee O death.

15
To the tally of my soul,
Loud and strong kept up the gray-brown bird,
With pure deliberate notes spreading filling the night.

Loud in the pines and cedars dim,
Clear in the freshness moist and the swamp-perfume,
And I with my comrades there in the night.

While my sight that was bound in my eyes unclosed,
As to long panoramas of visions.

And I saw askant the armies,
I saw as in noiseless dreams hundreds of battle-flags,
Borne through the smoke of the battles and pierc'd with missiles I saw
  them,
And carried hither and yon through the smoke, and torn and bloody,
And at last but a few shreds left on the staffs, (and all in silence,)
And the staffs all splinter'd and broken.

I saw battle-corpses, myriads of them,
And the white skeletons of young men, I saw them,
I saw the debris and debris of all the slain soldiers of the war,
But I saw they were not as was thought,
They themselves were fully at rest, they suffer'd not,
The living remain'd and suffer'd, the mother suffer'd,
And the wife and the child and the musing comrade suffer'd,
And the armies that remain'd suffer'd.

16
Passing the visions, passing the night,
Passing, unloosing the hold of my comrades' hands,
Passing the song of the hermit bird and the tallying song of my soul,
Victorious song, death's outlet song, yet varying ever-altering song,
As low and wailing, yet clear the notes, rising and falling, flooding the
    night,
Sadly sinking and fainting, as warning and warning, and yet again
    bursting with joy,
Covering the earth and filling the spread of the heaven,
As that powerful psalm in the night I heard from recesses,
Passing, I leave thee lilac with heart-shaped leaves,
I leave thee there in the door-yard, blooming, returning with spring.

I cease from my song for thee,
From my gaze on thee in the west, fronting the west, communing with
    thee,
O comrade lustrous with silver face in the night.

Yet each to keep and all, retrievements out of the night,
The song, the wondrous chant of the gray-brown bird,
And the tallying chant, the echo arous'd in my soul,
With the lustrous and drooping star with the countenance full of woe,
With the holders holding my hand nearing the call of the bird,
Comrades mine and I in the midst, and their memory ever to keep, for
    the dead I loved so well,
For the sweetest, wisest soul of all my days and lands—and this for his
    dear sake,
Lilac and star and bird twined with the chant of my soul,
There in the fragrant pines and the cedars dusk and dim.

Lilac
Syringa vulgaris

T. S. ELIOT

The Waste Land

For Ezra Pound
il miglior fabbro

I. THE BURIAL OF THE DEAD

April is the cruellest month, breeding
Lilacs out of the dead land, mixing
Memory and desire, stirring
Dull roots with spring rain.
Winter kept us warm, covering
Earth in forgetful snow, feeding
A little life with dried tubers.
Summer surprised us, coming over the Starnbergersee
With a shower of rain; we stopped in the colonnade,
And went on in sunlight, into the Hofgarten,
And drank coffee, and talked for an hour.
Bin gar keine Russin, stamm' aus Litauen, echt deutsch.
And when we were children, staying at the archduke's,
My cousin's, he took me out on a sled,
And I was frightened. He said, Marie,
Marie, hold on tight. And down we went.
In the mountains, there you feel free.
I read, much of the night, and go south in the winter.

  What are the roots that clutch, what branches grow
Out of this stony rubbish? Son of man,
You cannot say, or guess, for you know only
A heap of broken images, where the sun beats,
And the dead tree gives no shelter, the cricket no relief,
And the dry stone no sound of water. Only
There is shadow under this red rock,
(Come in under the shadow of this red rock),

And I will show you something different from either
Your shadow at morning striding behind you
Or your shadow at evening rising to meet you;
I will show you fear in a handful of dust.

> *Frisch weht der Wind*
> *Der Heimat zu*
> *Mein Irisch Kind,*
> *Wo weilest du?*

"You gave me hyacinths first a year ago;
"They called me the hyacinth girl."
—Yet when we came back, late, from the Hyacinth garden,
Your arms full, and your hair wet, I could not
Speak, and my eyes failed, I was neither
Living nor dead, and I knew nothing,
Looking into the heart of light, the silence.
Oed' und leer das Meer.

  Madame Sosostris, famous clairvoyante,
Had a bad cold, nevertheless
Is known to be the wisest woman in Europe,
With a wicked pack of cards. Here, said she,
Is your card, the drowned Phoenician Sailor,
(Those are pearls that were his eyes. Look!)
Here is Belladonna, the Lady of the Rocks,
The lady of situations.
Here is the man with three staves, and here the Wheel,
And here is the one-eyed merchant, and this card,
Which is blank, is something he carries on his back,
Which I am forbidden to see. I do not find
The Hanged Man. Fear death by water.
I see crowds of people, walking round in a ring.
Thank you. If you see dear Mrs. Equitone,
Tell her I bring the horoscope myself:
One must be so careful these days.

  Unreal City,
Under the brown fog of a winter dawn,
A crowd flowed over London Bridge, so many,

I had not thought death had undone so many.
Sighs, short and infrequent, were exhaled,
And each man fixed his eyes before his feet.
Flowed up the hill and down King William Street,
To where Saint Mary Woolnoth kept the hours
With a dead sound on the final stroke of nine.
There I saw one I knew, and stopped him, crying: "Stetson!
"You who were with me in the ships at Mylae!
"That corpse you planted last year in your garden,
"Has it begun to sprout? Will it bloom this year?
"Or has the sudden frost disturbed its bed?
"Oh keep the Dog far hence, that's friend to men,
"Or with his nails he'll dig it up again!
"You! hypocrite lecteur!—mon semblable,—mon frère!"

GALWAY KINNELL

Farewell

after Haydn's Symphony in F-sharp Minor
                    for Paul Zweig (1935–1984)

The last adagio begins.
Soon a violinist gets up and walks out.
Two cellists follow, bows erect, cellos dangling.
The flutist leaves lifting the flute high to honor it for blowing
        during all that continuous rubbing.
The bassoonist goes, then the bass fiddler.
The fortepiano player abandons the black, closeted contraption and
        walks away shaking her fingertips.
The orchestra disappears—
by ones, the way we wash up on this unmusical shore,
and by twos, the way we enter the ark where the world goes on
        beginning.
Before leaving each player blows
the glimmer off the music-stand candle,
where fireweed, dense blazing star, flame azalea stored it summers
        ago,
puffing that quantity of darkness into the hall
and the same portion of light
into the elsewhere where the players reassemble and wait
for the oboist to come with her reliable A,
as first light arrives in a beech and hemlock forest,
setting the birds sounding their chaotic vowels,
so they can tune,
and then play
the phrases inside flames wobbling on top of stalks in the field,
and in fireflies' greenish sparks of grass-sex,
and in gnats whining past in a spectral bunch,
and in crickets who would saw themselves apart to sing,

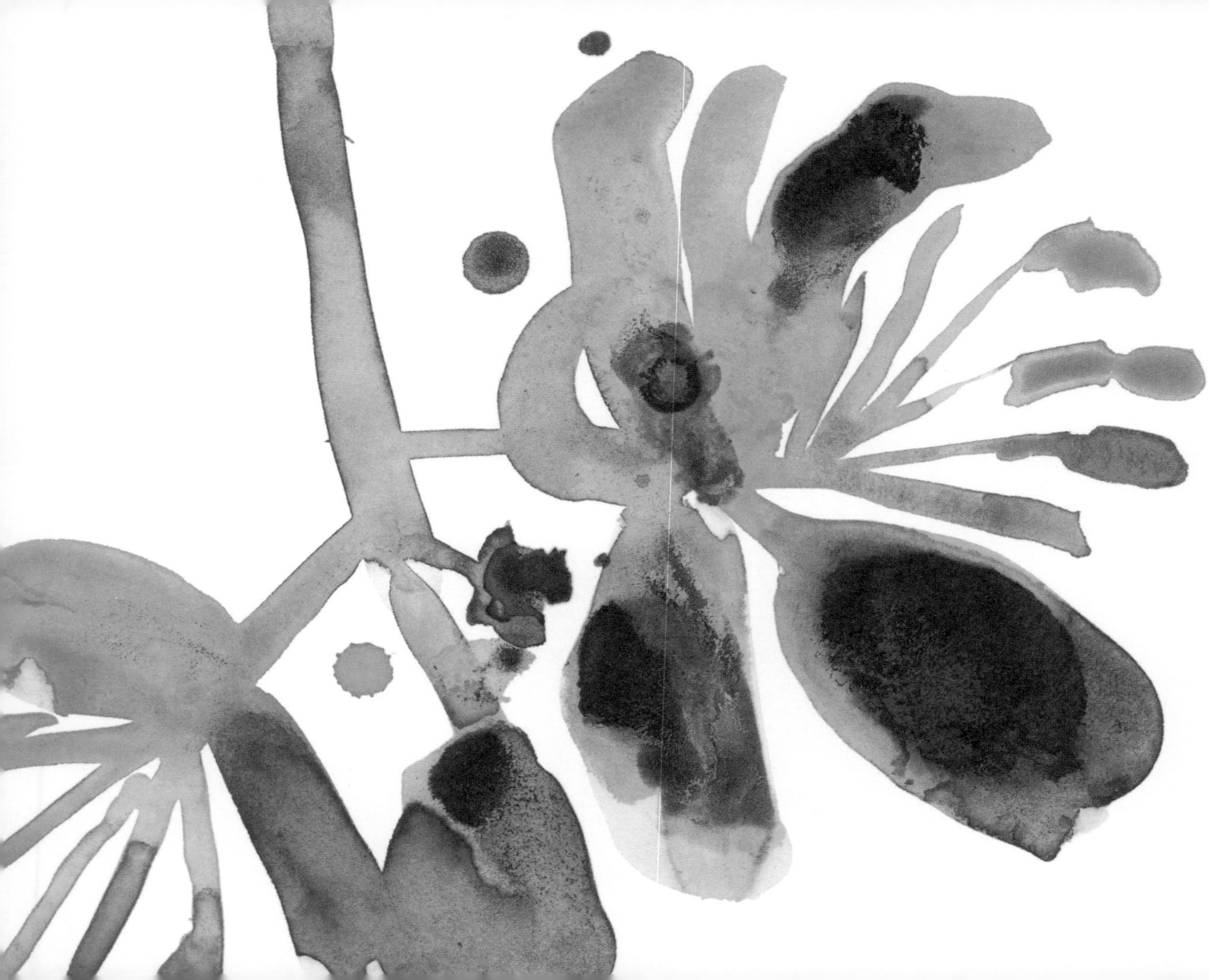

Fireweed
Chamaenerion angustifolium

and in the golden finch perched in the mountain ash, whose roots
　　push into the mouths of the emptied singers.
Now all the players have gone but two violinists,
who sit half facing each other, friends who have figured out what
　　they have figured out by sounding it upon the other,
and scathe the final phrases.
By ones and twos, our powers rise and go,
to lie jangled up in stacks
in woodsheds waiting until a new winter
to spring again in crackling orange voices; and only two are left.
In the darkness above the stage I imagine
the face of my old friend Paul Zweig
—who went away, his powers intact, into Eternity's Woods alone,
　　under a double singing of birds—
looking down and saying something like,
"Let the limits of knowing stretch and diaphanise:
knowledge increasing into ignorance gives the falling-trajectory its
　　grace."
The bow-hairs still cast dust on the bruised wood.
Everything on earth, born
only moments ago, abruptly tips over
and is dragged by mistake into the chaotic inevitable.
Goodbye, dear friend.
Even the meantime, which is the holy time
of being on earth in overlapping lifetimes, ends.
This is one of its endings.
The violinists scrape one more time,
the last of the adagio flies out through the f-holes.
The audience straggles from the hall and at once disappears.
For myself I go on foot on Seventh Avenue
down to the little, bent streets of the West Village.
From ahead of me comes the *hic* of somebody drunk
and then the *nunc* of his head bumping against a telephone pole.

A Flower Passage

(in memory of Joe Shank, the diver)

Even if you were above the ground this year,
You would not know my face.
One of the small boys, one of the briefly green,
I prowled with the others along the Ohio,
Raised hell in the B&O boxcars after dark,
And sometimes in the evening
Chawed the knots out of my trousers
On the river bank, while the other
Children of blast furnace and mine
Fought and sang in the channel-current,
Daring the Ohio.

Shepherd of the dead, one of the tall men,
I did not know your face.
One summer dog day after another,
You rose and gathered your gear
And slogged downhill of the river ditch to dive
Into the blind channel. You dragged your hooks
All over the rubble sludge and lifted
The twelve-year bones.

Now you are dead and turned over
To the appropriate authorities, Christ
Have mercy on me, I would come to the funeral home
If I were home
In Martins Ferry, Ohio.
I would bring to your still face a dozen
Modest and gaudy carnations.

But I am not home in my place

Where I was born and my friends drowned.
So I dream of you, mourning.
I walk down the B&O track
Near the sewer main.
And there I gather, and here I gather
The flowers I only know best.
The spring leaves of the sumac
Stink only a little less worse
Than the sewer main, and up above that gouged hill
Where somebody half-crazy tossed a cigarette
Straight down into a pile of sawdust
In the heart of the LaBelle Lumber Company,
There, on the blank mill field, it is the blind and tough
Fireweeds I gather and bring home.
To you, for my drowned friends, I offer
The true sumac, and the foul trillium
Whose varicose bloom swells the soil with its bruise;
And a little later, I bring
The still totally unbelievable spring beauty
That for some hidden reason nobody raped
To death in Ohio.

RITA DOVE

Evening Primrose

Poetically speaking, growing up is mediocrity.
—Ned Rorem

Neither rosy nor prim,
nor cousin to the cowslip
nor the extravagant fuchsia—
I doubt anyone has ever
picked one for show,
though the woods must be fringed
with their lemony effusions.

Sun blathers its baronial
endorsement, but they refuse
to join the ranks. Summer
brings them in armfuls,
yet, when the day is large,
you won't see them fluttering
the length of the road.

They'll wait until the world's
tucked in and the sky's
one ceaseless shimmer—then
lift their saturated eyelids
and blaze, blaze
all night long
for no one.

An Encounter

Once on the kind of day called "weather breeder,"
When the heat slowly hazes and the sun
By its own power seems to be undone,
I was half boring through, half climbing through
A swamp of cedar. Choked with oil of cedar
And scurf of plants, and weary and over-heated,
And sorry I ever left the road I knew,
I paused and rested on a sort of hook
That had me by the coat as good as seated,
And since there was no other way to look,
Looked up toward heaven, and there against the blue,
Stood over me a resurrected tree,
A tree that had been down and raised again—
A barkless spectre. He had halted too,
As if for fear of treading upon me.
I saw the strange position of his hands—
Up at his shoulders, dragging yellow strands
Of wire with something in it from men to men.
"You here?" I said. "Where aren't you nowadays
And what's the news you carry—if you know?
And tell me where you're off for—Montreal?
Me? I'm not off for anywhere at all.
Sometimes I wander out of beaten ways
Half looking for the orchid Calypso."

SUSAN BARBA

Second Nature

> "Where is the poet in all this, I wondered."
> —a reviewer

In the woods,
more preposition than noun,
bare arms breaking the fine finish
lines of spiders, the first upright
to pass this morning on the cutoff,
a gerund now and then depending
on a body self-sequestered since—
the names of months no longer
signify, revised to when the reign of
say, viburnum

heady pom poms
that succored with their scent
a blur of hummingbird,
of smaller antennaed humming
bird moths, pausing bees and a person,
racking my brain to associate
that scent, that sweetness, with something,
giving up to scent alone
for itself, bereft
of metaphor,
breathing breathing
the sweetness—

past, surplanted when?
just yesterday? last year?
by lilac visibly coterminous,
tightlipped purple nubs

but undetectable olfactorily
while the poms pirouetted on branches
now blown brown on the granite
block, the branches clothed
with furry heart-shaped leaves
as if nothing glorious had happened
and not much does here now
except the visitations of a bird or two
I think an indigo
bunting briefly but can't be
sure, the action's mostly

in the lilacs, some of the old
crowd, bees, and some new
yellow swallowtails, black
fly nymphs, young mosquitoes
drunk on lilac wine,
like longing, clusters
of my old associates, associations,
Kronstadt, Norwich, moths,
the moon I trust in walking
into my bedroom behind clouds
nearly hitting breaking
the glass I carry every night
before me like a dark lamp on the bedpost
after colliding with the black dog
not to evoke depression
just to name an animal I live with
the true diagnosis
"a sensation of whirling
"and loss of balance
"associated particularly when looking down from a great height
"or caused by disease
"affecting the inner ear or vestibular nerve;
"giddiness; a sensation of motion
"when no motion is occurring
"relative to the earth's gravity"

Lady's slipper orchid
Cypripedium parviflorum

gidig the old word was
a dizziness of common fate,
no matter where I stand
relative to

even the plants
though I was counting
bloodroot, bitterroot, trillium
as if I could create a codex of,
an almanac of
days the visible is
indivisible from the unseen,
each leaf each flowering
part of the sudden exponential
green, vertiginous,
though just now on the approach
I saw something rare
a lady's slipper
that stood out on account
of the veined pink sac of the ephemeral,
the pert unexpected
surprise of its aorta
an invitation to alacrity.

What Beauty Does

My memory of a perfect scent: pine, sage, and cypress;
My friends' faith in the power of rough and winding paths
to take me up a mountain and bring me back.

Specimens plucked from that mountain's pastures:
Indian paintbrush, sego lily, ordinary wildflowers.

How I got them is a story of friendship and passion
Nancy, now a doctor, once a shy sophomore in college
Her husband Mike, the second, better one, and their obsession
with the Great Outdoors—hence an Idaho address.

Boise's Northend is a throwback to neighborhoods American—nice homes
Next to two-story garden apartments down the street from a mansion.
Bikes and dogs and hand-pushed lawn mowers.
Where they dwell is a bungalow that spirits Memphis, Tennessee
circa 1971:

The Who blasting off a turntable, marijuana-scented air, boys with long hair,
girls wearing their boyfriends' blue jeans, bourbon and acid.
Paperbacks, record albums, text books piled up—azaleas on the parkway;
a howl of buzzing bees late spring just before graduation.

Their bungalow has dueling computers and a real backyard.
While Nancy and Mike's boxes are slowly being unpacked,
Their bicycles are carefully racked inside their front door.

Everyone is a thief out West. If you leave your bikes on the porch
They disappear. If you find water, someone else will divert it.
There are those who fight about the wind. Others the sun.

All angling for rights—mineral, water, air—that only comes with political
    power.

Oh, my friends who love to hike, to ski, to bike and me, they love
Are driving me from Boise to Ketchum through mountain and valley beauty.

High desert heat is clear, dry and when your body rises out of a chilly car,

BLAM.

From there you enter another air conditioning zone:
a general store at the edge of mountain lore.

This place has everything from Bibles to good bourbon.

I almost bought a foot long sausage. I almost bought a gun.
I did buy cowboy postcards, mostly made for fun.
Food and security. Winter just over the ridge, four weeks hence.

I used to watch *Death Valley Days*.
Death was hinted, but not shown—the wagon turned over,
The wagon train a going.

O, those long-suffering white people fearful of Indians and scared of bandits,
desperate for shade, for water, for land flowing milk and honey.

Hard-bitten men and sad-eyed women trekking.
How grand those verdant acres were to be.
What they got was land just green enough for wandering herds of long-horned
    beasts
and no where to farm, no where to hide.

Today, the wind machines whip around: BIG ENERGY.

Horses gambol and graze on that patch of land or this keen slope.
No wheat and corn, not even dope grows here.
But silver, gold, treasures unknown lode these mountains
inviting speculation, misery, and bad legislation.

A few miles up from Sun Valley, we enter a trail.
Mike and Nancy smile and cajole.

Indian paintbrush
Castilleja spp.

Straw hat and baseball cap attest to sun's plenty.
Their walking sticks to the rocks' ready
challenge to ankles and limbs.
Our water pouches are overflowing.
What were my friends thinking?

We slip and slide on the side of this mountain and step aside
for the sculpted women in tank tops and biker shorts—trotting as fast as
Nancy and Mike's favorite dog
She runs ahead following the blonde beauties until all is shadow.
We greet each glade with glee.

I am the novice hiker. I am afraid of falling into thin air.
One large Black woman with a bum knee. What were they thinking?

She will love the smell. Pine, sage, and cypress.
She will love the sound. Wind shakes aspens. Water crinkles rock
She will love the sight. Wildflowers—whites, yellows, purples and reds:
Indian paintbrush, sego lily, the wily cinquefoil.

When friends give you what you need, what more can you ask?
Oh the pleasure in a mountain's power to quiet a panicked heart.
The glade refined.
Hawk's home, wolf's dream, bears far away.

Stewards of American beauty—these are the paths my friends make in wild
    places
—the rise and fall of future walks.

I salute their obsession for Idaho's red undulating hills.
Whose mountain ranges east to west like those in the Himalayas

says a guidebook, but ours is a different story—in this young mountain,
on these new hills, circumspect is the American West.

Where people steal
a drop of ore,
a native flower,
a piece of splendor
day in and day out.

GARY SNYDER

Mimulus on the Road to Town

Out of cracks in the roadcut rockwalls,
clumps of peach-colored mimulus
spread and bloom,
       stiffly quiver in the hot
log-truck breeze-blast
always going by—
they never die.

Mimulus, monkeyflower
Mimulus guttatus

Rexroth's Cabin

On the way to • to the site of his • cabin, his temple • refurbished from
the plundered • temple of another religion • a religion of fishermen •
on the Tokelalume aka • Lagunitas Creek in Devil's • Gulch, the path into
the forest flagged • flagged on either side with orange • sticky monkey
flowers • innumerable stubby, macho • fence lizards rush in bursts •
ahead of you like heralds as • you come up the trail, but • half a mile
in, a single • Western skink, its neon-blue tail hauled upright behind
it • races diagonally crosstrail and disappears • beneath thimbleberry
brambles mantled • with shredded spiderweb

in the epic literature of India • which all those years ago • he was reading, lying • on this greywacke slab • above the ebulliently plashing •
creek, his head in shade, his • lanky body warm • legs crossed in the
sun's • maple light breaking through • tree limbs pajamaed in moss
• and stretching awkwardly out • out over the gulch • from a steep
hillside held in place • only by radial green explosions • of bracken,
Maidenhair fern, and • a pair of red-spiked black caterpillars • which
crawl onto his leather boots • set side by side in the rampant pipevine
the • caterpillars have been devouring • in all that epic literature of
India • no more than three colors • are mentioned

See? He is here and not here. Not • unlike you yourself. Or the water
• striders in the creek • rowing in punctuated contractions • against
the drift. What • you see in the clear absolute of the water • as you
stand on some paleostump at the bank • under an electric insect whine
• distributed perfectly throughout the canopy, • what you see below •
in the pellucid water is a cluster of • six Gothic black shadowdots
• cast onto the streambed • below the thin, sand-colored • bodies of
the actual water striders • who are bowed all but invisibly above • the
tensile surface of the stream

Not here. And here. And though you • you have hiked the dirt path through the forest • as he did before you were born • to the familiar place, the confluence • of two modest falls, to the ground truth • the little clearing where he snored • and fried two eggs for breakfast and sat • cross-legged on a slab of rock scribbling • into the future that holds you in it, • you are only still arriving • still • arriving • no trace of the cabin left, and yet • his presence is not • decomposable, your mind • merges with what is not • your mind, your happiness • is radiant and you squat, listening • in the tangible density of what is and isn't there • as you become your • shadow fluidly contiguous • with the shadows of trees

Mimulus, monkeyflower
Mimulus guttatus

Water hyacinth
Eichhornia crassipes

JAMES MERRILL

The Water Hyacinth

When I was four or so
I used to read aloud
To you—I mean, recite
Stories both of us knew
By heart, the book held close
To even then nearsighted
Eyes. It was morning. You,
Still in your nightgown
Over cold tea, would nod
Approval. Once I caught
A gay note in your quiet:
The book was upside down.

Now all is upside down.
I sit while you babble.
I watch your sightless face
Jerked swiftly here and there,
Set in a puzzled frown.
Your face! It is no more yours
Than its reflected double
Bobbing on scummed water.
Other days, the long pure
Sobs break from a choked source
Nobody here would dare
Fathom, even if able.

With you no longer able,
I tried to keep apart,
At first, or to set right
The stories you would tell.
The European trip,
The fire of 1908—

I could reel them off in sleep,
Given a phrase to start;
Chimneys of kerosene
Lamps only you could clean
Because your hands were small ...
I have them all by heart

But cannot now find heart
To hinder them from growing
Together, wrong, absurd.
Do as you must, poor stranger.
There is no surer craft
To take you where you are going
—A story I have heard
And shall over and over
Till you are indeed gone.
Last night the mockingbird
Wept and laughed, wept and laughed,
Telling it to the moon.

Your entire honeymoon,
A ride in a rowboat
On the St. Johns River,
Took up an afternoon.
And by that time, of course,
The water hyacinth
Had come here from Japan,
A mauve and rootless guest
Thirsty for life, afloat
With you on the broad span
It would in sixty years
So vividly congest.

JORIE GRAHAM

Of Forced Sightes and Trusty Ferefulness

Stopless wind, here are the columbine seeds I have
collected. What we would do with them is
different. Though both your trick and mine flowers blue
and white

with four stem tails and yellow underpetals. Stopless
and unessential, half-hiss, half-
lullaby, if I fell in among your laws,
if I fell down into your mind, your snow, into the miles

of spirit-drafts you drive, frenetic multitudes,
out from the timber to the open ground and back to no
avail, if I fell down, warmblooded, ill, into your endless
evenness,

into this race you start them on and will not let them win ... ?
If I fell in?
What is your law to my law, unhurried hurrying?
At my remove from you, today, in your supremest

calculation, re-
adjustment, are these three birds scratching for dead
bark beetles, frozen seeds, too late for being here yet only
            here,
in the stenchfree

cold. This is another current, river of rivers, this thrilling
third-act love. Who wouldn't want to stay
behind? They pack the rinds away, the blazing applecores,
the frantic shadow-wings scribbling the fenceposts, window-

panes. Meanwhile you turn, white jury, draft, away,
deep justice done.
I don't presume to cross the distances, the clarity,
but what grows in your only open hands? Or is

digressive love,
row after perfect greenhouse row,
the garden you're out of for good, wind of the theorems,
of proof, square root of light,

chaos of truth,
blinder than the mice that wait you out
        in any crack?
This is the best I can do now for prayer—to you,
for you—these scraps I throw

my lonely acrobats
that fall
of your accord
right to my windowsill: they pack it away, the grains, the

accidents, they pack it deep into the rent
heart of the blue
spruce, skins in with spiky needles.... Oh
        hollow
charged with forgetfulness,

through wind, through winter nights, we'll pass,
steering with crumbs, with words,
making of every hour
a thought, remembering

by pain and rhyme and arabesques of foraging
the formula for theft
under your sky that keeps
sliding away

married to hurry
and grim song.

Wolfsbane
Aconitum delphiniifolium

JOAN NAVIYUK KANE

Hyperboreal

Arnica nods heavy-headed on the bruised slope.
Peaks recede in all directions, in heat-haze,
Evening in my recollection.

The shield at my throat ornamental and worse.
We descended the gully thrummed into confusion
With the last snowmelt a tricklet into mud, ulterior—

One wolfbane bloom, iodine-hued, rising on its stalk
Into the luster of air: June really isn't June anymore,
Is it? A glacier's heart of milk loosed from a thousand

Summer days in extravagant succession,
From the back of my tongue, dexterous and sinister.

JUNE JORDAN

Letter to the Local Police

Dear Sirs:

I have been enjoying the law and order of our
community throughout the past three months since
my wife and I, our two cats, and miscellaneous
photographs of the six grandchildren belonging to
our previous neighbors (with whom we were very
close) arrived in Saratoga Springs which is clearly
prospering under your custody

Indeed, until yesterday afternoon and despite my
vigilant casting about, I have been unable to discover
a single instance of reasons for public-spirited concern,
much less complaint

You may easily appreciate, then, how it is that
I write to your office, at this date, with utmost
regret for the lamentable circumstances that force
my hand

Speaking directly to the issue of the moment:

I have encountered a regular profusion of certain
unidentified roses, growing to no discernible purpose,
and according to no perceptible control, approximately
one quarter mile west of the Northway, on the southern
side

To be specific, there are practically thousands of
the aforementioned abiding in perpetual near riot
of wild behavior, indiscriminate coloring, and only
the Good Lord Himself can say what diverse soliciting
of promiscuous cross-fertilization

Wild rose
Rosa acicularis

As I say, these roses no matter what the apparent
background, training, tropistic tendencies, age
or color, do not demonstrate the least inclination
toward categorization, specified allegiance, resolute
preference, consideration of the needs of others, or
any other minimal traits of decency

May I point out that I did not assiduously seek out
this colony, as it were, and that these certain
unidentified roses remain open to viewing even by
children, with or without suitable supervision

(My wife asks me to append a note as regards the
seasonal but nevertheless seriously licentious
phenomenon of honeysuckle under the moon that one may
apprehend at the corner of Nelson and Main

However, I have recommended that she undertake direct
correspondence with you, as regards this: yet
another civic disturbance in our midst)

I am confident that you will devise and pursue
appropriate legal response to the roses in question
If I may aid your efforts in this respect, please
do not hesitate to call me into consultation

Respectfully yours,

ANN TOWNSEND

The Enclosure Act

She examined the swampland and desired to drain it.

Her realtor's sign was a noble gesture on the roadside,
like a heraldic banner of the society of homes.

She had the capacity of mind to visualize, as they say, the
    end result.

Stipple leaf, wild rose, briar, briar, minnows,
quack grass, volunteer corn, an errant empty beer bottle,
    prairie remnant,
the soft depressions left where the plow passed,
the squeak sound of the realtor's sign elaborating in the
    wind.

What she saw were ranch condos fledged by white fencing,
and on and on. She had a capacity for longing, and an urge
    to fill it up.

A bird lit on the sign, bounced twice, and flew.
She was gaining weight, at this rate.

She could feel her stomach pressing against the buttons of
    her jeans.

At this rate, the jive of the wind would make a pasture of
    it. She saw it fenced,
the fence imposing a human face on the land.

Her boots sank in the mud. Time to fill it up.

AMY CLAMPITT

The Field Pansy

Yesterday, just before the first frost of the season,
I discovered a violet in bloom on the lawn—a white one,
with a mesh of faint purple pencil marks above the hollow
at the throat, where the petals join: an irregular, a waif,
out of sync with the ubiquity of the asters of New England,

or indeed with the johnny-jump-ups I stopped to look at,
last week, in a plot by the sidewalk: weedily prolific
common garden perennial whose lineage goes back to
the bi- or tri-colored native field pansy of Europe:
ancestor of the cloned ocher and aubergine, the cream-white,

the masked motley, the immaculate lilac-blue of the pansies
that thrive in the tended winter plots of tidewater Virginia,
where in spring the cutover fields at the timber's edge,
away from the boxwood and magnolia alleys, are populous
with an indigenous, white, just faintly suffused-with-violet

first cousin: a link with what, among the hollows of the
great dunes of Holland, out of reach of the slide and hurl
of the North Sea breakers, I found growing a summer ago—a
field pansy tinged not violet but pink, sometimes approaching
the hue of the bell of a foxglove: a gathering, a proliferation

on a scale that, for all its unobtrusiveness, seems to be
worldwide, of what I don't know how to read except as an
urge to give pleasure: a scale that may, for all our fazed
dubiety, indeed be universal. I know I'm leaving something out
when I write of this omnipresence of something like eagerness,

this gushing insouciance that appears at the same time capable
of an all but infinite particularity: sedulous, patient, though
in the end (so far as anyone can see) without consequence.
What is consequence? What difference do the minutiae
of that seeming inconsequence that's called beauty

add up to? Life was hard in the hinterland, where spring arrived
with a gush of violets, sky-blue out of the ground of the woodlot,
but where a woman was praised by others of her sex for being
Practical, and by men not at all, other than in a slow reddening
about the neck, a callowly surreptitious wolf-whistle: where the mode

was stoic, and embarrassment stood in the way of affect:
a mother having been alarmingly seen in tears, once only
we brought her a fistful of johnny-jump-ups from the garden,
"because you were crying"—and saw we'd done the wrong thing.

Violets

I had no thought of violets of late,
The wild, shy kind that spring beneath your feet
In wistful April days, when lovers mate
And wander through the fields in raptures sweet.
The thought of violets meant florists' shops,
And bows and pins, and perfumed papers fine;
And garish lights, and mincing little fops
And cabarets and songs, and deadening wine.
So far from sweet real things my thoughts had strayed,
I had forgot wide fields, and clear brown streams;
The perfect loveliness that God has made—
Wild violets shy and Heaven-mounting dreams.
And now—unwittingly, you've made me dream
Of violets, and my soul's forgotten gleam.

WILLIAM CARLOS WILLIAMS

The Flowers Alone

I should have to be
Chaucer to describe
them—
Loss keeps
me from such a
catalogue—

But!

—low, the
violet, scentless as
it is here! higher,
the peartree in full
bloom through which
a light falls as
rain—
And that is gone—

Only, there remains—

Now!
the cherry trees
white in all back
yards—
And bare as
they are, the coral
peach trees melting
the harsh air—
excellence
priceless beyond
all later
fruit!

And now, driven, I
go, forced to
another day—

Whose yellow quilt
flapping in the
stupendous light—

Forsythia, quince
blossoms—

and all
the living hybrids

Violet, field pansy
Viola bicolor

FRANCISCO X. ALARCÓN

In Xochitl In Cuicatl

cada árbol	every tree
un hermano	a brother
cada monte	every hill
una pirámide	a pyramid
un oratorio	a holy spot
cada valle	every valley
un poema	a poem
in xochitl	*in xochitl*
in cuicatl	*in cuicatl*
flor y canto	flower and song
cada nube	every cloud
una plegaria	a prayer
cada gota	every rain
de lluvia	drop
un milagro	a miracle
cada cuerpo	every body
una orilla	a seashore
al mar	a memory
un olvido	at once lost
encontrado	and found
todos juntos:	we all together:
luciérnagas	fireflies
de la noche	in the night
soñando	dreaming up
el cosmos	the cosmos

WILLIAM BARTRAM

Introduction to *Travels Through North and South Carolina, Georgia, East and West Florida, the Cherokee Country, the Extensive Territories of the Muscogulges, or Creek Confederacy, and the Country of the Chactaws*

The attention of a traveller should be particularly turned, in the first place, to the various works of Nature, to mark the distinctions of the climates he may explore, and to offer such useful observations on the different productions as may occur. Men and manners undoubtedly hold the first rank—whatever may contribute to our existence is also of equal importance, whether it be found in the animal or vegetable kingdom; neither are the various articles, which tend to promote the happiness and convenience of mankind, to be disregarded. How far the writer of the following sheets has succeeded in furnishing information on these subjects, the reader will be capable of determining. From the advantages the journalist enjoyed under his father John Bartram, botanist to the king of Great Britain, and fellow of the Royal Society, it is hoped that his labours will present new as well as useful information to the botanist and zoologist.

This world, as a glorious apartment of the boundless palace of the sovereign Creator, is furnished with an infinite variety of animated scenes, inexpressibly beautiful and pleasing, equally free to the inspection and enjoyment of all his creatures.

Perhaps there is not any part of creation, within the reach of our observations, which exhibits a more glorious display of the Almighty hand, than the vegetable world: such a variety of pleasing scenes, ever changing throughout the seasons, arising from various causes, and assigned each to the purpose and use determined.

It is difficult to pronounce which division of the earth, between the polar circles, produces the greatest variety. The tropical division certainly affords those which principally contribute to the more luxurious scenes of splendour, as Myrtus communis, Myrt. caryophyllata, Myrt. pimenta, Caryophyllus aromaticus, Laurus cinnam. Laurus camphor, Laurus

Persica, Nux mosch. Illicium, Camellia, Punica, Cactus melo-cactus, Cactus grandiflora, Gloriosa superba, Theobroma, Adansonia digitata, Nyctanthes Psidium, Musa paradisica, Musa sapientum, Garcinia mangostana, Cocos nucifera, Citrus, Citrus aurantium, Cucurbita citrullus, Hyacinthus, Amaryllis, Narcissus, Poinciana pulcherrima, Crinum, Cactus cochinellifer.

But the temperate zone (including by far the greater portion of the earth, and a climate the most favourable to the increase and support of animal life, as well as for the exercise and activity of the human faculties) exhibits scenes of infinitely greater variety, magnificence, and consequence, with respect to human economy, in regard to the various uses of vegetables.

For instance; Triticum Cereale, which affords us bread, and is termed, by way of eminence, the staff of life, the most pleasant and nourishing food to all terrestrial animals. Vitis vinifera, whose exhilarating juice is said to cheer the hearts of gods and men. Oryza, Zea, Pyrus, Pyrus malus, Prunus, Pr. cerafus, Ficus, Nectarin, Apricot, Cydonia. Next follow the illustrious families of forest-trees, as the Magnolia grandiflora and Quercus sempervirens, which form the venerated groves and solemn shades, on the Mississippi, Alatamaha and Florida; the magnificent Cupressus disticha of Carolina and Florida; the beautiful Water Oak,[1] whose vast hemispheric head presents the likeness of a distant grove in the fields and savannas of Carolina; the gigantic Black Oak,[2] Platanus occidentalis, Liquidambar styraciflua, Liriodendron tulipera, Fagus castanea, Fagus sylvatica, Juglans nigra, Juglans cinerea, Jug. pecan, Ulmus, Acer saccharinum, of Virginia and Pennsylvania; Pinus phœnix, Pinus tœda, Magnolia acuminata, Nyssa aquatica, Populus heterophylla, and the floriferous Gordonia lasianthus, of Carolina and Florida; the exalted Pinus strobus, Pin. balsamica, Pin. abies, Pin. Canadensis, Pin. larix, Fraxinus excelsior, Robinia pseudacacia, Guilandina dioica, Æsculus Virginica, Magnolia acuminata, of Virginia, Maryland, Pennsylvania, New Jersey, New York, New England, Ohio, and the regions of Erie and the Illinois; and the aromatic and floriferous shrubs, as Azalea coccinea, Azalea rosea, Rosa, Rhododendron, Kalmia, Syringa, Gardenia, Calycanthus, Daphne, Franklinia, Styrax, and others equally celebrated.

In every order of nature we perceive a variety of qualities distributed amongst individuals, designed for different purposes and uses; yet

---

1   Quercus hemispherica.
2   Quercus tinctoria.

it appears evident, that the great Author has impartially distributed his favours to his creatures, so that the attributes of each one seem to be of sufficient importance to manifest the divine and inimitable workmanship. The pompous Palms of Florida, and glorious Magnolia, strike us with the sense of dignity and magnificence; the expansive umbrageous Live Oak[3] with awful veneration; the Carica papaya seems supercilious with all the harmony of beauty and gracefulness; the Lilium superbum represents pride and vanity; Kalmia latifolia and Azalea coccinea, exhibit a perfect show of mirth and gaiety; the Illicium Floridanum, Crinum Floridanum, Convallaria majalis of the Cherokees, and Calycanthus floridus, charm with their beauty and fragrance. Yet they are not to be compared for usefulness with the nutritious Triticum, Zea, Oryza, Solanum tuberosum, Musa, Convolvulus Batata, Rapa, Orchis, Vitis vinifera, Pyrus, Olea; for clothing with Linum Cannabis, Gossypium, Morus; for medicinal virtues with Hyssopus, Thymus, Anthemis nobilis, Papaver somniferum, Quinquina, Rheum rhabarbarum, Pisum, &c. Though none of these most useful tribes are conspicuous for stateliness, figure, or splendour, yet their valuable qualities and virtues excite love, gratitude, and adoration to the great Creator, who was pleased to endow them with such eminent qualities, and reveal them to us for our sustenance, amusement, and delight.

But there remain of the vegetable world several tribes that are distinguished by very remarkable properties, which excite our admiration, some for the elegance, singularity, and splendour of their vestment, as the Tulipa, Fritillaria, Colchicum, Primula, Lilium superbum, Kalmia, &c.: others astonish us by their figure and disposal of their vesture, as if designed only to embellish and please the observer, as the Nepenthes distillatoria, Ophrys insectoria, Cypripedium calceolus, Hydrangia quercifolia, Bartramia bracteata, Viburnum Canadense, Bartsia, &c.

Observe these green meadows how they are decorated; they seem enamelled with the beds of flowers. The blushing Chironia and Rhexia, the spiral Ophrys with immaculate white flowers, the Limodorum, Arethusa pulcherrima, Sarracenia purpurea, Sarracenia galeata, Sarracenia, lacunosa, Sarracenia flava. Shall we analyze these beautiful plants, since they seem cheerfully to invite us? How greatly the flowers of the yellow Sarracenia represent a silken canopy? the yellow pendant petals are the curtains, and the hollow leaves are not unlike the cornucopia

---

3   Quercus sempervirens.

or Amalthea's horn; what a quantity of water a leaf is capable o contain-ing, about a pint! taste of it—how cool and animating—limpid as the morning dew: nature seems to have furnished them with this cordated appendage or lid, which turns over, to prevent a too sudden and copious supply of water from heavy showers of rain, which would bend down the leaves, never to rise again; because their straight parallel nerves, which extend and support them, are so rigid and fragile, the leaf would inevitably break when bent down to a right angle; therefore I suppose the waters which contribute to their supply, are the rebounding drops or horizontal streams wafted by the winds, which adventitiously find their way into them, when a blast of wind shifts the lid: see these short stiff hairs, they all point downwards, which direct the condensed vapours down into the funiculum; these stiff hairs also prevent the varieties of insects, which are caught, from returning, being invited down to sip the mellifluous exudation, from the interior surface of the tube, where they inevitably perish; what quantities there are of them! These latent waters undoubtedly contribute to the support and refreshment of the plant: perhaps designed as a reservoir in case of long continued droughts, or other casualties, since these plants naturally dwell in low savannas liable to overflows, from rain water: for although I am not of the opinion that vegetables receive their nourishment only through the ascending part of the plant, as the stem, branches, leaves, &c.; and that their descending parts, as the roots and fibres, only serve to hold and retain them in their places: yet I believe they imbibe rain and dews through their leaves, stems, and branches, by extremely minute pores, which open on both surfaces of the leaves and on the branches, which may communicate to little auxiliary ducts or vessels; or, perhaps the cool dews and showers, by constricting these pores, and thereby preventing a too free perspiration, may recover and again invigorate the languid nerves of those which seem to suffer for want of water, in great heats and droughts; but whether the insects caught in their leaves, and which dissolve and mix with the fluid, serve for aliment or support to these kind of plants, is doubtful. All the Sarracenias are insect catchers, and so is the Drossea rotundifolia.

But admirable are the properties of the extraordinary Dionea mus-cipula! A great extent on each side of that serpentine rivulet is occupied by those sportive vegetables—let us advance to the spot in which nature has seated them. Astonishing production! see the incarnate lobes expand-ing, how gay and sportive they appear! ready on the spring to intrap

Yellow pitcherplant
Sarracenia flava

incautious deluded insects! what artifice! there behold one of the leaves just closed upon a struggling fly; another has gotten a worm; its hold is sure, its prey can never escape—carnivorous vegetable! Can we after viewing this object, hesitate a moment to confess, that vegetable beings are endued with some sensible faculties or attributes, familiar to those that dignify animal nature; they are organical, living, and self-moving bodies, for we see here, in this plant, motion and volition.

What power or faculty is it, that directs the cirri of the Cucurbita, Momordica, Vitis, and other climbers, towards the twigs of shrubs, trees and other friendly support? we see them invariably leaning, extending, and like the fingers of the human hand, reaching to catch hold of what is nearest, just as if they had eyes to see with; and when their hold is fixed, to coil the tendril in a spiral form, by which artifice it becomes more elastic and effectual, than if it had remained in a direct line, for every revolution of the coil adds a portion of strength; and thus collected, they are enabled to dilate and contract as occasion or necessity requires, and thus by yielding to, and humouring the motion of the limbs and twigs, or other support on which they depend, are not so liable to be torn off by sudden blasts of wind or other assaults: is it sense or instinct that influences their actions? it must be some impulse; or does the hand of the Almighty act and perform this work in our sight?

The vital principle or efficient cause of motion and action, in the animal and vegetable[4] system, perhaps may be more familiar than we generally apprehend. Where is the essential difference between the seed of peas, peaches, and other tribes of plants and trees, and the eggs of oviparous animals, as of birds, snakes, or butterflies, spawn of fish, &c.? Let us begin at the source of terrestrial existence. Are not the seeds of vegetables, and the eggs of oviparous animals fecundated, or influenced with the vivific principle of life, through the approximation and intimacy of the sexes? and immediately after the eggs and seeds are hatched, does not the young larva and infant plant, by heat and moisture, rise into existence, increase, and in due time arrive to a state of perfect maturity? The physiologists agree in opinion, that the work of generation in viviparous animals, is exactly similar, only more secret and enveloped. The mode of operation that nature pursues in the production of vegetables, and oviparous animals, is infinitely more uniform and manifest, than that which is or can be discovered to take place in viviparous animals.

---

4   Vid. Sponsalia plantarum, Amœn. Acad. 1. n. 12. Linn.

The most apparent difference between animals and vegetables is, that animals have the powers of sound, and are locomotive, whereas vegetables are not able to shift themselves from the places where nature has planted them: yet vegetables have the power of moving and exercising their members, and have the means of transplanting and colonising their tribes almost over the surface of the whole earth; some seeds, for instance, grapes, nuts, smilax, peas, and others, whose pulp or kernel is food for animals, will remain several days without being injured in stomachs of pigeons and other birds of passage; by this means such sorts are distributed from place to place, even across seas; indeed some seeds require this preparation by the digestive heat of the stomach of animals, to dissolve and detach the oily, viscid pulp, or to soften the hard shells. Small seeds are sometimes furnished with rays of hair or down; and others with thin light membranes attached to them, which serve the purpose of wings, on which they mount upward, leaving the earth, float in the air, and are carried away by the swift winds to very remote regions before they settle on the earth; some are furnished with hooks, which catch hold of the wool and hair of animals passing by them, and are by that means spread abroad; other seeds ripen in pericarpes, which open with elastic force, and shoot their seed to a very great distance round about; some other seeds, as of the Mosses and Fungi, are so very minute as to be invisible, light as atoms, and these mixing with the air, are wafted all over the world.

The animal creation also excites our admiration, and equally manifests the almighty power, wisdom, and beneficence of the Supreme Creator and Sovereign Lord of the universe; some in their vast size and strength, as the mammoth, the elephant, the whale, the lion, and alligator; others in agility; others in their beauty and elegance of colour, plumage, and rapidity of flight, having the faculty of moving and living in the air; others for their immediate and indispensable use and convenience to man, in furnishing means for our clothing and sustenance, and administering to our help in the toils and labours of life: how wonderful is the mechanism of these finely formed self-moving beings, how complicated their system, yet what unerring uniformity prevails through every tribe and particular species! the effect we see and contemplate, the cause is invisible, incomprehensible; how can it be otherwise? when we cannot see the end or origin of a nerve or vein, while the divisibility of matter or fluid, is

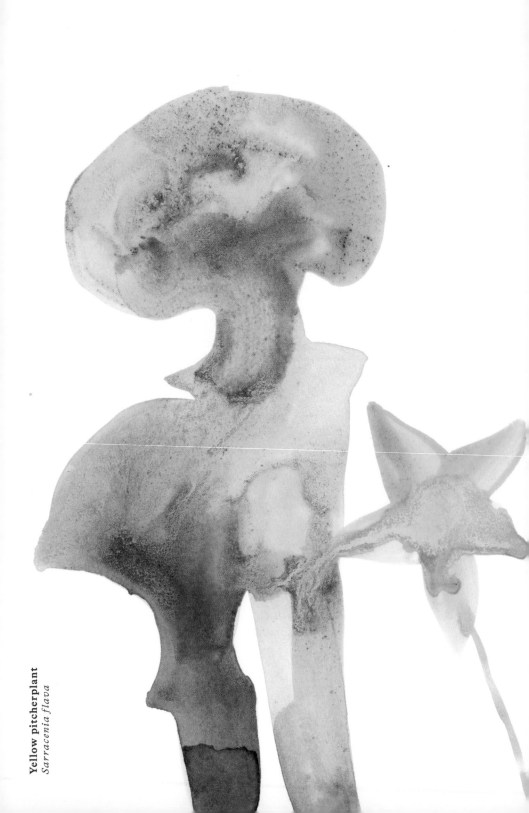

Yellow pitcherplant
Sarracenia flava

infinite. We admire the mechanism of a watch, and the fabric of a piece of brocade, as being the production of art; these merit our admiration, and must excite our esteem for the ingenious artist or modifier; but nature is the work of God omnipotent; and an elephant, nay even this world, is comparatively but a very minute part of his works. If then the visible, the mechanical part of the animal creation, the mere material part, is so admirably beautiful, harmonious, and incomprehensible, what must be the intellectual system? that inexpressibly more essential principle, which secretly operates within? that which animates the inimitable machines, which gives them motion, impowers them to act, speak, and perform, this must be divine and immortal?

I am sensible that the general opinion of philosophers has distinguished the moral system of the brute creature from that of mankind, by an epithet which implies a mere mechanical impulse, which leads and impels them to necessary actions, without any premeditated design or contrivance; this we term instinct, which faculty we suppose to be inferior to reason in man.

The parental and filial affections seem to be as ardent, their sensibility and attachment as active and faithful, as those observed in human nature.

When travelling on the east coast of the isthmus of Florida, ascending the south Musquito river, in a canoe, we observed numbers of deer and bears, near the banks, and on the islands of the river: the bears were feeding on the fruit of the dwarf creeping Chamærops; (this fruit is of the form and size of dates, and is delicious and nourishing food:) we saw eleven bears in the course of the day, they seemed no way surprised or affrighted at the sight of us. In the evening, my hunter, who was an excellent marksman, said that he would shoot one of them for the sake of the skin and oil, for we had plenty and variety of provisions in our bark. We accordingly, on sight of two of them, planned our approaches as artfully as possible, by crossing over to the opposite shore, in order to get under cover of a small island; this we cautiously coasted round, to a point, which we apprehended would take us within shot of the bears; but here finding ourselves at too great a distance from them, and discovering that we must openly show ourselves, we had no other alternative to effect our purpose, but making oblique approaches. We gained gradually on our prey by this artifice, without their noticing us: finding ourselves near enough, the hunter fired, and laid the target dead on the spot where she stood; when presently the other, not seeming the least moved at the report of our piece, approached the dead body, smelled, and pawed it, and appearing in agony, fell to weeping and looking upwards, then towards us, and cried out like a child. Whilst our boat approached very near, the hunter was loading his rifle in order to shoot the survivor, which was a young cub, and the slain supposed to be the dam. The continual cries of this afflicted child, bereft of its parent, affected me very sensibly; I was moved with compassion, and charging myself as if accessary to what now appeared to be a cruel murder, endeavoured to prevail on the hunter to save its life, but to no effect! for by habit he had become insensible to compassion towards the brute creation: being now within a few yards of the harmless devoted victim, he fired, and laid it dead upon the body of the dam.

If we bestow but very little attention to the economy of the animal creation, we shall find manifest examples of premeditation, perseverance, resolution, and consummate artifice, in order to effect their purpose. The next morning, after the slaughter of the bears, whilst my companions were striking our tent, and preparing to re-embark, I resolved to make a little botanical excursion alone: crossing over a narrow isthmus of sand hills, which separated the river from the ocean, I passed over a pretty high hill, its summit crested with a few palm trees, surrounded with an Orange grove: this hill, whose base was washed on one side by the floods of the Musquitoe river, and on the other side by the billows of the ocean, was about one hundred yards diameter, and seemed to be an entire heap of sea shells. I continued along the beach a quarter of a mile, and came up to a forest of the Agave vivipara (though composed of herbaceous plants, I term it a forest, because their scapes or flower-stems arose erect near 30 feet high): their tops regularly branching in the form of a pyramidal tree, and these plants growing near to each other, occupied a space of ground of several acres: when their seeds are ripe they vegetate, and grow on the branches, until the scape dries, when the young plants fall to the ground, take root, and fix themselves in the sand: the plant grows to a prodigious size before the scape shoots up from its centre. Having contemplated this admirable grove, I proceeded towards the shrubberies on the banks of the river, and though it was now late in December, the aromatic groves appeared in full bloom. The broad-leaved sweet Myrtus, Erythrina corallodendrum, Cactus cochinellifer, Cacalia suffruticosa, and particularly, Rhizophora conjugata, which stood close to and in the salt water of the river, were in full bloom, with beautiful white sweet scented flowers, which attracted to them two or three species of very beautiful butterflies, one of which was black, the upper pair of its wings very long and narrow, marked with transverse stripes of pale yellow, with some spots of a crimson colour near the body. Another species remarkable for splendour, was of a larger size; the wings were undulated and obtusely crenated round their ends, the nether pair terminating near the body, with a long narrow forked tail; the ground light yellow, striped oblique-transversely, with stripes of pale celestial blue, the ends of them adorned with little eyes encircled with the finest blue and crimson, which represented a very brilliant rosary. But those which were the most numerous were as white as snow, their wings large, their ends lightly crenated and ciliated, forming a fringed border, faintly marked with little black crescents, their points downward, with a cluster of little brilliant orbs of blue and crimson, on the nether wings near the body: the numbers were incredible, and there seemed to be scarcely a flower for each fly, multitudinous as they were, besides clouds of them hovering over the mellifluous groves. Besides these papiles, a variety of other insects come in for a share, particularly several species of bees.

As I was gathering specimens of flowers from the shrubs, I was greatly surprised at the sudden appearance of a remarkably large spider on a leaf, of the genus Araneus saliens: at sight of me he boldly faced about, and raised himself up, as if ready to spring upon me; his body was about the size of a pigeon's egg, of a buff colour, which, with his legs, were covered with short silky hair; on the top of the abdomen was a round red spot or ocelle encircled with black. After I had recovered from the surprise, observing that the wary hunter had retired under cover, I drew near again, and presently discovered that I had surprised him on predatory attempts against the insect tribes. I was therefore determined to watch his proceedings. I soon noticed that the object of his wishes was a large fat bomble bee (apis bombylicus), that was visiting the flowers, and piercing their nectariferous tubes: this cunning intrepid hunter conducted his subtil approaches with the circumspection and perseverance of a Siminole when hunting a deer, advancing with slow steps obliquely, or under cover of dense foliage, and behind the limbs, and when the bee was engaged in probing a flower, he would leap nearer, and then instantly retire out of sight, under a leaf or behind a branch, at the same time keeping a sharp eye upon me. When he had now gotten within two feet of his prey, and the bee was intent on sipping the delicious nectar from a flower, with his back next the spider, he instantly sprang upon him, and grasped him over the back and shoulder, when for some moments they both disappeared. I expected the bee had carried off his enemy, but to my surprise, they both together rebounded back again, suspended at the extremity of a strong elastic thread or web, which the spider had artfully let fall, or fixed on the twig, the instant he leaped from it: the rapidity of the bee's wings, endeavouring to extricate himself, made them both together appear as a moving vapour, until the bee became fatigued by whirling round, first one way and then back again: at length, in about a quarter of an hour, the bee quite exhausted by his struggles, and the repeated wounds of the butcher, became motionless, and quickly expired in the arms of the devouring spider, who, ascending the rope with his game, retired to feast on it under cover of the leaves; and perhaps before night, became himself the delicious evening repast of a bird or lizard.

Fragrant bedstraw
Galium triflorum

ELIZABETH BISHOP

North Haven

In memoriam: Robert Lowell

I can make out the rigging of a schooner
a mile off; I can count
the new cones on the spruce. It is so still
the pale bay wears a milky skin, the sky
no clouds, except for one long, carded horse's-tail.

The islands haven't shifted since last summer,
even if I like to pretend they have
—drifting, in a dreamy sort of way,
a little north, a little south or sidewise,
and that they're free within the blue frontiers of bay.

This month, our favorite one is full of flowers:
Buttercups, Red Clover, Purple Vetch,
Hawkweed still burning, Daisies pied, Eyebright,
the Fragrant Bedstraw's incandescent stars,
and more, returned, to paint the meadows with delight.

The Goldfinches are back, or others like them,
and the White-throated Sparrow's five-note song,
pleading and pleading, brings tears to the eyes.
Nature repeats herself, or almost does:
repeat, repeat, repeat; revise, revise, revise.

Years ago, you told me it was here
(in 1932?) you first "discovered *girls*"
and learned to sail, and learned to kiss.
You had "such fun," you said, that classic summer.
("Fun"—it always seemed to leave you at a loss . . .)

You left North Haven, anchored in its rock,
afloat in mystic blue ... And now—you've left
for good. You can't derange, or re-arrange,
your poems again. (But the Sparrows can their song.)
The words won't change again. Sad friend, you cannot change.

To the Lapland Longspur

I
Oh thou northland bobolink,
Looking over Summer's brink
Up to Winter, worn and dim,
Peering down from mountain rim,
Something takes me in thy note,
Quivering wing, and bubbling throat;
Something moves me in thy ways —
Bird, rejoicing in thy days,
In thy upward-hovering flight.
In thy suit of black and white,
Chestnut cape and circled crown,
In thy mate of speckled brown;
Surely I may pause and think
Of my boyhood's bobolink.

II
Soaring over meadows wild
(Greener pastures never smiled);
Raining music from above,
Full of rapture, full of love;
Frolic, gay and debonair,
Yet not all exempt from care,
For thy nest is in the grass,
And thou worriest as I pass:
But nor hand nor foot of mine
Shall do harm to thee or thine;
I, musing, only pause to think
Of my boyhood's bobolink.

Cranesbill
Geranium spp.

III

But no bobolink of mine
Ever sang o'er mead so fine,
Starred with flowers of every hue,
Gold and purple, white and blue;
Painted-cup, anemone,
Jacob's-ladder, fleur-de-lis,
Orchid, harebell, shooting-star,
Crane's-bill, lupine, seen afar,
Primrose, poppy, saxifrage,
Pictured type on Nature's page—
These and others here unnamed,
In northland gardens, yet untamed,
Deck the fields where thou dost sing,
Mounting up on trembling wing;
While in wistful mood I think
Of my boyhood's bobolink.

IV

On Unalaska's emerald lea,
On lonely isles in Bering Sea,
On far Siberia's barren shore,
On north Alaska's tundra floor,
At morn, at noon, in pallid night,
We heard thy song and saw thy flight,
While I, sighing, could but think
Of my boyhood's bobolink.

Unalaska, July 18, 1899

Nature's Garden for Victory and Peace

Agricultural Research and Experiment Station,
Tuskegee Institute
February 14, 1942

"And God said, Behold, I have given you every herb
bearing seed, which is upon the face of all the earth,
and every tree, in teh which is the fruit of a tree
yielding seed; to you it shall be for meat."
—Genesis 1:29.

Since the article appeared in the *Alabama Journal*, Tuesday, February 10,
1942, by Mr. W. T. Maynor, captioned "Don't Worry If War Causes
Shortage of Green Vegetables, Weeds Are Good To Eat" the large number
of letters that continue to come in asking for more information makes
us feel that here is an opportunity to render a service much needed at
the present time, and equally applicable to our coming rehabilitation
program.

COMPOSITE FAMILY

In the group idea in arrangement it is hoped that it will assist the housewife in the preparation of these vegetables as every member of a group
(with but few exceptions) have some food or medicinal properties in
common with the entire group, therefore, their preparation would be
similar in some respects.

DANDELION (Taraxacum officinale). This is the ordinary dandelion
of our dooryard, field and road sides, with which we are more or less
familiar. It is very tender and delicious now (February 20), and may be
served in a variety of appetizing ways. (Use leaves only).

    1. Wash, prepare, and cook exactly the same as turnip or
collard greens.

    2. Prepare the same as spinach with hard boiled eggs.

    3. A simple, plain and appetizing salad may be made thus:

1 pint of finely shredded young dandelion leaves
1 medium sized onion, finely chopped
2 small radishes, finely chopped
1 tablespoon of minced parsley
1 tablespoon of sugar (can be left out)
Salt and pepper to taste

Moisten thoroughly with weak vinegar or mayonnaise, mix, place in salad dish and garnish with slices of hard boiled egg and pickled beets. This is only one of the many delicious and appetizing salads that will readily suggest themselves to the resourceful housewife.

Aside from the dandelions' value for food, it is well known and highly prized for its many curative properties.

OX-EYE DAISY (Chrysanthemum leucanthemum). The young, tender leaves make a splendid addition to any green leafy salad. It is very appetizing when mixed with the dandelion and prepared in the same way.

WILD LETTUCE (Lactuca, several varieties). These several interesting plants are all members of the lettuce family, have milky juice and when young and tender taste very much like our cultivated lettuce to which it bears some slight resemblance in appearance; others are prickly and resemble a thistle; all are good for food.

Cook the same as turnip greens. When very young and tender the smooth sorts make an excellent uncooked salad, if prepared the same as dandelions.

Its medicinal virtues are similar to the cultivated lettuce and the dandelion. It is excellent when prepared like spinach. When blanched they become very crisp and much richer in flavor than the cultivated sorts. Blanching is easily done by turning a box or any other form of shade over them.

CHICORY (Cichorium intybus). Prepared the same as wild lettuce, before it begins to stem. The roots are very often peeled, dried and roasted a coffee brown. Some prefer it to real coffee; others mix it in various proportions to suit their taste.

Dandelion roots are often used in the same way.

HAWK WEEDS, FLORA'S PAINT BRUSH, etc. (Hieracium, Sp.) There are a number of varieties in this group, reminding one of the dandelion or wild lettuce at first sight. All the species around here are edible. Cook the same as the dandelion.

GIANT THISTLE (Elephantopus tomentosus). Grows plentifully down here, is a winter annual, forming a round mat of leaves fully 15 or 20 inches in diameter, very spiny, leaves dark green on top and woolly beneath with long white hairs.

This plant is delicious when young cooked just like turnip greens or mixed in with other greens. Take only the young tender leaves. Nearly all the leaves can be used if the sharp spines are clipped off with a pair of scissors before cooking.

RABBIT TOBACCO (Antennaria plantaginifolia). The young leaves are delicious cooked like turnip greens or mixed with other greens. It has a mild medicinal value. The young, tender leaves and shoots are very appetizing when used in a mixed salad as recommended for the dandelion.

BUCKWHEAT FAMILY (Polygonaceae)

Twenty-one varieties are found in the United States. The ones listed here are not only edible but contain well known medicinal values.

CURLED DOCK (Rumex Crispus). This is often called our native rhubarb; grows in abundance almost everywhere and is one of the very best of our wild greens; relished almost universally. Cook the same as turnip greens. Many like it prepared the same as spinach. The root of this plant is highly prized as a blood medicine.

WESTERN DOCK (Rumex occidentalis). An unusually fine vegetable. Prepare the same as the above. Many declare it is much richer than any of the docks.

FIELD or SHEEP SORREL (Rumex acetosella). This one is especially prized for salads, making cooling drinks, and pies similar to the Oxalis. Use when the stems are about ⅔ grown.
I have eaten in one way or another, nearly all of the 21 varieties and found them delicious and appetizing. The young, tender leaves and stems of all are delicious in uncooked salads.

GOOSEFOOT FAMILY (Chenopodiaceae)

These vegetables must be eaten and their effects on the system noted to be appreciated. The name, Lamb's Quarters, indicates something of the esteem in which they were held centuries ago.

LAMB'S QUARTERS (Chenopodium album). A wild vegetable, familiar to almost everyone. Many claim that they like it much better than spinach, when prepared the same way. It is good boiled with meat the same as mustard, collards or turnip greens, and equally good when mixed with other greens.

BEETROOT (Beta vulgaris). Our cultivated beets belong to this group. Many housewives, dietitians do not know the leaves and stems are quite as fine as spinach when prepared in the same way. They improve the flavor of other greens when mixed with them and cooked like turnip greens. They also make an appetizing salad when steamed or boiled until tender, drained and served with mayonnaise, French or any other dressing you wish. A little shredded onion, a spring of parsley, chow-chow or mixed pickle of any kind aid much in the preparation of this versatile food stuff.

I think you will like the many combinations better than spinach. The pickled leaf stems are especially fine when served with cold meats. The entire spinach family are especially rich in iron and other mineral salts.

THE MUSTARD FAMILY (Brassicaceae)

Just a few of this large and outstanding group of edible and medicinal plants will be mentioned here.

PEPPER-GRASS (Lepidium species). There are several varieties of this common dooryard and garden plant. It belongs to the mustard family and can be cooked in the same way. It is delicious when prepared as an uncooked salad, the same as recommended for dandelion. The three that are of special interest here can be easily recognized by their heart-shaped seed vessels and peppery odor and taste of the leaves.

SHEPHERD'S PURSE (Capsella bursa pastoris), is a member of this great family and highly prized for its palatability and real dietetic value.

BLACK MUSTARD (Brassica nigra), originally was cultivated, but now in many sections of the United States has become weedy. It is highly prized for its seed and also as a vegetable, eaten raw, or cooked with other greens it is most highly prized.

WATER GRASS (Nasturtium officinale). This plant is too well known to need description here. As a pot herb, garnishing salads, etc. it has but few equals.

There are many different types growing in both swamps and upland.

CULTIVATED RADISH (Raphanus sativus). The young leaves and tender stems are quite an addition to mixed greens.

HORSE RADISH (Cochleria armoracia). The young tender leaves are very fine in uncooked salad, and equally desirable when cooked with other greens.

STOCK (Matthiola incana). The young tender leaves are appetizing mixed with an uncooked salad or boiled with mixed greens. Stock is cultivated both in the greenhouse and the outside for its beautiful flowers and attractive foliage.

PRIMROSE FAMILY (Onagracea)

EVENING PRIMROSE (Enothera biennis). There are several varieties of this splendid wild vegetable. All the winter annuals of this group that form a round mat of leaves during the fall and early spring are highly edible, piquant, and possess mild medicinal value.

WILD PRIMROSE (Primula). At this time of the year, these plants form round discs on the ground nearly as large as a saucer. They are often called pig or butter weeds. The leaves are light green in color, and the roots near the crown usually of a reddish cast when cut. Cooked like turnip greens they are so rich in flavor that the name butter weed is given them. The medicinal virtue of the primrose is well known.

AMARANTH FAMILY (Amaranthacea)

In many localities both the smooth and spiny varieties are used as pot herbs; the roots of some are red similar to beets, and are prized for garnishing salads, pickling, etc.

CARELESS WEEDS (Amaranthus). These are often called pig weeds; the two most commonly used are the smooth and the thorny. When young and tender, both are very choice as a vegetable.

Cook leaves and stems, the same as turnip greens. Their medicinal value is said to be similar to that of beet leaves.

Evening primrose
Oenothera biennis

POKEWEED FAMILY (Phytolaccaceae)

Persons who are fond of spinach and find it hard to get will be glad to know that the leaves and stems of the poke weed when taken very young and prepared like spinach can hardly be detected from it.

POKEWEED (Phytolacca decandra). A plant with which we are all acquainted, and relish when cooked. The leaves and young, tender shoots are the choice parts. They should be boiled for two or three minutes in water that has been slightly salted. That water should be drained off and thrown away, then proceed to cook the same as turnip greens. The tender stems are delicious when the leaves are removed, scalded in salt water, and afterwards creamed like asparagus. There is no better vegetable. Its medicinal virtues are many and varied.

WOOD SORREL FAMILY (Oxalidaceae)

SOUR GRASS (Oxalis, two kinds). This is the old-fashioned sheep sorrel with which most people are familiar. It makes a pie similar to apple or rhubarb, and is very appetizing.

Take the leaves and tender stems, wash clean and cook in a little water until tender; pass through a fine sieve to remove any hard stems. The after procedure is exactly the same as for stewed apple pie. Thicken, if necessary with a little flour or corn starch; bake with upper and lower crust. It makes a splendid salad when prepared the same as recommended for the dandelion. It is also excellent when served as a sauce when stewed the same as apple sauce. Many attractive combinations can be made with gelatine.

SOUP. We hope every person who likes something new, novel, delicious, nourishing and appetizing will try this soup. Thoroughly clean and wash about two quarts of the leaves, boil slowly until tender (preferably in a porcelain or granite ware vessel); rub through a sieve, add your favorite seasoning and three cups of soup stock to it; thicken with one table-spoonful of butter and one of flour rubbed together, and stir this into a teacupful of boiling hot milk. Add to the soup stirring it vigorously to prevent curdling. Let boil up and serve at once with croutons or toasted crackers.

POTATO FAMILY (Solanaceae)

IRISH POTATO, WHITE POTATO, etc. (Solanum tuberosum). The tender shoots and leaves are a fine addition to add to a pot of mixed greens, greatly improving the flavor.

HORSE NETTLE, BULL NETTLE, SANDBRIER, TREAD SALVE, etc. (*Solanum Carolinense*). The young, tender tops add much to a pot of mixed greens.

MINT FAMILY (Menthaceae)

The following are pot herbs, used in the preparation of foods largely for their flavoring qualities:
PENNYROYAL (Hedeoma pulegioides)
LEMON BALM, GARDEN BALM, SWEET BALM, etc. (Melissa officinalis)
PEPPERMINT (Mentha piperita)
SPEARMINT (Mentha spicata)
BEE BALM, OSWEGO TEA, etc. (Monarda didyma)
WILD BERGAMOT, HORSEMINT, etc. (Monarda fistulosa)
HORSEMINT (Monarda punctata)
CATNIP, CATMINT, etc. (Nepeta cataria)

PEA FAMILY (Papilionaceae)

PURPLE MEDIC, ALFALFA, LUCERNE, etc. (*Medicago sativa*). The young, tender leaves and stems are especially good when mixed with other greens, and especially piquant and appetizing made into a salad, thus: Wash and prepare the alfalfa similar to that of lettuce, garnish the whole with shredded onion, radishes, pickled beets, carrots, etc. Serve with mayonnaise or French dressing.

This salad lends itself to an almost endless variety of artistic combinations in the way of ribbons, spots, layers, jellied, etc. The nutritional value of alfalfa is too well known to need further discussion here.

CLOVER
CLOVER FLOWERS
RED CLOVER (Trifolium pratense)
WHITE CLOVER (Trifolium repens)
The flower heads of these two varieties have held first place in delicate and fancy salads for many years. Serve in mixed salads or separately as fancy dictates. They lend themselves admirably to any type of mild dressing.

MILK WEED FAMILY (Asclepiadaceae)

SWAMP MILK WEED (Asclepias incarnata)
COMMON SILK WEED (Asclepias syriaca)
Have always held a high place as a delicious food; cut just before the leaves are half grown, prepare like asparagus tips. They improve all mixed greens. They are also choice boiled or steamed until tender and

served with mayonnaise or French dressing; and they are equally fine in any mixed salad.

They are good also in a puree of vegetables, bouillon cubes or gelatinized vegetables.

LILY FAMILY (Liliaceae)

ONIONS. The following have been exceptionally palatable and appetizing when used in the ordinary way:

WILD GARLIC (Allium canadense)

WILD ONION (Allium mutabile)

WILD ONION often called garlic (Allium vineale)

All of the above have been relished and found appetizing in the early spring when the tops are tender, prepared as follows: Take a few pieces of fat bacon, cut in small pieces, fry until nearly done, and while the grease is very hot stir in the finely cut onion tops, and let cook until done. Have ready two or three eggs that have been salted and peppered to taste; stir these quickly into the bacon and onions, being careful not to let the eggs get too hard, and serve at once.

Some like cheese grated over the eggs before frying.

The roots of these onions can be used if desired. They are equally fine in uncooked salads, garnishing, boiling with mixed greens, and in soups and purees of vegetables.

PINK FAMILY (Caryophyllaceae)

CHICK WEEDS (Stellaria).

CHICK WEED, STAR WORT (Stellaris media). This delicate little plant can be used in a number of ways. It gives to green salads a very mild and pleasing taste; is equally good when cooked the usual way with mixed greens.

One of its outstanding and almost uncanny values is the way it lends itself to garnishing vegetable, meat and salad dishes as well as other forms of table decoration.

Select only the fresh, tender ends. Keep in cold water or refrigerator until ready to use. If properly done it never fails to get much favorable comment on its unusual beauty.

LAUREL FAMILY (Lauraceae)

SASSAFRAS (*Sassafras officinale*). The medicinal value of this tree is almost as old as the beginning of time. Oil of sassafras has many uses in the arts and trades, aside from the delicious tea furnished by the roots, the young, tender stems and leaves are becoming a real article of commerce.

They are cut, dried, and ground to a fine powder and used in soups, broths, and is growing in popularity for such purposes. It is especially useful in the preparation of gumbo of various kinds. It can be cooked with the soup, etc.; or put in a salt shaker and placed on the table to be used at will, like salt and pepper. It is most wholesome and appetizing.

PLANTAIN FAMILY (Plantaginaceae)

DOORYARD PLANTAIN, etc. (Plantago major). The young, tender leaves of this plant is highly prized for food when cooked like turnip greens, or mixed with other greens.

The seeds are used in medicine.

Plantago cordata, Plantago rugelii, and Plantago lanceolata are all good when cooked like turnip greens or mixed with other greens.

VALERIAN FAMILY (Valerianaceae)

WILD LAMB SALAD, CORN SALAD, etc. (Valerianella radiata). There are six varieties of this choice vegetable scattered throughout the United States. The one named above grows freely in Alabama and is so highly prized cooked like turnip greens alone or mixed with others. It is cultivated in some sections. It is equally desirable served like lettuce, with shredded onion, radishes, pickled beets, cucumber, etc.

GERANIUM FAMILY (Geraniaceae)

WILD GERANIUM, ALUM ROOT, etc. (*Geranium maculatum*). The small plants are palatable when mixed with other greens and cooked with them.

PURSLANE FAMILY (Portulacaceae)

PURSLANE, PUSSLEY, etc. (Portulaca oleracea). This plant is familiar to almost everyone, and is highly prized when prepared like spinach, cooked with other greens, or it is equally acceptable as a raw salad.

MORNING GLORY FAMILY (Convolvulaceae)

SWEET POTATO (Ipomea batatas). The young, tender vines and leaves of the sweet potato are especially rich and palatable cooked like spinach. They are equally good mixed and boiled with other greens.

This bulletin is becoming so large that it seems wise to bring it to a close right here.

Evening primrose
Oenothera biennis

LUCILLE CLIFTON

flowers

here we are
running with the weeds
colors exaggerated
pistils wild
embarrassing the calm family flowers   oh
here we are
flourishing for the field
and the name of the place
is Love

ROBERT CREELEY

The Flower

I think I grow tensions
like flowers
in a wood where
nobody goes.

Each wound is perfect,
encloses itself in a tiny
imperceptible blossom,
making pain.

Pain is a flower like that one,
like this one,
like that one,
like this one.

CAMILLE DUNGY

Letter to America: Diversity, a Garden Allegory with Suggestions for Direct Action

Dear America,

When we first moved into our house, the yard was tame and orderly. There were three aspen trees in the rear corners of the backyard, but mostly the plant life consisted of severely trimmed juniper bushes and a substantially weed-free lawn. Beds of river rocks, so uniform in size and shape as to seem manufactured, edged these expanses of green. It was a well-manicured yard.

This was the first thing about the house I set out to change.

I've been pulling rock for four years now. Every spring before the heat comes on and again in the fall before the cold settles, I rip out a new section of river rock and landscaping fabric. This is a slow process. The rock and plasticized landscaping fabric deplete the soil. Efforts to reduce natural diversity nearly always result in some form of depletion, and this certainly has been true in my yard. What I find beneath those repressed beds would be of little use to a garden. It's hard clay I have to amend with the compost I produce from kitchen scraps and fallen leaves. I also add topsoil hauled in from a landscaping supply store called Hageman Earth Cycle. I love the environmental vision inscribed in the name "Earth Cycle." I also love climbing their small hills of topsoil to shovel some into my wheelbarrow and haul with me back home. It's the full-bodied participation in promoting an ecologically vibrant landscape that excites me.

I try to salvage native earthworms I find under the river rocks, tossing the wrigglers back into my newly-enriched beds. The work might go more quickly if I hired a Bobcat to scoop the rock,

Coneflower
Echinacea angustifolia

but I work slowly, extracting and replanting desirable vegetation whose roots have grown into the landscaping fabric. I spare centipedes and pill bugs, do my best to avoid spiders. Once, I found an anthill teeming with creatures who were busy tunneling into the difficult dirt. I left them where they were. Proceeding this way, it may take me 12 hours to prepare a satisfactory three-square-foot plot. I'll sow this with wildflower seed, perennial starts, tulip bulbs, and irises' gangly rhizomes. Within months, I will enjoy a riot of color where once there was nothing but a hard, grey expanse.

In the center of my lawn, and also in poorly irrigated corners that had been overtaken by crabgrass and purslane, I've started more flowerbeds. Making these, too, is a difficult process, but not the kind of process that takes place on my knees as does the reclamation of the rock beds. The object on the lawn is to turn turf into rich soil. I cover the grass with layer on layer of cardboard, kitchen scraps, topsoil, compost, newspaper, and mulch. At the end of the long winter, I'll turn it all with a shovel and pitchfork. Then I will plant my seeds. I begin around Halloween and must wait until nearly June before I can start to see any results. The process of changing my environment from homogenous to diverse is rewarding, but slow.

Because I garden by scattering seed, I never quite know what's going to appear, or where. If, as Michael Pollan writes, "a lawn is nature under totalitarian rule," my yard reveals a very different sort of possibility. My property yields an explosion of color come mid-summer. You never know exactly what you'll find on my little patch, or whom.

The August we moved into this house, I found canister upon canister of herbicides and pesticides on the worktable in the garage. That first summer, very few pollinators braved the poisoned turf. They'd flit from one rare dandelion to the next, then buzz away, seemingly forlorn. But this year I've counted numerous species of bee, more than two dozen different kinds of birds, and a slew of moths and butterflies, including monarchs. I've planted milkweed in many places around the yard. I've planted other native plants as well. In some of this year's reclaimed beds, I planted handfuls of sunflower seeds left over from last year's crop. These have grown as high as 13 feet, delighting many species of neighbors, humans included.

The brilliant goldfinches that hang out near our feeders eat my sunflower petals. I would prefer if they didn't eat my sunflower petals, but the sunflowers are there for them as much as they are there for me, and I'm learning that birds eat flower petals, not just the seeds from the middle of the plants. Next year, to continue to attract these beautiful birds, I'll sow more sunflower seeds. The sunflowers, *and* the birds who eat them, fill me with joy I could not have imagined.

The covenant for our homeowners' association specifies that what I've done around my house is technically prohibited. There should be fewer wildflowers in my yard. Banish the milkweed. Banish the tall grass. Banish the front yard onion patch, the sad squash trials. When the sunflowers have finished flowering, rather than leave the dried stalks and seed heads for birds to perch and munch on as they stock up for their winter migrations, I should pull all remnants of the summer plants out of the ground. There should be nothing brown like that around the yard. Nothing that might be construed as aesthetically unsavory.

Did I mention that my family is the only black family on our block? That we're some of the only black people in our neighborhood? That, in fact, we're one of the few black families in our entire town? I say this now because it may help you to understand that my resistance to the particular brand of suburban American monoculture my HOA promotes is also a resistance to a culture that has been set up to exclude people like me. A culture that—through laws and customs that amount to toxic actions and culturally constructed weeding—has effectively maintained homogenous spaces around houses like mine.

But, I'm lucky. My neighbors claim to be grateful I've moved in and cultivated the most heterogeneous environment on our street. And the bees love the flowers. And the sunflowers shade the low-growing plants at their bases, some of which flower and some of which don't. A whole new ecosystem is thriving in my yard. Hardly anyone used to visit, but now it is alive and full of action. Birds I don't see on any of the neighboring lawns have taken up regular habitation around our place. Several mating pairs chose spots in our various trees and bushes to nest and raise their young. The worms I so carefully preserved provide tasty snacks for robins. I released 9,000 ladybugs to help with an aphid infestation on my rudbekia plants. Now I've seen an increase in creatures feeding on the healthy black-eyed susans (and probably on some ladybugs as well). Swallowtails, painted ladies, and the occasional monarch pass through the garden in late summer. When our aspens succumbed to the scale that struck many of the trees in the neighborhood this year and we had to cut them down, there were still plenty of places for bugs and birds and squirrels to congregate, places that did not exist before I began the work of diversifying the landscape I found in my backyard.

Though it fills me with joy to be surrounded by such vibrancy, keeping up with all of this isn't easy. This spring, it was as if every dandelion in the county called its neighbor to join them in our yard. I spent countless hours with my old-fashioned weed remover, pulling weeds at the root. It occurs to me, doing this work, that one of the reasons we prefer homogeneity is that it can seem much easier. There is a man who comes to my house and fixes things. He's handy, smart, and strong. He has an eye for order and structure, and I defer to him when it comes time to decide what type of stain to use on the deck. He recently offered to help me out with the weeds. A couple applications of chemical herbicide and my yard will surely look neat as a magazine photo. I will admit I have been tempted. My flowerbeds are spectacular, but the mounds of clover and bindweed scattered around the unimproved sections detract from the overall grandeur of my lot. It's difficult to strike a balance between acceptance and dominance. I have to come to terms with the fact that maintaining a poison-free yard will mean revising some of my opinions about what plants I want around me and which I do not.

This is one of the key glories of cultivating diversity: when we cultivate diversity, we learn things we never knew we might want to know. Things we may even *need* to know one day. Neither our river rocks nor our turf grass are edible, but the dandelions, purslane, sunflowers, coneflowers, California poppies, and curly dock I either cultivate or tolerate all have some nutritive value. The vibrant variety in my yard can provide sustenance in all kinds of ways!

Our first winter in this house was hard on me. The killing frosts did what they do and then there were the months without flowers. February came, then March, and then April and, because of all that rock and turf, there was nothing to look at but gray and more gray until May came and, with it, some green. As I've spent the past years planting bulbs and seeds, and as I've put in perennial starts, and as I've swapped plant cuttings with friends, planting plots in their honor, and as I've divided and rearranged tubers, and as I've cultivated the diversity of my garden, I have grown happier earlier and earlier each spring. I didn't know I was that dependent on color, on variety, on watching so many different kinds of life being lived but, evidently, I am.

Yours,
Camille

Quentin Compson at the Natural History Museum, Harvard University

You won't have allergies here.
The flowers are made of glass,
your little spine will become a maple tree.
The orchids, posing like eavesdroppers—
they will make you their Queen.

We will make love on Russian glass,
pickled seeds, roots and stamens,
the translucent xylem of the flowers
pricking our spines.

Couldn't you die here?
Don't speak of Father.
Look to the cashew trees.

Remember the wild orchids in the New England wood?
Their veiny leaves and cuticles fresh with vanilla.
These are not fresh, but they inhale.
They can smell your minty breath,
they can bow to your sighs,
they will make soil of your shoulders
and grow you arms.

Caddy, surrounded by glass.
Caddy, surrounded by glass, a little tree inside her.
Caddy, surrounded by glass, smells like trees.

Couldn't you die here, Caddy?
In all this glass?

PAUL GOODMAN

Pagan Rites

Creator Spirit come
by whom
I'll say what is real
and so away I'll steal.

When my only son
fell down and died on Percy mountain
I began
to practice magic like a pagan.

Around the open grave we ate
the blueberries that he brought
from the cloud, and then we
buried his bag with his body.

Upon the covered grave
I laid the hawkweed that I love
that withered fast
where the mowers passed.

I brought also a tiny yellow
flower whose name I do not know
to share my ignorance
with my son. (But since

then I find in the book
it is a kind of shamrock
Oxalis corniculata,
Matty, sorrel of the lady.)

Blue-eyed grass with its gold hexagon
beautiful as the gold and blue
double in Albireo
that we used to gaze on

when Matty was alive
I laid on Matty's grave
where two robins were
hopping here and there;

and gold and bluer than that blue
or the double in Albireo
bittersweet nightshade
the deadly alkaloid
I brought for no other reason
than because it was poison.

Mostly, though, I brought some weed
beautiful but disesteemed,
plantain or milkweed,
because we die by the wayside.

(And if spring comes again
I will bring a dandelion,
because he was a common weed
and also he was splendid.)

But when I laid my own forehead
on the withering sod
to go the journey deep,
I could not fall asleep.

I cannot dream, I cannot quit
the one scene in the twilight
that is no longer new yet does
not pass into what was.

Last night the Pastoral Symphony
of Handel in the key of C
I played on our piano
out of tune shrill and slow

because the shepherds were at night
in the field in the starlight
when music loud and clear
sang from nowhere.

Will magic and the weeks placate
the soul that in tumbling fright
fled on August eighth?
The first flock is flying south

and a black-eyed susan
is livid in the autumn rain
dripping without haste or strain
on the oblong larger than a man.

Creator Spirit come
by whom
I say that which is real
and softly away I steal.

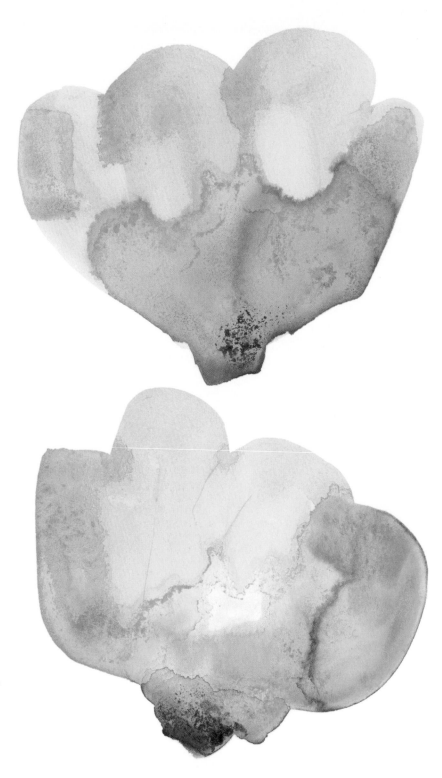

California poppy
Eschscholzia californica

ROBERT HASS

Spring Rain

Now the rain is falling, freshly, in the intervals between sunlight,
a Pacific squall started no one knows where, drawn east as the drifts of
warm air make a channel;
it moves its own way, like water or the mind,
and spills this rain passing over. The Sierras will catch it as last snow
flurries before summer, observed only by the wakened marmots at ten
thousand feet,
and we will come across it again as larkspur and penstemon sprouting
along a creek above Sonora Pass next August,
where the snowmelt will have trickled into Dead Man's Creek and the
creek spilled into the Stanislaus and the Stanislaus into the San Joaquin and the San Joaquin into the slow salt marshes of the bay.
That's not the end of it: the gray jays of the mountains eat larkspur
seeds, which cannot propagate otherwise.
To simulate the process, you have to soak gathered seeds all night in
the acids of coffee
and then score them gently with a very sharp knife before you plant
them in the garden.
You might use what was left of the coffee we drank in Lisa's kitchen
visiting.
There were orange poppies on the table in a clear glass vase, stained
near the bottom to the color of sunrise;
the unstated theme was the blessedness of gathering and the blessing
of dispersal—
it made you glad for beauty like that, casual and intense, lasting as long
as the poppies last.

BERNADETTE MAYER

Renaming Things

Flowers ... plants
Clover ... lovers
Thistle ... stick-in-the-mud
Goldenrod ... ne'er-do-well
Unidentifiable shrub ... isis' blood
Grass ... cheveux de spectre
Celandine ... cowering DNA
Woodland sunflower ... how strange
Field fern ... bronze idol
Bramble bush ... attacker of Bernadette
Poison ivy ... ménage à trois
Grass ... hector's lunch
Wild aster ... smart mouth pucker
Dandelion ... liminal lettuce
Yarrow ... the bobby mcgee
Thimble berry ... tom's tart
Bloodroot ... dragon buddies
Sycamore ... quark ladder
Dragonflies ... braidkissers
Butterfly ... indigo tourism

(with the members of the Rootdrinker workshop)

.

Bloodroot
Sanguinaria canadensis

ELEANOR PERÉNYI

Wild Flowers

Study a book on wild flowers (I can commend *Wildflowers of Eastern America* by Klimas and Cunningham) or for that matter walk out into the woods and fields, and you wonder why you go to the trouble of sowing seed, ordering plants, when the countryside is alive with flowers that are identical with or sometimes superior to their domesticated cousins. Wild bluebells (*Mertensia viginica*), bee balm (*Monarda*), the common bleeding heart, Jacob's-ladder, false indigo, passion-flower and lots of others differ in no important respect from cultivated varieties. Still others are uniquely themselves and therefore unobtainable except in the wild, among them our native orchids: the exquisite pink lady's-slipper that really looks more like a little satchel to carry satin dancing shoes than the shoes themselves; the white fringed orchis (*Habenaria blephari-glottis*), hooded plumes collected on a spike; the rosebud orchid, poised like a hummingbird on its stalk; the three-bird orchis. Cattleyas grown under glass are coarse by comparison. The golden *Iris Pseudacorus*, wild blue flag, *Iris prismatica* and the crested dwarf iris make all but certain Japanese and Siberian varieties look vulgar. Wild flowers are never vulgar. One and all they have an elegance and restraint to their design that ought to give the hybridists pause as they go about their work: Fabergé would have been proud to produce the nodding bells of *Clematis viorna*, purple enameled on green gold; Grinling Gibbons pleased to have carved the wild-ginger flower, a three-cornered brown box whose petals open to reveal the surprise at the bottom—pistils incised like a cameo. Wood lilies are so refined in their beauty that if Jan de Graaff, for one, hadn't been born, I would say that they too couldn't be improved upon.

There was a time when one could have looted all this natural beauty without compunction. It had, in fact, to be done, or we would have had no flowers to grow in our gardens, since all are descended from some wild variety that caught somebody's eye. But—it can't be too often emphasized—that time has gone. No longer is it permissible to venture forth with a trowel and a view to improving a naturalistic patch in one's own garden. Remoteness of the site is no justification, rather the opposite.

To remove a plant from a spot where "no one will notice" is a greater risk than to dig up something by the roadside. The chances are excellent that the hidden specimen is the rare one, perhaps the only example to have survived for miles around, while the one by the roadside is nothing more than an escapee from a lost farm. Even then, one should proceed with caution. I can remember, and it isn't longer than twenty years ago, when Turk's-cap lilies abounded in this part of New England. Now they are gone, raped, many of them, by passing motorists who treated them as cut flowers and didn't even plant the bulbs when they got home. They are of course on the endangered species list—as are all the orchids I mention. But those who go out to bag wild flowers are hardly ever the same people who know or care about endangered species.

A middle ground exists between the extremes of letting all wild flowers strictly alone and robbing them indiscriminately, and I tread it uneasily. What if you happen to know that a certain area is threatened with "development" and the wild flowers in it are sure to be destroyed? I am thinking of a miniature swamp close by one of our back roads where each June a lake of *Iris prismatica* comes into bloom, and every time I pass it I whisper to myself, why not? The tide of tacky little houses has all but reached this point and if not this year, then next or the year after, the iris will be gone. Why not, in the meantime, dig up a few and preserve them, as it were, in my garden? The problem is exactly analagous to that of what to do with wild animals. If man is going to destroy their habitats, making survival impossible, is it or isn't it a good idea to preserve and try to breed a few specimens in zoos? Any answer you can think of is repulsive. Extinction is almost too awful to contemplate, but are a few survivors preserved in memoriam any better? I don't know. So far, I have left the *Iris prismatica* to its fate.

The decision, I have to confess, isn't exclusively on moral grounds. Like wild animals, wild plants often sicken and die in captivity. Nobody understands exactly what combination of soil and soil bacteria, of moisture, light, heat or cold are responsible for their success in a given place; whereas with domesticated plants all these factors are to some extent predictable in their effect. Those wild flowers that grow from bulbs or tubers are the least risky to tamper with. Usually they can be transplanted with fair hopes that they will accommodate themselves to a new environment. The commoner ferns are equally adaptable. With others, the issue is in doubt. Wild flowers seem tough a priori to the ignorant: If they weren't, they wouldn't have managed so well without the helping hand of man. So goes the reasoning and it is false. Wild flowers do best when they are allowed to make their own choices about where and how they will grow, and the best that man can do is try to emulate those conditions. As often as not, he fails, and the lover of wild flowers would do better to join a conservationist society than to try to start his own sanctuary for endangered species.

Some nurserymen offer wild flowers by mail. To be consistent, I suppose one should inquire into precisely how the plants were obtained, and if it were admitted that those on the endangered list were collected in the wild, refuse to order them. I've not gone to that length, and have done fairly well with the few I have ordered. Trilliums seem to transplant easily, as do Virginia bluebells, wild columbines and Jack-in-the-pulpit. But with me it has been precisely the threatened orchids that fare badly—likewise the fringed and closed gentians and trout lilies (also called dogtooth violet, *Erythronium americanum*), all on the list. None of these can I claim to have "saved," so probably shouldn't have sent for them in the first place. As I say, I don't know the answer to this dilemma.

Dogtooth violet
Erythronium americanum

MICHAEL HOFMANN

Idyll

The windows will reflect harder, blacker, than before,
and fresh cracks will appear in the yellow brick.

There is no milkman or paper boy, but presumably
the lurid pizza flyers and brassy offers of loans

will continue to drop through the letter box.
The utilities will be turned off one by one,

as the standing orders keel over or lose their address,
though there was never that much cooking or bathing or

phoning went on here anyway—the fridge will stop its buzz,
the boiler its spontaneous combusting—till there is nothing

but a mustiness of gas. The dust will coil and thicken
ultimately to hawsers around pipes and wires;

ever more elaborate spiders' webs will sheet off the corners;
rust stains and mildew and rot will spread chromatically

below the holes in the roof, radiate from the radiators;
eventually mosses and small grasses and even admirable

wild flowers, hell, an elder or buddleia, push their heads
through the chinks between the boards; a useless volume of books—

who could ever read that many—will keep the moths entertained,
generations of industrious woodlice and silverfish

will leave their corpses on the clarty work-surfaces,
and a pigeon or two will hook its feet over the tarnished sink

and brood vacantly on its queenly pink toes.

KATIE PETERSON

The Government

Years later, the same argument
about what to eat and drink
for hours. Those in elected
positions whirl around those positions
like petals on a flower. At night,
the story of the accident gets told again, this time,
the greatest dramatic pause follows the rescuer
walking away. I say it has been years,
years, I say, to any flower that will
listen, to our excuses for lilies, a flower
I've never actually seen.

Wildflower

Some—the ones with fish names—grow so north
they last a month, six weeks at most.
Some others, named for the fields they look like,
last longer, smaller.

And these, in particular, whether trout or corn lily,
onion or bellwort, just cut
this morning and standing open in tapwater in the kitchen,
will close with the sun.

It is June, wildflowers on the table.
They are fresh an hour ago, like sliced lemons,
with the whole day ahead of them.
They could be common mayflower lilies of the valley,

day lilies, or the clustering Canada, large, gold,
long-stemmed as pasture roses, belled out over the vase—
or maybe Solomon's seal, the petals
ranged in small toy pairs

or starry, tipped at the head like weeds.
They could be anonymous as weeds.
They are, in fact, the several names of the same thing,
lilies of the field, butter-and-eggs,

toadflax almost, the way the whites and yellows juxtapose,
and have "the look of flowers that are looked at,"
rooted as they are in water, glass, and air.
I remember the summer I picked everything,

flower and wildflower, singled them out in jars
with a name attached. And when they had dried as stubborn

Toadflax
Linaria vulgaris

as paper I put them on pages and named them again.
They were all lilies, even the hyacinth,

even the great pale flower in the hand of the dead.
I picked it, kept it in the book for years
before I knew who she was,
her face lily-white, kissed and dry and cold.

Tácheeh

boys swim in lake water
                        coming thunder
            they hold the other
try to hear a heartbeat
                splash apart
hands petal on the shore
                        a spine
their bodies lap and tenor
                    they press their lips together
their torch skin
                            a distant sunset
                    distant headlight
            distant city
distant brushfire

———

they burrow roads for hot wheels
            discover entire towns

in damp soil
            roll tiny cars
back and forth to even roadways
            pack dirt with feet

shine die-cast metals with their shirts

            goose bumps
dot lower backs
                    fingers
            wander beneath jeans

damp air curves

in around the navel

        they discover their names
as bottle caps beneath them
        the letters teethed

———

just boys still
veined hands latched to their necks

each eye a coal pearl
        for grandfathers returned to water

mothers held in their hair
        cousins at teeth

one carries his name
        like a cold sore

on their knees on vinyl tile
mistaken for water

on the kitchen floor
        after painting an ode

to sky bit down
on scar tissue in inner cheek

just another war
        wars in arm hair
in the tomatoes

        instead of a burning
their names become a cornfield

fingers lupine
        beardtongue
bee plant in harrow grasses

pronghorn in wild rose
        truck radio more sego lily
and pigweed spewing

        from open mouth
boys watch ricegrass shimmer in smoke

fires everywhere around them
        arms stretch in sap and bark
hair now meadow

limbs tangle into snakeweed
burning burning burning burning

they know becoming a man
means knowing how to become charcoal

staccato of ash
holding a match to their skin

trying not to light themselves on fire

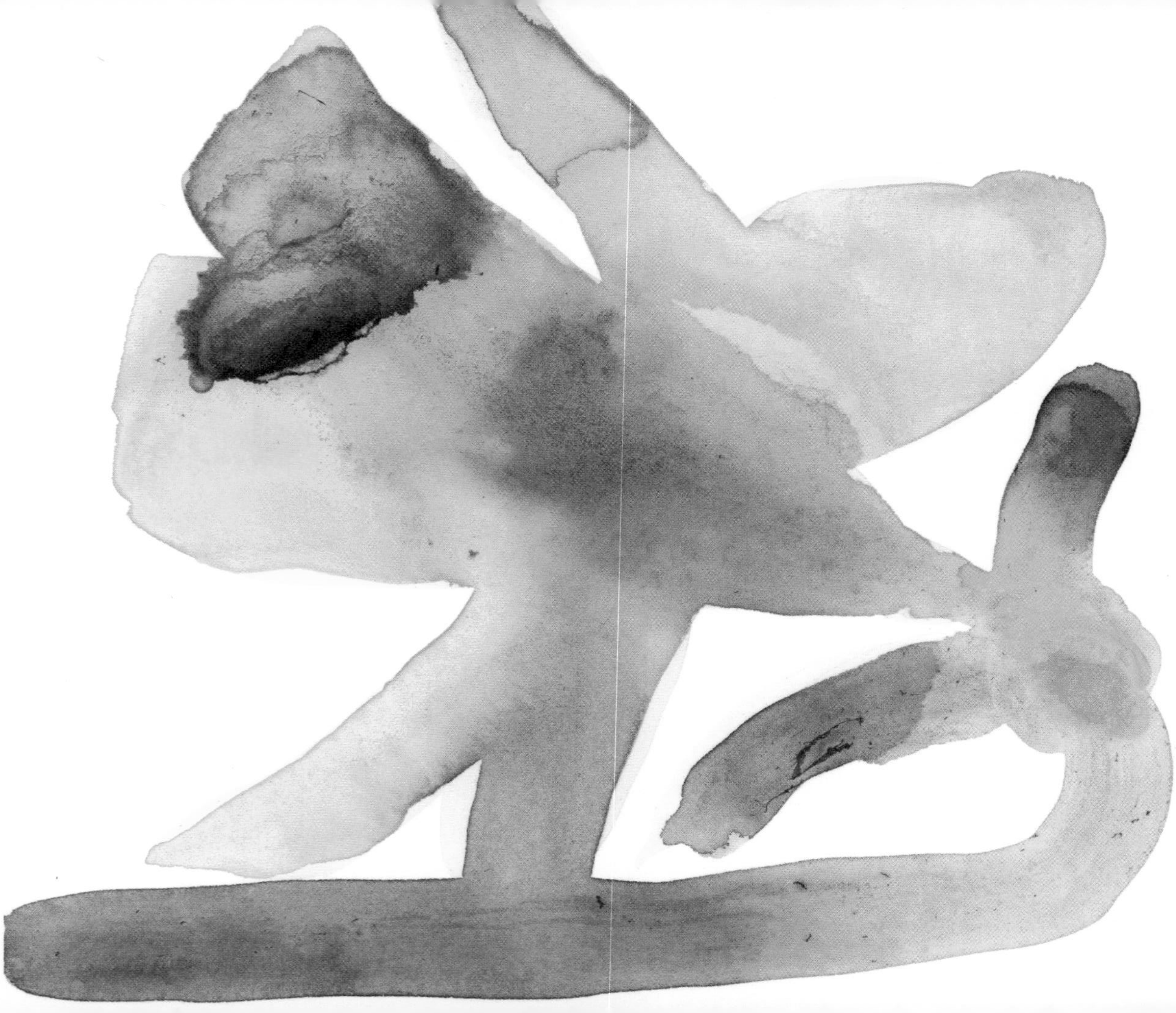

Narcissus
Narcissus pseudonarcissus

GARY SNYDER

For the Children

The rising hills, the slopes,
of statistics
lie before us.
The steep climb
of everything, going up,
up, as we all
go down.

In the next century
or the one beyond that,
they say,
are valleys, pastures,
we can meet there in peace
if we make it.

To climb these coming crests
one word to you, to
you and your children:

stay together
learn the flowers
go light

Batsaki, Yota, Sarah Burke Cahalan, Anatole Tchikine, eds. *The Botany of Empire in the Long Eighteenth Century*. Washington, D.C.: Dunbarton Oaks Research Library and Collection, 2016.

Blunt, Wilfred. *The Art of Botanical Illustration: An Illustrated History*. New York: Dover Publications, 1994.

Bynum, Helen and William. *Botanical Sketchbooks*. New York: Princeton Architectural Press, 2017.

Christenhusz, Maarten J.M., Michael F. Fay, and Mark W. Chase. *Plants of the World: An Illustrated Encyclopedia of Vascular Plants*. Chicago: University of Chicago Press, 2017.

Dana, Mrs. William Starr. *How to Know the Wild Flowers*. New York: Scribner, 1893.

Elliman, Ted and New England Wild Flower Society. *Wildflowers of New England*. Portland, OR: Timber Press, 2016.

Marris, Emma. *Rambunctious Garden: Saving Nature in a Post-Wild World*. New York: Bloomsbury USA, 2011.

Parker, Peter. *A Little Book of Latin for Gardeners*. London: Little, Brown, 2018.

Pavord, Anna. *The Naming of Names: The Search for Order in the World of Plants*. New York: Bloomsbury, 2005.

Rickett, H. W. *Wild Flowers of America*. New York: Crown Publishers, Inc., 1953.

Scarry, Elaine. *On Beauty and Being Just*. Princeton: Princeton University Press, 1999.

Thoreau, Henry David. *Thoreau's Wildflowers*. Edited by Geoff Wisner. New Haven and London: Yale University Press, 2016.

Indian pipe
Monotropa uniflora

ACKNOWLEDGMENTS

I began my journey back to flowers thanks to a friend, Michael McCarthy, whose own encounters with nature and joy led him to the Oak Spring Garden Foundation in Upperville, Virginia, for a talk on meadow restoration. There he and Dr. Peter Crane, Oak Spring's esteemed director, spoke about what seemed to be a paucity of American wildflower writing. In his work as a naturalist, writer, and environmental journalist, Mike turns as often to the British poets as to the authors of scientific studies to build the case for conservation. Back home he wrote to me with a question, which was really an idea that became a call to action. This florilegium would not exist without him. Furthermore, I am indebted to the kind encouragement and expertise of Peter Crane and the indispensable generosity of Oak Spring Garden Foundation, whose support enabled the inclusion of the texts collected here, as well as the commission of the initial illustrations.

So many people assisted in the creation of this anthology, and I am grateful to them all, namely: Helen Houghton, Arete Warren, and Liza Bennett for invaluable early conversations; Jane Hirshfield and Elizabeth Coleman for helpful advice regarding permissions; Tony Willis, Kimberley Fisher, and Nancy Collins at Oak Spring Garden Foundation Library, and Catherine Muckerman and Stephanie Murdaugh for their assistance with accounting; Jay Flaherty and Nico and Ellen Walsh for their perpetual interest and encouragement; Alec and Sally Walsh, for the generous use of their house, where I wrote the introduction; Ari Solotoff, Joy Naifeh, and Marie J. Harvat of Solotoff Law for their counsel; Helen Vendler for her wisdom; Lydia Davis for her generous correspondence; the Cambridge Public Library, the Cook Memorial Library, Widener Library, and all the librarians who kept books circulating during the pandemic and allowed research and reading to continue; Victoria Fox, permissions director extraordinaire; Rebecca Nagel at the Wylie Agency for her poised and dedicated representation; Michael Sand for his belief in this book and his keen attention, Deb Wood for her gorgeous design, and everyone at Abrams; and, especially, Leanne Shapton for saying yes. To my family: thank you for the books, the talks, the time, the walks, for all the manifestations of your love and support; and finally, my deepest thanks to all the writers herein for your words.

"The Waste Land" (Part I) from *The Waste Land* by T. S. Eliot. New York: Boni and Liveright, 1922. UK and British Commonwealth rights granted by Faber and Faber Ltd.

"The Rhodora" from *Early Poems of Ralph Waldo Emerson* by Ralph Waldo Emerson. New York, Boston: Thomas Y. Crowell & Company, 1899.

"Quentin Compson at the Natural History Museum, Harvard University" by Megan Fernandes. Copyright © 2015 by Megan Fernandes. First appeared in *The Kingdom and After* (Tightrope Books, 2015). Reprinted with permission of the author.

"An Encounter" from *Mountain Interval* by Robert Frost. New York: Henry Holt and Company, 1916.

"Rexroth's Cabin" from *Twice Alive*, by Forrest Gander. Copyright © 2019, 2020, 2021 by Forrest Gander. Reprinted by permission of New Directions Publishing Corp.

"Ending the Estrangement" from *Catalog of Unabashed Gratitude* by Ross Gay. Copyright © 2015. Reprinted by permission of the University of Pittsburgh Press.

"The South Wind and the Maiden of the Golden Hair" and "Doodooshaaboojiibik" from *Plants Have So Much to Give Us, All We Have to Do Is Ask: Anishinaabe Botanical Teachings*, edited by Wendy Makoons Geniusz. Copyright © 2015 by Mary Siisip Geniusz. Used by permission of University of Minnesota Press.

"May Apple, or American Mandrake (*Podophyllum peltatum*)" from *Stalking the Wild Asparagus* by Euell Gibbons. Copyright © 1962 by Euell Gibbons. Reproduced with permission of Rowman and Littlefield Publishing Group Inc. through PLSclear.

"Sunflower Sutra" from *Collected Poems, 1947–1980* by Allen Ginsberg. Copyright © 1984 by Allen Ginsberg. Used by permission of HarperCollins Publishers.

"The Wild Iris" from *The Wild Iris* by Louise Glück. Copyright © 1992 by Louise Glück. Used by permission of HarperCollins Publishers. UK and British Commonwealth rights excluding Canada granted by Carcanet Press.

"Pagan Rites" from *North Percy* by Paul Goodman. Copyright © 1968 by Paul Goodman. Reprinted with the permission of The Permissions Company, LLC, on behalf of Black Sparrow Books, an imprint of David R. Godine, Publisher, Inc.

"Of Forced Sightes and Trusty Ferefulness" from *The Dream of the Unified Field: Selected Poems, 1974–1994* by Jorie Graham. Copyright © 1995 by Jorie Graham. Used by permission of HarperCollins Publishers. UK and British Commonwealth rights excluding Canada granted by Carcanet Press.

"Too Bright to See" from *Too Bright to See / Alma* by Linda Gregg. Copyright © 1985 by Linda Gregg. Reprinted with the permission of The Permissions Company, LLC, on behalf of Graywolf Press, graywolfpress.org.

Thoreau, edited by Damion Searls. Copyright © 2009 by Damion Searls. Used by permission of New York Review Books.

"November Cotton Flower" from *Cane* by Jean Toomer. New York: Boni and Liveright, 1923.

"The Enclosure Act" from *The Coronary Garden* by Ann Townsend. Copyright © 2005 by Ann Townsend. Reprinted with the permission of The Permissions Company, LLC, on behalf of Sarabande Books, Inc., www.sarabandebooks.org.

"Green Thoughts in a Green Shade" from *Onward and Upward in the Garden* by Katharine S. White. Copyright © 1958, 1959, 1960, 1961, 1962, 1965, 1966, 1967, 1968, 1970, 1970 by E. B. White, Executor of the Estate of Katharine S. White. Reprinted by permission of ICM Partners.

"When Lilacs Last in the Dooryard Bloom'd" from *Sequel to Drum-Taps: When Lilacs Last in the Dooryard Bloom'd and other poems* by Walt Whitman. Washington: Gibson Brothers, 1865.

"Wild Flowers" from *Specimen Days; and Collect* by Walt Whitman. Philadelphia, PA: Rees Welsh & Co., 1882.

"The Mayflowers" from *Poems of nature: poems subjective and reminiscent: religious poems* by John Greenleaf Whittier. Boston, New York: Houghton, Mifflin and Company, 1892.

"Signatures" from *Collected Poems 1943–2004* by Richard Wilbur. Copyright © 2004 by Richard Wilbur. Reprinted by permission of HarperCollins Publishers. All rights reserved.

"Chicory and Daisies"; "Spring and All (Part I)"; "The Flowers Alone"; "The Red Lily" from *The Collected Poems: Volume I, 1909–1939* by William Carlos Williams. Copyright © 1938 by New Directions Publishing Corp. Reprinted by permission of New Directions Publishing Corp. UK and British Commonwealth rights excluding Canada granted by Carcanet Press.

"A Flower Passage" from *Above the River: The Complete Poems* by James Wright, introduction by Donald Hall. Copyright © 1990 by Anne Wright. Reprinted by permission of Farrar, Straus and Giroux. All rights reserved.

"Lechuguilla" from *Hey, Marfa* by Jeffrey Yang. Copyright © 2018 by Jeffrey Yang. Reprinted with the permission of The Permissions Company, LLC, on behalf of Graywolf Press, graywolfpress.org.

FRANCISCO X. ALARCÓN (1954–2016) was a Chicano poet and teacher, raised in California and Guadalajara, Mexico. He published numerous books of poetry, Spanish language textbooks, and bilingual books for children. He was an advocate for bilingual education, and taught Spanish at the University of California, Davis, where he was the director of the Spanish for Native Speakers program.

A. R. AMMONS (1926–2001) was a formally inventive poet with an abiding interest in ecology and scientific discourse. Born in North Carolina, he lived much of his life in Ithaca, New York, and taught at Cornell University. He won the National Book Award for Poetry in 1973 for *Collected Poems, 1951–1971* and again in 1993 for *Garbage*.

DAVID BAKER's newest book of poems is *Whale Fall*. The longtime poetry editor of *The Kenyon Review*, he is now a professor emeritus of English at Denison University, where he continues to teach.

SUSAN BARBA is the author of two collections of poetry, *Fair Sun* and *geode*. In addition to editing *A Literary Field Guide to American Wildflowers*, she is coeditor of *I Want to Live: Poems of Shushanik Kurghinian*. She works as a senior editor for New York Review Books and lives in Cambridge, Massachusetts.

WILLIAM BARTRAM (1739–1823) was an early American botanist, and the son of John Bartram, King George III's botanist. Accompanying his father on specimen-collecting trips through Pennsylvania, New York, and Florida, Bartram grew adept at sketching and writing about flora and fauna. His *Travels Through North and South Carolina, Georgia, East and West Florida* brought him international renown and admiration from writers such as Wordsworth, Coleridge, and Chateaubriand.

JILL BIALOSKY is the author of five collections of poetry, most recently, *Asylum*; four novels, including the forthcoming *The Deceptions*; and two works of nonfiction, *History of a Suicide: My Sister's Unfinished Life* (a *New York Times* bestseller) and *Poetry Will Save Your Life*. She was honored in 2014 for her distinguished contribution to poetry by the Poetry Society of America. She is a vice president and executive editor at W. W. Norton & Company.

ELIZABETH BISHOP (1911–1979) was a major poet of the twentieth century. She received the Pulitzer Prize in 1956 for *Poems: North & South*, and the National Book Award in 1965 for *Questions of Travel* and again in 1970 for *The Complete Poems*.

NELTJE BLANCHAN (1865–1918) was a writer of popular nature guides about birds and wildflowers and an early advocate for wildlife conservation.

JERICHO BROWN is the author of *Please*, *The New Testament*, and *The Tradition*, which was awarded the 2020 Pulitzer Prize in Poetry. He is the Charles Howard Candler Professor of English and Creative Writing and the director of the Creative Writing Program at Emory University.

JOSEPH BRUCHAC is a writer, storyteller, and Nulhegan Abenaki citizen. He has written more than a hundred books for adults and children, and, in 1999, he received the Lifetime Achievement Award from the Native Writers' Circle of the Americas.

WILLIAM CULLEN BRYANT (1794–1878) was a popular poet, an abolitionist, and, for nearly fifty years, the editor in chief of the *New York Evening Post*.

JOHN BURROUGHS (1837–1921) was well-known for his essays on nature, in addition to his poetry and literary criticism. He was a lifelong friend of Walt Whitman and the author of the first Whitman biography.

STEPHANIE BURT is a professor of English at Harvard University, coeditor of poetry at the *Nation*, and the recipient of a 2016 Guggenheim Fellowship for poetry. Her work appears regularly in the *New York Times Book Review*, the *New Yorker*, the *London Review of Books*, and other journals. She lives in Massachusetts.

GEORGE WASHINGTON CARVER (c. 1861–1943) was an agricultural chemist and agronomist who advanced crop diversification and soil conservation. His promotion of peanut and sweet potato products, in place of cotton, greatly benefited the lives of farmers in the South, especially Black sharecroppers. Born into slavery, Carver went on to study botany at Iowa State University, from which he earned his master's degree. He directed the department of agriculture at the Tuskegee Institute (now University) from its founding in 1896 until his death.

CYRUS CASSELLS is the 2021 Texas Poet Laureate. Among his honors are a Guggenheim Fellowship, the National Poetry Series, a Lambda Literary Award, and a Lannan Literary Award. His latest book is *The World That the Shooter Left Us*.

AMY CLAMPITT (1920–1994) was born in New Providence, Iowa, and spent much of her life in New York City as an editor and librarian. She published her first full-length volume of poetry, *The Kingfisher*, in 1983, at the age of sixty-three. She went on to publish four more books and became a highly regarded poet.

LUCILLE CLIFTON (1936–2010) was a celebrated poet, writer, and children's book author. Her many awards include four Pulitzer Prize nominations and the National Book Award for Poetry for *Blessing the Boats: New and Selected Poems, 1988–2000*.

HENRI COLE was born in Fukuoka, Japan. He has published ten collections of poetry, most recently *Blizzard*, and a memoir, *Orphic Paris*. He teaches at Claremont McKenna College and lives in Boston.

ROBERT CREELEY (1926–2005) was a poet and prose writer who was associated early on with the innovative Black Mountain Poets. He was an ambulance driver for the American Field Service in India and Burma during World War II. He published numerous volumes of poetry, as well as prose, and received the Bollingen Prize in 1999 and the Lannan Lifetime Achievement Award in 2001.

LYDIA DAVIS's most recent books have been *Essays Two* (Farrar, Straus and Giroux, 2021), on translation, foreign languages, and the city of Arles; and *Night Train* (New Directions), translations from the Dutch of stories by A. L. Snijders. She is at present compiling another book of stories, while at the same time working within a task force toward the greening and greater climate resilience of her village as part of New York State's Climate Smart Communities program.

NATALIE DIAZ is the author of the poetry collections *When My Brother Was an Aztec* and *Postcolonial Love Poem*, which was awarded the Pulitzer Prize in Poetry in 2021. She is Mojave and an enrolled member of the Gila River Indian Tribe. She teaches in the Arizona State University Creative Writing MFA program.

EMILY DICKINSON (1830–1886) is one of the most significant figures in American poetry. A prolific poet, she wrote nearly two thousand poems, of which fewer than a dozen were published during her lifetime.

DEBORAH DIGGES (1950–2009) was the author of five volumes of poetry, including *Rough Music*, which was awarded the Kingsley Tufts Poetry Award, and two memoirs about adolescence, her son's and her own.

RITA DOVE is a poet, writer, and playwright. She received the Pulitzer Prize in Poetry in 1987 for *Thomas and Beulah*, the National Humanities Medal, and the Fulbright Lifetime Achievement Medal, among other honors. She served as the US Poet Laureate from 1993 to 1995.

ALICE DUNBAR-NELSON (1875–1935) was a writer, teacher, and lifelong advocate for civil rights and the women's suffrage movement.

CAMILLE T. DUNGY is the author of four collections of poetry, most recently *Trophic Cascade*, the winner of the Colorado Book Award, and the essay collection *Guidebook to Relative Strangers: Journeys into Race, Motherhood and History*, a finalist for the National Book Critics Circle Award. She has edited three anthologies, including *Black Nature: Four Centuries of African American Nature Poetry*. She is a University Distinguished Professor at Colorado State University.

T. S. ELIOT (1888–1965), a renowned modernist poet, playwright, and literary critic, received the Nobel Prize in Literature in 1948 and is best known for *The Waste Land* (1922), one of the most influential poems of the twentieth century.

RALPH WALDO EMERSON (1803–1882), an essayist, poet, and philosopher, was a central figure in the American literary tradition known as Transcendentalism. Referred to as the "Sage of Concord," Emerson was a major influence on Henry David Thoreau and an early supporter of Walt Whitman.

MEGAN FERNANDES is a writer living in NYC. Her work has been published in *The New Yorker*, *The American Poetry Review*, *Ploughshares*, and *The Common*, among many other publications. Her second book of poetry, *Good Boys*, was published by Tin House in 2020.

ROBERT FROST (1874–1963) was a greatly admired poet of the twentieth century who wrote primarily about rural New England. He received four Pulitzer Prizes for his poetry and was awarded the Congressional Gold Medal in 1960.

FORREST GANDER is a poet, translator, essayist, and novelist. His book *Be With* won the 2019 Pulitzer Prize for Poetry and was long-listed for the National Book Award. He is the Adele Kellenberg Seaver Professor of Literary Arts and Comparative Literature at Brown University.

ROSS GAY is the author of a collection of essays, *The Book of Delights*, and four books of poetry, including *Catalog of Unabashed Gratitude*, the winner of the 2015 National Book Critics Circle Award and the 2016 Kingsley Tufts Poetry Award. He is a founding board member of the Bloomington Community Orchard, a nonprofit, free-fruit-for-all food justice and joy project, and he teaches at Indiana University.

MARY SIISIP GENIUSZ (1948–2016) was of Cree and Métis descent and worked as an *oshkaabewis*, a traditional Anishinaabe apprentice, of the late Keewaydinoquay Peschel, an ethnobotanist and Anishinaabeg Elder of the Crane Clan. She taught university courses on ethnobotany, American Indian studies, and American multicultural studies at University of Wisconsin–Milwaukee, University of Wisconsin–Eau Claire, and Minnesota State University–Moorhead.

EUELL GIBBONS (1911–1975), who grew up foraging for food by necessity in East Texas during the Dust Bowl era, became a proponent of wild foods and the author of multiple, widely popular books about wild plant and animal food sources.

ALLEN GINSBERG (1926–1997) was a visionary poet and central figure of the Beat movement. A political activist, a proponent of gay rights, and a Buddhist, Ginsberg was, in the words of poet J. D. McClatchy, "as much a social force as a literary phenomenon."

LOUISE GLÜCK is the author of thirteen books of poetry, most recently *Winter Recipes from the Collective*. She was awarded the Nobel Prize in Literature in 2020.

PAUL GOODMAN (1911–1972), born and raised in New York City, was a sociologist, psychologist, anarchist, and public intellectual. He wrote fiction, poetry, and literary criticism and is best known for his book *Growing Up Absurd*.

JORIE GRAHAM is the author of numerous collections of poetry, including *The Dream of the Unified Field: Selected Poems, 1974–1994*, which won the Pulitzer Prize in Poetry. She is the Boylston Professor of Rhetoric and Oratory at Harvard University.

LINDA GREGG (1942–2019) was the author of nine books of poetry, beginning with *Too Bright to See* in 1981. She was awarded the American Book Award for *All of It Singing: New and Selected Poems*.

ROBERT HASS is a poet, translator and essayist. His most recent books are *Summer Snow*, a collection of poems, and the prose volume, *A Little Book on Form: An Exploration into the Formal Imagination of Poetry*. His poetry collection *Time and Materials* was awarded the Pulitzer Prize in Poetry and the National Book Award. He served as Poet Laureate of the United States from 1995 to 1997 and is a professor of English at UC Berkeley.

ROBERT HAYDEN (1913–1980) was born and raised in Detroit and studied poetry with W. H. Auden at the University of Michigan. He taught at Fisk University for over twenty years and published nine collections of poetry, as well as essays and children's literature. In 1976 he was the first Black American poet to be appointed a Poetry Consultant to the Library of Congress.

MICHAEL HOFMANN has published five books of poems, three books of essays, and numerous translations from the German, including work by Benn, Roth, Brecht, Döblin, and Kafka. He teaches at the University of Florida.

DEVIN JOHNSTON is the author of seven books of poetry, most recently *Mosses and Lichens: Poems*. He teaches literature and creative writing at Saint Louis University and is one of the coordinators of the university's Prison Education Program. He is also an editor for Flood Editions, an independent nonprofit publisher.

PATRICIA SPEARS JONES is a poet, writer, and educator who has published five books of poetry and served as the first African American program coordinator for The Poetry Project at St. Mark's Church. She was awarded the Jackson Poetry Prize in 2017, and her most recent book is *A Lucent Fire: New and Selected Poems*.

JUNE JORDAN (1936–2002) was a celebrated poet, writer, teacher, and activist committed to the civil rights, feminist, LGBTQ, and anti-war movements during the twentieth century. She published numerous volumes of poetry, children's books, and essays; she wrote plays and libretti as well, and was a regular political columnist for the *Progressive*. She taught at UC Berkeley, where she founded Poetry for the People, from 1989 until her death.

JOAN NAVIYUK KANE is Inupiaq with family from King Island (Ugiuvak) and Mary's Igloo (Qawairaq). Her publications include the newly published *Dark Traffic*, *The Cormorant Hunter's Wife*, *Hyperboreal*, and *Milk Black Carbon*. She is a faculty member of the graduate creative writing program at the Institute of American Indian Arts, and she teaches at Tufts University and Harvard University, in addition to serving as the 2021 Mary Routt Chair of Creative Writing and Journalism at Scripps College.

ROBIN WALL KIMMERER is a mother, scientist, decorated professor, and enrolled member of the Citizen Potawatomi Nation. She is the author of *Braiding Sweetgrass: Indigenous Wisdom, Scientific Knowledge and the Teachings of Plants*, and *Gathering Moss: A Natural and Cultural History of Mosses*. She lives in Syracuse, New York, where she is a SUNY Distinguished Teaching Professor of Environmental Biology, and the founder and director of the Center for Native Peoples and the Environment.

GALWAY KINNELL (1927–2014) was a poet and translator. After serving in the US Navy during World War II, he attended Princeton University, where he was roommates with the poet W. S. Merwin. He taught in France, Spain, and Iran, and worked to register southern Black voters with the Congress for Racial Equity (CORE). He received the National Book Award and the Pulitzer Prize for Poetry for his *Selected Poems* in 1983.

YUSEF KOMUNYAKAA served in the US Army as a correspondent and as managing editor of the *Southern Cross* during the Vietnam War, for which he received a Bronze Star. He has published numerous books of poetry, including *Neon Vernacular: New and Selected Poems 1977–1989*, which won the Pulitzer Prize for Poetry and the Kingsley Tufts Poetry Award. He is a senior faculty member in the NYU Creative Writing Program.

LI-YOUNG LEE was born in Jakarta, Indonesia, and immigrated to the United States with his Chinese-born parents in 1964. He has published five books of poetry, and a memoir, *The Winged Seed: A Remembrance*, for which he received an American Book Award.

ALDO LEOPOLD (1886–1948) was a writer, a forester, a naturalist, a professor of wildlife management, and an early advocate of ecologically based conservation. He cofounded The Wilderness Society in 1935. His best-known book is *A Sand County Almanac: And Sketches Here and There*.

BEN LERNER's most recent book is *Gold Custody*, a collaboration with the artist Barbara Bloom.

DENISE LEVERTOV (1923–1997) was born in Ilford, England, and immigrated to the United States in 1948. She was a poet, editor, essayist, translator, and educator. She was active in the anti-war movement during the Vietnam War and in the anti-nuclear movement. A prolific writer, she was the author of numerous books of poetry and prose and received the Lannan Literary Award for Poetry.

MERIWETHER LEWIS (1774–1809) was born in Albemarle County, Virginia. He served in the army and then as President Thomas Jefferson's private secretary. He was appointed captain, with William Clark as second lieutenant, of the first US government–sponsored expedition to explore the territory west of St. Louis, much of which was still held by Native nations, after the Louisiana Purchase in 1803. Throughout the expedition both Lewis and Clark kept detailed journals of their geographical, scientific, and anthropological observations, which are valued for their historical interest.

SANDRA LIM was born in Seoul, South Korea. She is the author of three poetry collections, *The Curious Thing*, *Loveliest Grotesque*, and *The Wilderness*, chosen by Louise Glück for the Barnard Women Poets Prize. She is an associate professor of English at the University of Massachusetts Lowell and also serves on the poetry faculty in the Warren Wilson College MFA Program for Writers. She lives in Cambridge, Massachusetts.

ALICE LOUNSBERRY (1873–1949) was a botanist who wrote about North American flora. Her field guides took a new approach of organizing species by ecosystem, and the three books she published with illustrations by the Australian painter Ellis Rowan, including *Southern Wild Flowers and Trees*, were a popular success.

BERNADETTE MAYER was born in Brooklyn, New York. She is the author of more than twenty-seven collections, including most recently *Works and Days*, as well as many artist-books and chapbooks. She served as the director of the St. Mark's Poetry Project, and has taught at many universities, including the New School for Social Research and Naropa University.

HERMAN MELVILLE (1819–1891) was a novelist and poet who began life as a sailor and went on to write nine novels, including his masterpiece *Moby-Dick* (1851), as well as stories and poems. He struggled with ill health and finances throughout his life due to the uneven reception of his work in the US, though he was celebrated in England; by the twentieth century he had become a canonical figure in American literature.

WILLIAM MEREDITH (1919–2007) was a poet and translator who served as an air force and naval pilot in World War II and in the Korean War. He published numerous books of poetry, including the Pulitzer Prize–winning *Partial Accounts: New and Selected Poems* in 1988 and the National Book Award–winning *Effort at Speech: New and Selected Poems* in 1997. He was an advocate for Bulgarian poetry, and he served as the Poetry Consultant to the Library of Congress from 1978 to 1980.

JAMES MERRILL (1926–1995), a poet, playwright, and translator, was recognized as a master of complex poetic forms. He received two National Book Awards, the Bollingen Prize in Poetry, and the Pulitzer Prize, among many other awards. He established the Ingram Merrill Foundation, a permanent endowment for the benefit of writers and artists.

W. S. MERWIN (1927–2019) was a prize-winning poet and a prolific translator. He opposed the war in Vietnam, and when he was awarded the Pulitzer Prize in 1971 for his book of poetry *The Carrier of Ladders*, he donated the prize money to the draft resistance movement. Having moved to Hawaii in 1976 to study Zen Buddhism, he stayed in Maui, where established over the next forty years a rare palm preserve, which is now permanently conserved through the Hawaiian Islands Land Trust.

MARIANNE MOORE (1887–1972) was a poet and a writer of literary reviews and essays. She was the editor of the modernist literary magazine *The Dial*, founded by Emerson and Margaret Fuller. She won the National Book Award, the Pulitzer Prize, and the Bollingen Prize for her *Collected Poems*.

GARY PAUL NABHAN, a first-generation Lebanese American, is an agricultural ecologist, ethnobotanist, Ecumenical Franciscan brother, and author whose work has focused primarily on the interaction of biodiversity and cultural diversity of the arid binational Southwest. He is considered a pioneer in the local food movement and the heirloom seed saving movement.

AIMEE NEZHUKUMATATHIL is the author of the illustrated collection of nature essays *World of Wonders: In Praise of Fireflies, Whale Sharks, and Other Astonishments*. She has four previous poetry collections: *Oceanic, Lucky Fish, At the Drive-In Volcano*, and *Miracle Fruit*. Her most recent chapbook is *Lace & Pyrite*, a collaboration of epistolary garden poems with the poet Ross Gay. She is a professor of English and creative writing in the University of Mississippi's MFA program.

ELEANOR PERÉNYI (1918–2009) was an editor and writer, best known for her book of essays, *Green Thoughts: A Writer in the Garden*. Her biography *Liszt: The Artist as Romantic Hero* was nominated for a National Book Award. Her memoir, *More Was Lost*, reissued by NYRB, is a fascinating account of her early marriage to a Hungarian baron in 1937 and their restoration of his country estate before the war severed their life together permanently.

KATIE PETERSON is the author of five books, including *Life in a Field* (2021) and *A Piece of Good News* (2019). Born in California, she is a former faculty member and current trustee of Deep Springs College, an experimental school in the high Mojave. She directs the MFA program in creative writing at UC Davis and lives in Berkeley, California, with her husband and daughter.

STANLEY PLUMLY (1939–2019) was a poet and writer, who published eleven books of poetry and several books of prose, devoting much of his writing to the life and work of John Keats. His book *Old Heart: Poems* was a finalist for the National Book Award, and he was named the poet laureate of Maryland, where he lived and taught at the University of Maryland at College Park.

D. A. POWELL is the author of *Cocktails* and *Chronic*, both finalists for the National Book Critics Circle Award in Poetry, and *Useless Landscape, or A Guide for Boys*, winner of the National Book Critics Circle Award in Poetry. He has taught at Columbia University, University of Iowa, and Harvard University, and is currently on the faculty at the University of San Francisco.

MARY KAWENA PUKUI (1895–1986) was born in Kaʻu, Hawaiʻi, to a native Hawaiʻian and a descendant of Anne Bradstreet, the first English poet to settle and publish in the North American colonies. She was a translator and researcher of the Hawaiʻian language and culture, an expert consultant for the Bishop Museum, and a teacher. She conducted extensive field research and collected native Hawaiʻian oral histories. She also compiled the first English-Hawaiʻian, Hawaiʻian-English dictionary and published a companion grammar book. Her work is an indispensable part of the Hawaiʻian anthropological record.

ENRIQUE SALMÓN is a Rarámuri, from the state of Chihuahua, Mexico. He is head of the American Indian Studies Program at Cal State University–East Bay. He holds a PhD in anthropology from Arizona State University and has published many articles on Indigenous ethnobotany, agriculture, nutrition, and traditional ecological knowledge. He is the author of *Eating the Landscape: American Indian Stories of Food, Identity and Resilience* and *Iwígara*.

JAMES SCHUYLER (1923–1991) was a poet, playwright, and novelist, who wrote regularly for *Art News* and was a member of the staff of the Museum of Modern Art. He received the Pulitzer Prize for Poetry in 1981 for *The Morning of the Poem*, and the Lambda Literary Award for Gay Poetry in 1993 for the posthumous publication of his *Collected Poems*.

LESLIE MARMON SILKO is a Laguna Pueblo, Mexican American, and Anglo American writer and poet. Her novels include *Ceremony, Gardens in the Dunes*, and *Almanac of the Dead*. She received a MacArthur Foundation "Genius" fellowship and the Native Writers' Circle of the Americas Lifetime Achievement Award. She is a professor at the University of Arizona at Tucson.

JAKE SKEETS is the author of *Eyes Bottle Dark with a Mouthful of Flowers*, winner of the National Poetry Series, Kate Tufts Discovery Award, American Book Award, and Whiting Award. He is from the Navajo Nation and teaches at Diné College.

GARY SNYDER is a poet, a translator, and an environmental activist who worked as a seaman, logger, trail-crew member, and forest lookout in California. He was an early member of the Beat Movement, and then moved to Japan to study Zen Buddhism. He taught at UC Berkeley, and UC Davis, where he is now a professor emeritus. He has received, among other awards, the Pulitzer Prize in Poetry in 1975 for *Turtle Island*, the National Book Critics Circle Award nomination in 2004 for *Danger on Peaks: Poems*, and numerous lifetime achievement awards, including the Shelley Memorial Award.

WALLACE STEVENS (1879–1955) was an esteemed poet and writer, an insurance lawyer, and later, an executive at the Hartford Accident and Indemnity Company, where he worked for much of his life. He received the Bollingen Prize for Poetry, the National Book Award in 1951 for *The Auroras of Autumn*, and both the National Book Award and Pulitzer Prize in 1955 for *The Collected Poems of Wallace Stevens*.

HENRY DAVID THOREAU (1817–1862) was one of the great literary prose writers of the nineteenth century. His book *Walden*, about his two-year sojourn at Walden Pond, is an iconic work of American literature. He worked as a handyman for Emerson and visited Walt Whitman in New York. Throughout his life he kept a journal of his musings and observations that came to roughly seven thousand pages in total, an ecological, philosophical, and cultural record of its time.

JEAN TOOMER (1894–1967) was a leading figure in the Harlem Renaissance, best known for his highly praised novel *Cane* (1923). He was a poet and prose writer, a follower of the Russian mystic George Gurdjieff, and a teacher of Gurdjieff's spiritual philosophy.

ANN TOWNSEND is the author of *Dear Delinquent*, *The Coronary Garden*, and *Dime Store Erotics*, and is the editor, with David Baker, of *Radiant Lyre: Essays on Lyric Poetry*. She is the cofounder of VIDA: Women in Literary Arts. A professor of English and director of Creative Writing at Denison University, she hybridizes modern daylilies at Bittersweet Farm in Granville, Ohio.

KATHARINE S. WHITE (1892–1977) was the first fiction editor at *The New Yorker*, where she discovered and published Vladimir Nabokov, John Updike, and Marianne Moore, among others. She married the writer E. B. White and moved to Maine, where she became a keen gardener and took up the genre of garden writing, while still editing fiction. Her garden pieces for *The New Yorker* were collected and published posthumously as *Onward and Upward in the Garden*.

WALT WHITMAN (1819–1892) was a revolutionary figure in American poetry, best known for his book *Leaves of Grass*, which was published in multiple editions throughout his life and after. A teacher, a freelance journalist, and an editor of a number of newspapers in Brooklyn and Manhattan, he worked as a nurse during the Civil War, writing the poems that were collected as *Drum-Taps*, along with his celebrated elegy for President Abraham Lincoln, "When Lilacs Last in the Dooryard Bloom'd."

JOHN GREENLEAF WHITTIER (1807–1892) was a poet, an abolitionist, and a journalist. He was a delegate to the National Anti-Slavery Convention and an editor for the Philadelphia-based *Pennsylvania Freeman*. He cofounded the *Atlantic Monthly* in 1857, and his collection *Poetical Works of 1869* was a popular success.

RICHARD WILBUR (1921–2017) was a poet and a prize-winning translator of French poetry and plays, especially the work of Molière. He wrote several books for children and was a lyricist as well. His collection *Things of This World: Poems* won the Pulitzer Prize and National Book Award in 1957, and his *New and Collected Poems* won the Pulitzer Prize in 1989. He served as US Poet Laureate and taught at universities and colleges throughout the country.

WILLIAM CARLOS WILLIAMS (1883–1963) was a poet, a playwright, a novelist, an essayist, and a physician. He was an early member of the Imagist movement, an innovator of the poetic idiom, and his book *Spring and All* was as influential a work of modernism as T. S. Eliot's *The Waste Land*. For four decades he ran a private medical practice in Rutherford, New Jersey, where he lived his whole life. He won the National Book Award for his *Selected Poems*, and for book three of his multivolume work, *Paterson*, as well as the Pulitzer Prize in Poetry for *Pictures From Brueghel*.

JAMES WRIGHT (1927–1980) was born in Martins Ferry, Ohio, and served in the US Army during World War II. He was a poet and translator, and he taught at the University of Minnesota, Macalester College, and Hunter College in New York City. He won the Pulitzer Prize in 1972 for his *Collected Poems*. His son Franz Wright was also a poet.

JEFFREY YANG is the author of the poetry collections *Hey, Marfa*; *Vanishing-Line*; and *An Aquarium*. He is the translator of Bei Dao's autobiography *City Gate, Open Up*, Ahmatjan Osman's *Uyghurland*, and Su Shi's *East Slope*, among others. He has also edited the poetry anthologies *Birds, Beasts, and Seas* and *Time of Grief*; a volume of Walt Whitman's poetry and prose, *The Sea Is a Continual Miracle*; and an expanded edition of Mary Oppen's *Meaning a Life: An Autobiography*.

Red trillium, red wake robin
Trillium erectum